EMPLOYMENT LAW IN EUROPE

SECOND EDITION

About Coopers & Lybrand

- This book was compiled by the Employment Law Unit of Coopers & Lybrand in the United Kingdom.
- Coopers & Lybrand is the largest firm of chartered accountants and management consultants in the United Kingdom with approximately 9 400 partners and staff.
- Its employment law practice focuses on those areas of employment which concern employers namely contracts, business transfers, terminations, compensation, remuneration, dismissals, redundancy and discrimination both in the United Kingdom and Europe.
- The Employment Law Unit forms part of a network of employment lawyers based in member firms of Coopers & Lybrand throughout Europe.
- Coopers & Lybrand International, based in Brussels provides a central resource for business and legal matters concerning the European Union.

EMPLOYMENT LAW
IN EUROPE

SECOND EDITION

A Country by Country Guide
for Employers

Coopers
&Lybrand

Gower

Published by
Gower Publishing Limited
Gower House
Croft Road
Aldershot
Hampshire GU11 3HR
England

Gower
Old Post Road
Brookfield
Vermont 05036
USA

British Library Cataloguing in Publication Data.
A catalogue record for this book is available from the British Library.

ISBN 0-566-07692-6

Printed and bound in Great Britain by
Hartnolls Limited, Bodmin, Cornwall

Contents

Introduction

This book has been written entirely by employment lawyers working for member firms of Coopers & Lybrand International throughout Europe.

It is a sign of the times that a book formerly dealing with employment law in Western Europe should be extended to include chapters on Eastern Europe. Europe has been dramatically extended since the first edition of this book was published in 1986. Then the term 'European employment law' could be used to refer to employment law in Western Europe; in 1986 it seemed unlikely that readers in the West would expect a book with that title to cover Central or Eastern Europe. This edition covers all of the countries in the European Union, including those countries which may soon join - Austria, Finland, Norway and Sweden - and the major countries of Central and Eastern Europe. The topics covered include health and safety requirements as well as individual and collective employment rights. Each chapter follows the same format to assist readers to make comparisons between the different countries.

Nowadays no book on employment law in Europe would be complete without an account of the law of the European Union. European Union social affairs and case law of the European Court of Justice have developed significantly since the last edition of this book. This chapter has therefore been greatly revised and extended.

All chapters describe the law as it was on 1 August 1994, some chapters take account of developments up until 30 November 1994.

Acknowledgements

The third edition of Employment Law in Europe has been edited by Leigh-Anne Buxton of Coopers & Lybrand, who has also written chapters on the United Kingdom and The European Union. We would like to thank Anne Tompkins for her assistance in editing and formatting this edition, together with the following member firms of Coopers & Lybrand International who wrote chapters on their respective countries:

Coopers & Lybrand GmbH	Austria
Coopers & Lybrand	Belgium
Coopers & Lybrand, Ioannou, Zampelas & Co	Cyprus
Coopers & Lybrand	Czech Republic
Coopers & Lybrand	Denmark
KHT-yhteisō Coopers & Lybrand Oy	Finland
Coopers & Lybrand, CLC Juridique et Fiscal	France
Coopers & Lybrand GmbH, Treuhand-Vereinigung Deutsche Revision AG	Germany
Ioannou - Zampelas & Co OE - Coopers & Lybrand	Greece
Coopers & Lybrand Kft	Hungary
Coopers & Lybrand	Ireland
Pirola Pennuto Zei & Associati	Italy
Coopers & Lybrand	Luxembourg
Coopers & Lybrand	Netherlands
Coopers & Lybrand Tax Services A.S.	Norway
Coopers & Lybrand Sp. z o.o.	Poland
Coopers & Lybrand, Limitada	Portugal
Coopers & Lybrand	Slovakia
Coopers & Lybrand, S.A.	Spain
Coopers & Lybrand, Öhrlings Reveko AB	Sweden
Schweizerische Treuhandgesellschaft - Coopers & Lybrand AG	Switzerland
Nas Yeminli Mali Müşavirlik A.Ş., Coopers & Lybrand International	Turkey
Coopers & Lybrand	United Kingdom

The European Union

Introduction

The European Union (EU) was established by the Maastricht Treaty on European Union (the Maastricht Treaty). This Treaty was ratified by the existing Member States of the European Community, namely Belgium, Denmark, France, Germany, Greece, Ireland, Italy, Luxembourg, the Netherlands, Portugal, Spain and the United Kingdom on 1 November 1993. Since then the Treaty of Rome has been ratified by Austria, Finland and Sweden. They will join the EU with effect from 1 January 1995.

The Maastricht Treaty not only amended the existing Treaties establishing the European Union, but introduced a protocol on social policy binding 11 out of the 12 existing Member States. The exception being the United Kingdom, who negotiated an 'opt out' clause in the Treaty, allowing the United Kingdom to 'opt out' of any new social policy matters.

This chapter is intended to give a brief introduction to the institutions, functions and law of the EU and outline the scope of EU employment law.

The European Union Institutions

The primary institutions of the EU are:

- the Council of Ministers;
- the European Commission;
- the European Parliament (EP);
- the European Court of Justice (ECJ).

The Council of Ministers

The Council of Ministers is the decision making institution within the European Union and is comprised of Ministers from the Member States. The identity of the ministers varies according to the subject matter of the meeting. Thus when employment law matters are being discussed the Council is made up of Ministers of Labour.

The Presidency of the Council of Ministers is held for six months by each of the Member States in turn.

The European Commission

The Commission consists of 17 members, with one member elected as President of the Commission. Before nominating members of the Commission, the national governments must firstly nominate the potential President of the Commission by common accord, after consulting the European Parliament. The other Commissioners are then nominated by Member State governments in consultation with the nominee for President. All nominees, including the President, must then be approved as a body by the EP before being appointed by common accord of the Member State governments. The Commission itself has the power to appoint one or two Vice Presidents.

Commissioners must be independent and act in the interests of the EU as a whole and not of any particular national interest. The larger states nominate two representatives and the smaller states one each, and each Commissioner, including the President, is appointed for a renewable term of five years.

The Commission is responsible for ensuring the proper functioning and development of the EU. This role takes a number of forms:

- policing by monitoring compliance with the Treaties, detecting breaches and enforcing the Treaties against defaulters (whether States, commercial undertakings or individuals);
- making recommendations or delivering opinions sought by the Council on matters relating to the Treaties;
- exercising executive powers conferred on it by the Council.

The Commission's influence is derived from its function in proposing new measures to the Council. Once its proposals are adopted it is responsible for forming the detailed rules with which to implement them.

The European Parliament

The European Parliament or European Assembly (EP) was established to provide an element of democratic accountability within the legislative and executive system. Elections have been held every five years since 1979 by nationals of the Member States, with representation being proportionate to population size. Since June 1994, the number of representatives in the EP have increased from 518 to 567, to take into account German reunification and possible future membership.

In addition to the EP's original 'advisory and supervisory powers', the Maastricht Treaty has extended these powers to include:

- the right to request the Commission to submit any proposals for legislation;
- to establish a Commission of Inquiry to investigate any alleged cases of contravention or maladministration in the implementation of EU law;
- to receive petitions from citizens of the Union concerning activities in the EU;
- to appoint an independent Ombudsman to deal with complaints of maladministration by EU institutions and organizations;
- the right of 'co-decision' with the Council on draft EU legislation on some issues;
- a role in the appointment of the Commission.

The European Court of Justice

Article 164 of the Treaty of Rome provides for a European Court of Justice (ECJ) to ensure that Member States observe Union law in their interpretation and application of the Treaties. Its powers can be grouped under four headings:

- judicial review;
- actions against the EU;
- actions against Member States;
- preliminary reference procedures.

The ECJ, which sits in Luxembourg, consists of 13 judges, appointed by agreement between Member States, one from each state and an additional judge nominated by the larger states in rotation.

Actions against Member States

There are two possible methods under the Treaty of Rome by which to take action against a Member State which fails to meet an obligation under the Treaty, namely:

- the ECJ may make a ruling if it finds that there has been a failure to implement a Treaty obligation, in any case put forward by the Commission. Where the Member State fails to take the necessary measures to comply with the ECJ's ruling, the Commission may bring a new case before the ECJ specifying the amount of a financial penalty;
- the ECJ is the final appellate Court in proceedings brought by one Member State against another. The proceedings can only be initiated after a process involving the Commission which tries to arbitrate between the States. It is rare for such an action to go as far as the ECJ.

Preliminary reference procedures

Article 177 provides a mechanism for national courts to refer problems of interpretation of EU law to the ECJ. This is important to establish uniform application of EU law across the European Union. The Treaty of Rome requires such references to be heard by the full court in plenary session, but pressure of work has led to a procedure of hearing cases in chambers.

Questions that may be referred include:

- interpretation of the Treaty of Rome;
- validity or interpretation of acts of the EU institutions;
- interpretation of EU legislation.

Judicial review

The ECJ is the supreme arbiter of EU law and its decisions can only be reversed by amendments to the Treaties themselves. Article 173 of the Treaty of Rome gives the ECJ the power in very restricted circumstances to annul acts by EU institutions which violate Union law.   Article 174 allows the ECJ to review any failure of the Commission or Council to act which amounts to an infringement of the Treaty.

Actions against the European Union

The ECJ has jurisdiction to decide actions brought by individuals against the EU in two situations, namely where:

- the EU is allegedly in breach of a contractual obligation. Such an action may be referred to a national court;
- damage is allegedly caused by the institutions or servants of the EU in performing their duties. These cases, which must be brought within five years, are decided on general principles common to the laws of Members States.

The sources of European Union law

EU law is derived from:

- the Treaties;
- EU legislation;
- decisions of the ECJ.

The Treaties

The European Union developed from two different founding Treaties which are the primary source of EU law, namely:

- the Treaty of Paris which established the European Coal and Steel Community in 1951; and
- the Treaty of Rome which established the European Economic Community and the European Atomic Energy Community in 1957.

These Treaties established the basic obligations of Member States and provide for the future development of the European Union by amendment and by legislation.   It is the Treaty of Rome which established the employment rights which are discussed later in this chapter.

European Union legislation

Article 189 of the Treaty of Rome provides for three forms of 'legislation':

- regulations;
- directives;
- decisions.

Regulations of the Council and the Commission have general application and are binding in their entirety. Once adopted they are automatically part of the national legal systems of Member States and do not require legislative or administrative implementation. They are 'directly applicable'.

Directives are made in the name of the European Community and are binding on Member States as to the result to be achieved. It is left to the national authorities to choose the form and method of application. A directive will usually contain a date by which it must be implemented by appropriate national legislation.

Decisions of the Council and Commission are binding in entirety upon those to whom they are addressed. A decision may be addressed to all States, one State, or to individuals.

Decisions of the European Court of Justice

The ECJ is responsible for interpreting EU law. Its judgments cannot be reversed by legislation, but only by Treaty amendment. Its views on the status of, and effect, of the Treaties and EU legislation therefore are definitive statements of European Union law.

The ECJ's influence in the development of employees' rights within the Union has been important due to its determination to implement the aspirations of the Treaty drafters.

The effect of European Union law

Certain provisions of EU legislation have direct applicability (for example Regulations). This means that they automatically become part of the domestic legal system of Member States without the need for formal enactment at national level. Some provisions (for example Regulations, Treaty provisions and Directives) may also be relied upon by the individual before national courts (the principle of 'direct effect'). The concept of direct applicability is found in Article 189 of the Treaty of Rome in relation to regulations but the principle of direct effect has been developed by the ECJ.

Any provision can have direct effect if it is sufficiently clear, precise, unconditional and self-contained and does not require any further measures by national authorities to give it effect. Provisions which have direct effect are sometimes further distinguished into those which have 'vertical' direct effect (in other words are enforceable by individuals but only against a Member State) and those which have 'horizontal' direct effect (in other words are enforceable by a private individual against another private individual).

An important example of a provision which has horizontal effect is Article 119 of the Treaty of Rome which incorporates the principle of equal pay for equal work. This was successfully enforced by an individual, a Belgian air hostess, against her employer, in *Defrenne v SABENA*[1].

It is important to be aware that domestic legislation must be interpreted in accordance with EU law whether the domestic legislation predates or postdates the relevant EU provision. The ECJ has held in *Marleasing SA v Le Commerical Internacional de Alimentacion SA*[2] that where a national court is asked to interpret its own national law, it must do so in the light of the wording and purpose of provisions regardless of when the law was enacted, in order to achieve the result sought by the European Community legislation.

Employment law in the European Union

EU employment law is already a complex subject in its own right. In the space available it is not possible to do more than indicate the scope of EU employment law and give some examples of its application.

European Community directives have been passed relating to:

- the principle of equal pay for equal work;
- the principle of equal treatment of men and women;
- preservation of employees' rights in the context of transfers of undertakings;
- protection of employees in redundancy and insolvency situations;
- freedom of movement by workers between Member States;
- rights in relation to health and safety at work;
- certain aspects on the organization of working time;
- protection of young people at work;
- European Works Councils.

In addition, particularly in the field of equal pay and equal treatment, decisions of the ECJ have had a dramatic impact on rights in relation to equal opportunities between men and women.

Equal pay for equal work and equal treatment

Article 119 - The principle of equal pay for equal work was established by Article 119 of the Treaty of Rome. As mentioned above Article 119 is directly applicable and directly enforceable by individuals in Member States even where it is contrary to the relevant domestic law.

Supplementary legislation - Article 119 has been complemented by subsequent directives. These are:

- Directive 75/117 ('the Equal Pay Directive') which extended the principle of equal pay in Article 119 to work of equal value.
- Directive 76/207 ('the Equal Treatment Directive') which makes sex based discrimination at work unlawful and requires equality of treatment in recruitment, vocational training, promotion and dismissals.
- Directive 79/7 on equal treatment in social security matters.
- Directive 86/378 aims to ensure equal treatment in occupational social security schemes.
- Directive 86/613 which extends the principle of equal treatment to the self-employed.

In addition, the Commission has adopted a Memorandum on equal pay for work of equal value to help redefine the issue for individuals and national courts, when interpreting Union law. Although the Memorandum does not carry legal weight, it acts as a guide by identifying those areas where the Commission considers Member States are failing to meet their obligations under EU law.

Equal Pay Directive

The purpose of the Equal Pay Directive is to facilitate the practical application of the principle of equal pay established by Article 119. It also extended the principle of equal pay for the same or like work to include equal pay for work of equal value. The principle has been further extended by the ECJ in a series of cases. In *Barber v Guardian Royal Exchange Assurance Group*[3], the ECJ established that benefits paid under an occupational pension scheme came within the definition of 'pay' for the purposes of Article 119. Later cases have held that

Article 119 can be relied upon to claim equality in the right to join an occupational pension scheme as from the date of the ruling in *Defrenne v SABENA* [4] (8 April 1976).

In these cases, the ECJ has held that the principle of equal pay outlaws indirect discrimination in addition to direct discrimination. In the case of *Kowalska v Freie und Hansestadt Hamburg* [5] the ECJ found that to exclude part-time workers from compensation payments on the grounds of an hours of work requirement amounted to indirect discrimination since a considerably smaller percentage of men than women work part-time.

In *Enderby v Frenchay Health Authority and Secretary of State for Health* [6] the ECJ held that it was not sufficient for an employer to show that significant pay differences between female dominated jobs and male dominated jobs arose from non-discriminatory methods such as collective bargaining processes.

The Equal Pay Directive has horizontal direct effect and so may be applied by and against individuals in Member States.

The Equal Treatment Directive

The concept of equal treatment although not expressly provided for in the Treaty of Rome is seen as an extension of the principle of equal pay. The Equal Treatment Directive was adopted under Article 235 which gives the Commission power to take measures which are necessary to achieve an EU objective where the Treaty has not expressly provided for it elsewhere.

The Directive not only provides for equal access to employment, vocational training, working conditions and promotion but also prohibits discrimination by reference to family or marital status.

The Equal Treatment Directive has also been the springboard for some far reaching ECJ decisions. In the *Dekker* [7] case, the Court held that to treat a woman less favourably than a man because she is pregnant is contrary to this directive. Another example is the ECJ's decision in *Marshall v Southampton Area Health Authority* [8] where different compulsory retirement ages for men and women were held to be unlawful.

Social Security Directive

The Directives on social security matters extended the principle of equal pay to schemes which provide protection against sickness, old age, early retirement, industrial accidents, occupational diseases and unemployment. It also applies to social benefits paid to employees. There is provision for some exceptions, for example, where differences are due to actuarial reasons. To some extent these provisions have been overtaken by the ECJ's decision in *Barber* [9] and other cases interpreting Article 119.

Preservation of employees' rights in the context of transfers of undertakings

The 1977 Acquired Rights Directive (Directive 77/187) was adopted to standardize the treatment of employees being transferred from one employer to another, as a result of a national or European business transfer. The Directive obliged Member States to introduce legislation to establish four principles:

- that rights and obligations under the contracts of employment of those employed in the business would bind the person acquiring the business ('the Transferee');
- that the transferee must observe and fulfil the provisions of any collective agreement entered into by the transferor;
- that any dismissals arising out of the transfer must be for economic or technical or organizational reasons; and
- that where the business transferred retains its autonomy the position of employee representatives must be preserved.

The Directive also required advance information of the transfer to be given to the employees' representatives.

A series of cases in the ECJ have made it clear that the Directive, and national legislation implementing it, apply to privatization and contracting out in both the public and private sectors. As a result of difficulties encountered by companies and public sector organizations, particularly in the United Kingdom and Germany, there has been considerable pressure to exclude outsourcing and other similar types of transfer from the scope of the Directive.

The Commission has recently proposed an amendment to the Acquired Rights Directive, which would apply only to undertakings, private or public, which carry out economic activities, whether or not the undertakings are operated with a view to making a profit. Once amended the Directive will distinguish between the transfer of 'an economic entity which retains its identity after the transfer' and the transfer of a mere 'activity of an undertaking'. Employees will be protected only if the economic entity in which they work is transferred, not if there is only the transfer of 'activity'.

Collective redundancies

The Directive on Collective Redundancies (No. 75/129) aims:

- to strengthen the position of workers affected by collective redundancies; and
- to standardize the treatment of redundant workers across the EU.

The Directive has led to legislation in Member States which requires employers to consult employee representatives prior to implementing redundancy to try to reach agreement on possible alternatives to redundancies and on mitigating its consequences. This entails giving the representatives full information. Notification must be given as soon as redundancies are contemplated and at least 30 days before the dismissals are effected. The timescale for notification and consultation depends on the number of proposed dismissals and the size of the undertaking involved.

Insolvency situations

The Insolvency Directive No. 80/987 sets out to establish uniform laws to protect employees in the event of the insolvency of the employer. It aims to guarantee payment of remuneration for a certain period prior to the insolvency. It also allows the Member States to put a ceiling on the liability of the guarantee funds.

Free movement of workers

The single market was established to allow free movement of trade, capital and labour between the Member States. Article 48 of the Treaty of Rome established the right of workers to seek work in Member States and, to move freely between them. This right was to be restricted only on grounds of public policy, security or public health.

It has proved difficult to establish these rights in practice. For example the Treaty did not provide for the differences in educational and vocational qualifications among the Member States, and it has been necessary to introduce directives to provide for mutual recognition of qualifications.

The right of free movement has given rise to a substantial amount of case law which made it a complex area of law in its own right.

Health and safety at work

The EC legislation on issues of health and safety is also a complex subject in its own right. Much of it is aimed at particular industries and work situation, for instance, construction sites or exposure to chemicals, and much of it is extremely detailed.

This area received much attention after the insertion of Article 118A into the Treaty of Rome by the Single European Act and is developing rapidly because given a broad consensus among most Member States on health and safety measures, qualified majority voting makes it easier for legislation to be passed.

Examples of measures which have been adopted include measures relating to:

- protection from exposure to radiation, chemical, physical and biological agents, asbestos, noise, carcinogens and Visual Display Units;
- provision of safety signs at work;
- information on health and safety at work;
- minimum operational requirements for the workplace (including fishing vessels), the use of equipment at work, the use of personal protective equipment;
- protection against risks arising in the coal and steel industries and 'extractive industries'.

Generally EU health and safety legislation does not give rise to directly enforceable rights. In other words in this area the rights of employees against their employers are determined by national law. However that EU recommendations may affect the interpretation of national law as the case of *Grimaldi v Fonds Des Maladies Professionnelles* [10] shows.

Working time

The Directive on working time has been adopted by the Council, although the United Kingdom abstained from voting on it. The United Kingdom has challenged the legal basis of the Directive, namely Article 118A which provides measures aimed at 'encouraging improvements, especially in the working environment, as regards the health and safety of workers', on the basis that the Directive is ultra vires. At the time of writing the UK's challenge to the Directive has not been decided by the ECJ.

The main provisions of the Directive provide for maxima and minima working time as follows:

- maximum 48 hour working week (including overtime);
- a minimum daily rest period of 11 consecutive hours per 24 hour period;
- a rest break for all workers with a working day of six hours or more;

- a minimum weekly uninterrupted rest period of 24 hours, plus the daily 11 hours (35 hours in total); and
- a minimum period of paid leave of four weeks per year.

Protection of young people at work

The Directive on the protection of young people at work aims at prohibiting work by children under the age of 15, or under the compulsory full-time schooling age of the Member State provided it is not less than 15.

Member States must also ensure that work by adolescents, who are defined as persons aged between 15 and 17 and who are no longer subject to compulsory full-time schooling, is strictly regulated and protected in accordance with the Directive.

European Works Councils

On 22 September 1994, the Council adopted the Directive on European Works Councils which was the first Directive to be adopted under the Social Protocol, and as a result will only apply to 'the eleven' that is all Member States, except the United Kingdom.

The companies affected are those with at least a 1 000 employees in the 11 Member States who employ at least 150 employees in each of two or more Member States.

The Directive obliges companies to establish a procedure for consulting employees on transnational issues such as transfers of production, closures, reductions in the size of establishments and collective dismissals. The purpose of the Directive is to provide European employees of multinational companies with information about management plans and decisions which may affect their employment, their terms of employment or their working conditions.

1. *Defrenne v SABENA (No 2)* [Case 43/75; [1976] ECR 455]

2. *Marleasing AS v La Comercial Internacional de Alimentacion SA* [Case 106/89; [1991] ECR 1-4135]

3. *Barber v Guardian Royal Exchange Assurance Group* [Case 262/88; [1990] ECR 1-1889]

4. *Defrenne v SABENA (No 2)* [Case 43/75; [1976] ECR 455]

5. *Kowalska v Freie und Hansestadt Hamburg* [Case 33/89; [1990] IRLR 447]

6. *Enderby v Frenchay Health Authority and Secretary of State for Health* [Case 127/92; [1992] IRLR 15]

7. *Dekker v Stichting Vormingscentrum voor Jong Volwassenen (VJV - Centrum) Plus* [Case 177/88; [1990] ECR 1-3941, [1992] ICR 325, [1991] IRLR 27]

8. *Marshall v Southampton and South West Hampshire Area Health Authority* [Case 152/84; [1986] ECR 723]

9. *Barber v Guardian Royal Exchange Assurance Group* [Case 262/88; [1990] ECR 1-1889]

10. *Grimaldi v Fonds Des Maladies Professionnelles* [Case 322/88; [1989] ECR 4407, [1991] 2 CMLR 265]

Austria

Introduction

The most important areas of Austrian labour law are regulated in detail by statute. There is no unified code and particularly in individual labour law there are many different statutes. These statutory provisions are mostly to the employee's advantage. This means that neither collective agreements, work agreements nor individual contracts of employment can contain terms diverging from statute which are less advantageous to the employee.

The Collective Employment Regulatory Act 1974 (*Arbeitsverfassungsgesetz - ArbVG*) regulates this collective creation of law (collective agreements and works agreements) works representation and conciliation law. Statutory provisions in collective labour law are for the most part binding on both parties. For instance, no form of employee participation can validly be agreed between employers and employees if it is not allowed for in the ArbVG.

Apart from statute, there are the following regulations:

General executive orders - These are of relatively minor significance. The constitution for the most part only permits the issue of executive orders in order to implement statutes.

Collective agreements - These mainly relate to the rights and duties incorporated in individual contracts of employment. A collective agreement has the same force as a statute. The main impact of a collective agreement is on wage settlements, but other things covered include hours of work, vacation rights, periods of notice, expense allowances and so on.

In practice, most collective agreements are concluded between the statutory employer associations and the trade unions (*Österreichischer Gewerkschaftsbund*).

Since employers' statutory associations, to which an employer must belong, usually conclude the agreements on their behalf, and because the ArbVG also specifies that such collective agreements extend to employees who do not belong to the body concluding it (outsiders), the Austrian collective agreements apply to the majority of employees and employers.

Work agreements - A works agreement is a written agreement between the owner of an establishment and the works council. The application of the works agreement is restricted to the establishment concerned. It can only regulate those matters allowed by statute or collective agreement.

Individual contracts of employment - An individual contract of employment is a contract under common law creating and, where it is possible, governing the individual employment relationship.

Employer's orders - Where the employee's duties are not regulated by statute, collective agreement, works agreement or individual contract of employment, an employer can specify them by giving orders (unilateral directives).

Individual employment regulations

Contracts

No special form is required for contracts of employment. They can be concluded verbally, in writing or by conclusive negotiation. Since the most important conditions of employment are regulated by statute and collective agreement (especially for blue-collar workers) their role can be restricted to specifying the type of work and the date when employment commences.   However, for employees at management level, individual agreements are usually concluded in writing specifying the following items:

- the parties to be bound by the contractual terms;
- the date on which employment with this employer began and whether any previous employment is to be regarded as continuous with the present employment;
- if the employment is for a fixed term, the expiry date;
- the rate of pay;
- any terms relating to hours of work, including normal working hours and overtime arrangements;
- entitlement to holidays if exceeding the statutory entitlement;
- the length of notice the employee is required to give and is entitled to receive in addition to the basic statutory minima;
- the employee's job title.

In exceptional cases the law specifies written forms of the employment contract, but usually only for certain sorts of agreement.   For instance, according to the Janitors Act 1970 (*Hausbesorgergesetz*) the waiving of the janitor's rights to the duty accommodation at his disposal must be in writing.

Wages and salaries

Minimum wage provision - The majority of employees and employers are governed by collective agreements on pay issues.   Wages specified by a collective agreement are minimum wages;   an individual agreement can only effectively specify more, not less, pay.

Works councils and employers can only determine incentive pay. Other payments can only be dealt with by a workers' agreement as allowed for by the collective agreement in force.

Method of payment - Unless otherwise specified by a collective, works or individual agreement, the place of payment is the establishment. Agreements providing for payment to be made by bank transfer to the employee's account are permissible and widespread.

Deductions from pay - With few exceptions, the only deductions from pay which an employer can make without the express agreement of the employee concerned are those in respect of income tax and national insurance contribution. The most common exception is usually a deduction in pursuance of a court order.

Itemized pay statement - Every employee has a right to an itemized pay statement, at or before the time payment is made, showing in writing the gross and the net amounts, amounts and purposes of any deductions, and the amount of payment.

Hours of work/shift work/overtime

The permissible working hours are eight hours per day and 40 hours per week, which are primarily regulated by Hours of Work Act 1969 (*Arbeitszeitegesetz - AZG*). This statute also contains provisions for work breaks and rest periods and specifies that additional payment must be made for overtime work. Special statutory regulations exist restricting the hours of work of women and young people. There are no special statutory limits on the working hours of management staff. Working hours can also be regulated by collective agreements, but longer working hours than provided for in the AZG can only be specified in special cases listed in the AZG itself.

Overtime is worked when the permissible normal daily or weekly working hours are being exceeded. This means that overtime is worked if an employee works longer on one day in a week but does not achieve the normal weekly number of working hours (40) because of time lost through illness.

Permissible overtime is limited to five hours weekly. A further 60 hours yearly are permissible in cases of an increased workload, but this must be so distributed that no more than ten hours are worked in a day and no more than a total of ten hours of overtime in any week.

Young persons or women may not work between 8pm and 6am. In exceptional cases the day's work may end later than 8pm (for example in the hotel and restaurant trade or theatrical performances) or begin earlier than 6am (for example in bakeries).

Child labour is prohibited. 'Child' is defined as a minor still subject to full-time compulsory education, at least to 1 July of the year in which it has its fifteenth birthday.

It is possible to work longer than a 40 hour week in exceptional cases. This applies to employees in trading establishments, drivers and assistant drivers and shift workers. In such cases, average weekly working hours must not exceed 40 hours over a specified period.

Holidays

Work ceases on paid public holidays, most of which are religious feast days. With a few exceptions, holiday entitlement is specified for all employees by the Holidays Act 1976 (*Urlaubsgesetz - UrlG*).

In the first year of work, there is only a right to paid holidays after the end of six months employment and in subsequent years with the beginning of each new work year. If employment ends within the first six months the employee receives compensation for 'unearned' vacation time.

Special regulations govern construction workers, who have a claim to vacation leave of 30 working days after 46 weeks and 36 working days after 1 150 unbroken weeks of employment at any given time. It is not necessary to have worked this time for the same employer and holiday pay is not necessarily paid by the individual employers because a fund exists for financing holiday pay.

Agreements between employers and employees providing for payment or other material reward in lieu of holidays are invalid. The statutory entitlement to vacation is specified in Table 1.

Table 1

Period of service	Entitlement
Up to 25 years	30 working days
From 25 years onwards	36 working days

For white-collar employees (*Angestellte*) and blue-collar workers (*Arbeiter*) normal wages are paid during the leave period. Additional payment of one month's salary (less income tax and national insurance) is due (thirteenth month salary). For construction workers payments during the holidays are paid by the Special fund (*Urlaubskassa*). Contributions are paid monthly by the employer and are based on the wages of the construction workers.

Maternity provisions

Protection of pregnant employees is contained in the Maternity Protection Act 1979 (*Mutterschutzgesetz - MschG*).

Pregnant women may not work in the eight weeks preceding the expected date of birth (calculated on the basis of a doctor's certificate) and for a further eight weeks after confinement, regardless of whether the child is born dead or alive. In the event of premature or multiple confinement, the period increases to 12 weeks. There is no right to wage payment; instead the employee receives social insurance benefits.

Pregnant women may not be given heavy physical work or work which is otherwise injurious, regardless of whether or not the danger is specific to pregnancy. Extra prohibitions on night work apply to pregnant women. With few exceptions they may not be employed between 8pm and 6am, or on Sundays or public holidays. Nor may pregnant employees do additional work beyond the statutory or collectively agreed working hours, and the weekly working hours may not under any circumstances exceed 40. Where no permissible work is available the employee has the right to full pay.

Time off

Members of a works council have the right to paid time off for further training and representative duties. In larger establishments one or more council members have the right to total exemption from work on full salary (one for over 150 employees, two for over 700, three for over 3 000).

Employees under notice of dismissal for reason of redundancy are entitled to time off with pay to look for alternative work or to make arrangements for training for future employment.

An employee has the right to continued wages in the case of incapacity due to illness or accident and also, in certain cases, if prevented from working for important personal reasons. These include, for instance, death of a close relative, birth of a child, accompaniment of a child to school where necessary, a change of home, essential appointments with an official body, and so on.

If an employee's dependant falls ill and must be looked after by the employee, the employee has the right to continue to receive pay up to a limit of his or her weekly working time in each work year.

Disciplinary and grievance procedures

The imposition of disciplinary measures is possible for a breach of duty on the part of the employee and as a means to deter any further breaches of duty. A disciplinary measure can only be imposed if provided for in a statutory collective agreement, works agreement or in the individual contract of employment.

Lay-off and guaranteed payments

An employee has a right to payment if he or she is prepared to work but is prevented from doing so by circumstances on the employer's side. This applies to every employee group and there is no time limit on the continuation of wage payment. Everything concerned with the technical running of the establishment, the delivery of materials and supply of resources, the order book and sales and the legality of the establishment's activities is part of the employer's sphere of responsibility. Events in the nature of a general disaster are not part of the employer's sphere of responsibility. If work is halted for such reasons there is no right to payment.

The employer never has the right to lay-off blue-collar workers or white-collar employees without pay.

Period of notice

Minimum periods of notice are specified for almost all employment relationships by statute or collective agreements.

For most blue-collar workers the Industrial Code specifies a 14 day period of notice for both contracting parties. However the rule is not binding. Collective agreements often contain different provisions related to length of employment with the present employer.

For white-collar employees different periods exist depending on whether the employer or the employee gives notice. Employers are bound by a six week period of notice, increasing to two months after the second year of employment, three months after the fifth, four months after the fifteenth and five months after the twenty-fifth, while a white-collar employee can terminate the employment with one month's notice regardless of the length of service.

Dismissal

An employer must inform the appropriate works council before giving any employee notice for the notice to be effective. The works council has the right to be consulted about the intended notice and to comment on it within five working days.

Afterwards the employer can issue the notice but the works council must again be notified. If the works council agrees to it, notice is final. If the works council expressly or implicity lodges a protest, the dismissal can be appealed by either the works council or by the employee.

An appeal to the conciliation authority against notice can only succeed if the notice of termination is socially unjustifiable.

Unlawful reasons for dismissal include:

- trade union or works council membership or activity;
- activities as a member of a mediation board;

- activities as an employee representative responsible for works safety;
- impending call up for national service.

Dismissal is unacceptable unless there are facts about the employee's person which are detrimental to the establishment's interests or economic requirements. This only applies to employees with more than six months' continuous service.

Special protection against unwarranted notice is afforded to particular groups of employees:

- works council members;
- pregnant employees;
- disabled persons;
- those involved in military service.

An employee has no right to a written statement of the reasons for dismissal; a verbal statement is sufficient.

At the request of an employee, the employer is obliged to issue a written certificate stating the length and type of work done. The statement may not contain anything prejudicing the employee in finding a new position.

Redundancy

Any employee who is declared redundant is entitled to a statutory redundancy payment from the unemployment (labour) office. The essential conditions are that the employee is capable and willing to work and is unemployed.

The minimum payment is 40 per cent of the last monthly salary, but there is a maximum absolute amount of ATS 12 225, which can be increased in line with family responsibilities. This is payable for a minimum of 12 weeks, and up to 30 weeks after five years' employment, if 156 weeks' unemployment insurance has been paid.

Severance pay is a special payment paid at the end of an employment relationship by the employer. It is only due after at least three years' employment. The legal claim on severance payment depends on years of employment, as shown in Table 2.

Table 2

Length of employment	Months' salary
3 years	2
5 years	3
10 years	4
15 years	6
20 years	9
25 year	12

Women employees who terminate employment within eight weeks after the birth of a child are entitled to receive 50 per cent of the severance payments up to a maximum of three months' salary, provided that the employment has lasted for at least five years.

There is no right to severance pay where the employment relationship is terminated by a summary dismissal where the employee is at fault, or by the employee giving notice (except in case of retirement).

Collective employment regulations

Collective labour law is divided into the law of trades representation (trades union federation, labour chamber) and the law of works representation.

Trades representation law provides for the so called 'collective creation of law', in particular collective agreements. It also includes the law of industrial disputes and rules providing state assistance in the settlement of the industrial disputes (conciliation law).

Collective creation of law

There are four regulatory instruments in the general collective creation of law which are similar to statutory laws. They are:

- collective agreements;
- works agreements;
- charters;
- minimum wage scales.

As a rule, all these regulating instruments can only specify minimum employment conditions, and therefore only restrain the freedom of contract to the advantage of the employee.

A collective agreement is a legally binding contract in civil law, based on the consensus of the contractual parties.

Works agreements are concluded at establishment level, the contractual parties being the individual employer (owner of the establishment) and the staff represented by the works council. Another form of collective law making is the state minimum wage scale. The state determines both the content of the instrument and the date it comes into force, but the initiative must come from the autonomous associations. In practice, particularly because it is strictly subordinate to collective agreements, the minimum wage is not of great significance.

Trade disputes

Industrial action includes every planned disturbance of the 'productive peace' by collective action intended to achieve a specific aim (including strikes and lockouts). Therefore action intended finally to end employment relationships or ruin the social opponent is not industrial action.

An intention to end the action when the objective is achieved defines an industrial action.

In a strike employees usually withdraw their labour without ending their employment relationship. However they can also resort to collective notice pending a change of contract.

A lockout is taken to mean a decision by one or more employers to withdraw work and earnings until the aim of the action has been achieved or abandoned. A lockout similarly does not end the employment relationship. However an employer can combine it with one of the generally permissible forms of termination.

Employee participation

Statutory works representation

In addition to trade unions and labour chambers, employees have a third representative organization, the works council, at enterprise or company level. Statutory work representation law is intended to restrict the employer's general right to issue orders, granting staff certain rights of co-participation. These refer to decisions such as planning a product, investment, prices, rationalization or closing down an establishment, as well as transferring and dismissing individual employees, starting and ending work, inspection methods, safety and security at work and so on.

A works council may be formed on staff initiative if the enterprise has at least five employees aged over 18. However employees who have a decisive influence on the management of the enterprise are expressly excepted. Separate works councils are appointed for blue-collar workers and white-collar employees if each of both groups consists of more than five employees. The number of works council members depends on the number of employees (Table 3).

The works council has the right to monitor the employer's compliance with compulsory laws safeguarding the interests of employees. In this connection the council has, amongst others, the following rights and responsibilities:

- to review all written materials on salaries payable to employees, including the documents needed to calculate salaries;

Table 3

Employees	Works council members
5 - 9	1
10 - 19	2
20 - 50	3
51 - 100	4
Each additional 100	one additional member
Exceeding 1 000	14
Each additional 400	one additional member

- to check that applicable collective agreements, works agreements and other labour law agreements are complied with by the employer;
- to ensure that legal provisions regarding the safety of employees and workers, social security and job training are complied with;
- to review personal files of each employee, provided that the employee has agreed to such review.

Employee consultation (co-determination)

According to Austrian practice, 'co-determination' exists if the staff have the right to decide an establishment issue on an equal footing with the management. The ArbVG establishes the different possible forms of co-determination very deliberately. The most important areas of co-determination concern social affairs. At the moment, co-determination in economic commercial affairs does not exist.

Compulsory co-determination gives the works council a right of co-decision which is not subject to binding mediation. Enforceable co-determination leaves an issue subject to binding mediation but does not hinder its regulation in other ways.

In personal matters the most important co-determination rights are concerned with dismissals.

A permanent change of workplace for an indefinite period exceeding 13 weeks is only subject to co-determination if it adversely affects the employee's pay or other work conditions. If the consent required from the works council is not given, the transfer is null and void, and the employee need not accept it.

Co-determination provisions also cover disciplinary measures.

Employee participation in the supervisory body

Participation is also provided for on the supervisory body of the stock corporation (*Aktiengesellschaft*), the limited liability company (*Gesellschaft mit beschränkter Haftung*) and cooperatives.

Stock corporations are required by law to have a supervisory board. For limited liability companies a supervisory board has only to be appointed if the average number of employees is more than 300. The works council has a right to delegate one member of the supervisory board for every two members elected by the shareholders.

Pensions, tax and insurance

Income tax and national insurance

Employers have a statutory obligation to deduct income tax and national insurance contributions from the earnings of their employees. The employer has to pay the income tax withheld and the national insurance contributions (employer's and employee's portion) within ten days of the end of the tax month. The employer is liable for any deductions that should have been made.

There are different national insurance contributions for white-collar employees and blue-collar workers.

The maximum insurable earnings are ATS 36 000. They add up to 17.65 per cent of earnings for white-collar employees and 18.20 per cent for blue-collar workers. Employee contributions amount to a monthly maximum of ATS 6 354 and 6 552 for other workers. The maximum employers' contributions are 20.85 per cent (ATS 7 506) and 24.20 per cent (ATS 8 712) respectively.

Sickness benefit

If an employee is prevented from working as agreed by illness or accident, the right to wage or salary payment is retained for a certain period, but there is no protection against losing a job because of illness. If incapacity to work is due to a work accident or occupational disease, the length of the period during which full wages continue to be paid depends on the length of employment with the same employer. There is an additional right to the payment of half the wage for a further four weeks in all cases.

For blue-collar workers the employer receives a refund of the paid wage during the illness from a special fund in the amount of the gross wage. For white-collar employees the continuance of the salary payments has to be absorbed by the employer.

Retirement pensions

The national insurance contribution includes contributions to the statutory old age pension fund. The state retirement pension becomes payable at age 65 for males and 60 for females. Early retirement is quite widespread for males at 60 and for females at 55. The employee may insist on a later retirement if he or she does not want to give up work.

In some large enterprises, employees receive pension payments from the employer in addition to the statutory old age pension. Unlike severance payments, this is not provided for statutorily but paid according to works agreements or individual agreements.

Health and safety

Places of work must be equipped and run as to avoid work associated accidents and illness. Employees must be informed of an existing danger. The employer must provide any necessary protective equipment, washing facilities, drinking water and toilets, and is also obliged to provide such equipment (for example, to reduce noise) for the use of employees during breaks.

Young and female employees must be protected from annoyance and damaging influence. Therefore the differences between the sexes are to be taken into account in the provision of sanitary facilities and, where applicable, living quarters.

An employer must provide for the protection of property such as is normally brought into the establishment by an employee (although the employer is not liable for any loss of such property).

Different types of establishment and work are covered in more detail by the Employees' Protection Act 1972 (*Arbeitnehmerschutzgestz - AschG*) and ministerial orders.

A special authority (the Work Inspection Office - *Arbeitsinspektorat*) is responsible for checking observance of the regulations.

Anti-discrimination regulations

Race and sex discrimination

The Equal Treatment Act 1979 (*Gleichbehandlungsgesetz - GleichbG*) expressly forbids differentiation according to gender. The Act refers to wage payments, fringe benefits and education and training. A general 'equal treatment' principle extends to other conditions of employment. A commission oversees enforcement.

Discrimination and trade unions

The ArbVG expressly forbids discrimination against both works council members and all personnel due to the exercise of their statutory works representation powers. In particular, works council members' activities must not be detrimental to their chances of career advancement. Discriminatory motives need only be made credible for this to apply. Special protection also exists against unwarranted dismissal.

Regulatory bodies

Statutory representative bodies are incorporated bodies with compulsory legal continuity and membership. As a rule they finance their activities by tax like contributions. They can only be disbanded by statute.

The Labour Chamber (*Arbeiterkammer*) and Chambers of Commerce (*Handelskammer*) are the two most important groups of statutory representative bodies in the employment arena.

On the employees' side, there is only one significant trade organization - the Federation of Trade Unions or (*Österreichischer Gewerkschaftsbund - OGB*). Within the Associations Act 1951 (*Vereinsgesetz*), the OGB has the following tasks:

- representing employee's economic and social interests;
- promoting union campaigns and improving employment conditions, where necessary by industrial action;
- concluding collective agreements;
- supporting individual employees, in particular in the event of legal disputes;
- influencing and participating in legislation;
- influencing social insurance.

Representation of employers' interests is carried out by the Chambers of Commerce, the statutory employers' representative bodies. Membership comprises all those entitled to run an undertaking in industry, trade, commerce, finance, credit, insurance, transport and tourism. Membership is automatic. The Chambers of Commerce particularly have the task of advising their members as employers and representing their interests vis-à-vis the state and their social opponents.

Mediation authority and reconciliation board

The mediation authority (*Einigungsamt*) is appointed by the Federal Minister of Social Administration on the recommendation of the employees' and the employers' statutory representatives.

The reconciliation board (*Schlichtungsstelle*) consists of a chairman appointed by the chairman of the mediation authority and four members, half each from employers and employees. The reconciliation board deals mainly with disputes arising in connection with works agreements.

Social partnership and subcommittees

In 1957 a voluntary forum of cooperation between employers and employees was created, the Wage and Price Parity Commission (*Paritätische Kommission für Lohn-und Preisfragen*).

The members of the Commission include the Chancellor, Ministers, the presidents of the Federal Chambers of Commerce, Labour and Agriculture, and of the Federation of Trade Unions (OGB).

Although the commissions, the sub-commissions and the subcommittees have no executive power, almost all industrial disputes are resolved within them. As a consequence Austria has practically no strikes.

The Subcommittee for Prices must approve price increases for goods and services offered by members of the Federal Chamber of Commerce.

The Subcommittee on Wages deals with all matters relating to increases of wages and salaries planned by the trade unions.

The Advisory Committee for Economic and Social Issues deals with economic and social matters and their impact on the Austrian economy.

Legal institutions

Labour courts, consisting of a judge, deputy judges and assessors nominated by employer and employee representative bodies judge legal disputes between employers and employees. Appeals against the decisions of labour courts can be taken to the respective state or circuit courts. The Supreme Court takes final jurisdiction in labour disputes.

Foreign employees

The employment of non-Austrians requires approval of the Local Labour Authorities (*Arbeitsamt*) unless the individual is a citizen of a country of the European Union or the European market.

Individuals who come from one of these countries will get a special identity card issued by a special authority for foreigners (*Fremdenpolizei*) which entitles them to reside and work in Austria.

For all other non-Austrians approval is granted if important public interests and the interests of the Austrian economy are not in conflict with such employment.

Approval is granted for a specific job and is valid for a limited period of time, no longer than one year. The following conditions are stipulated:

- salary provisions and working conditions must not be worse than for Austrian employees having comparable responsibilities and qualifications;
- in case of reduction in the number of jobs available, the employer must terminate the employment of non-Austrian employees first.

Recruitment and training

Recruitment

There are no regulations and provisions for employee recruitment.

Apprenticeships

An apprenticeship is an employment relationship which serves the purpose of educating trainees in a particular profession. Apprenticeship is regulated in detail by the Vocational Training Act 1969 (*Berufsausbildungsgesetz - BAG*). Apprentices are employees being trained according to a training contract by an employer entitled to train apprentices in one of the occupations named in the list of apprentice professions. Among other things the BAG specifies the length of an apprenticeship. As a rule it lasts for three years.

Other training relationships

It is possible to agree training relationships other than apprenticeships. These training relationships are not especially treated by law and include the 'unpaid trainee' category. Unpaid trainees are people being trained in a business establishment but neither in an apprenticeship profession nor for later employment in the establishment - they simply wish to acquire skills and knowledge for other purposes.

Finally many collective agreements also recognise the term 'on the job trainee'. These are employees who are trained for a certain length of time in specific activities so they can then receive better payment on the grounds of their consequently better qualifications. Their contractual relationship is a normal employment relationship.

This chapter was written by Renate Höfer, Coopers & Lybrand GmbH, Austria.

Belgium

Individual employment regulations

Contracts

Individual contracts of employment are essentially governed by the Law on Contracts of Employment 1978 (*loi du 3 juillet 1978 relative aux contrats du travail*). The legislation distinguishes between various types of contracts depending on the nature of the work. There continues to be a fundamental distinction between blue-collar workers who perform work that is chiefly manual and white-collar employees who are involved in mainly intellectual activities. There are also special rules applying to commercial travellers, domestic servants and student workers who are covered by an Act governing individual contracts of employment. Where there is no distinction between blue-collar workers and white-collar employees, the text will refer to the term 'employees'.

A contract of employment occurs where the employee gives an undertaking to the employer to perform work in return for remuneration in a position subordinate to or under the direction and authority of the employer. A contract of employment may contain provisions which are more favourable to the employee than those specified in the legislation as long as they do not restrict the employee's rights or extend the employee's obligations. Provisions which are considered to be less advantageous to the employee will be null and void at law.

The legislation does not generally require contracts to be in writing, although specific types of contract and certain provisions must be in writing at a time not later than the start of the employment relationship. Written contracts must be provided for persons working on a part-time basis, persons employed under fixed term contracts or contracts for a specified task, apprenticeship contracts and contracts for professional sportsmen. The contract of employment must never be concluded 'for life', and if there is a trial period, the duration of the trial period should be specified in writing.

Where a fixed term contract or contract for a specified task is not recorded in writing, it shall be subject to the same conditions as a contract concluded for an unspecified period. Conversely, if the parties enter into two or more successive fixed term contracts without any interruption between them, the contract will be deemed to be a contract of employment for an unspecified period, unless the employer can prove that the contract or contracts were justified by the nature of the work or other valid reasons.

However, the Law of 30 March 1994 offers the possibility to conclude successive fixed term contracts until 31 December 1997, on the condition that the parties conclude fixed term contracts of at least three months, with a global duration of employment of a maximum of two years.

If the preliminary authorization of the competent authority is obtained, parties can clonclude successive fixed term contracts of at least six months, with a global duration of employment of a maximum three years.

Wages and salaries

Minimum wage provision - In April 1994 the guaranteed minimum monthly pay for employees over 21 amounted to Bfrs 40 843 gross. This amount changes in line with the consumer price index, and is regularly adapted by the National Labour Council. There are higher minima in certain sectors of industry, depending on the employee's skills and age.

Method of payment - In principle wages must be paid either in cash or through a financial institution if so agreed in writing. Payment in kind is strictly limited and in principle may not exceed 20 per cent of the local gross wage. The nature of payments in kind is also strictly controlled.

Wages must be paid for blue-collar workers, at least twice a month, with a maximum interval of 16 days and for white-collar employees at least once a month.

Deductions from pay - Deductions from pay are only made in exceptional circumstances. The most important deductions allowed are for employee's social security contributions, professional withholding tax and repayment of advanced salary payments.

Salary freeze - For the 1994 year, no salary increases or supplementary benefits may be attributed if they have not already been provided for in a collective labour agreement, which was registered with the Ministry of Employment on or before 15 November 1993.

For 1995 and 1996, no individual or collective labour agreement or agreement between employer and employee may be concluded, and no unilateral decision may be taken by the employer, which provides for a salary increase or new benefits in cash, in kind or in whatever form.

Specific clauses of the legislation provide for freezes in extra-legal pensions.

A series of increases are not considered as going against the salary freeze. The allowed increases are:

- scale increase obtained following seniority or age;
- increase resulting from a normal promotion or individual change of category;
- increase resulting from an increase in worked overtime;
- increase resulting from spreading an allowed increase in 1994 over 1995 and 1996.

The existing merit rating systems may be continued, but no new systems may be introduced.

Hours of work/shift work/overtime

The legal limits on working hours are eight hours per day, or 40 hours per week, except where these limits are reduced or increased by the law or collective labour agreements. Overtime is also strictly regulated. Some systems of flexible working hours have been introduced by law.

Night work is only permitted in certain companies, or for certain types of work. There are specific regulations for women and young employees. In principle, Sunday work is prohibited. There are some exceptions specified in the law, depending on the industrial sector and the organization of work (shifts).

Holidays

On the following statutory holidays work is forbidden: New Year's Day, Easter Monday, Ascension Day, Whit Monday, National Day (21 July), Assumption, All Saints' Day (1 November), 11 November and Christmas Day. Days off in lieu must be granted to employees when one of these holidays falls on a Sunday or another day of inactivity.

Annual leave is determined according to the days of effective work performed during the calendar year before. An employee with a complete calendar year of service is entitled to 20 days' holiday the following calendar year.

Dates for collective annual leave can be determined for sectors by joint committees. If no such decision exists the dates for collective holidays are determined by the 'works council' or by an agreement between the employer and the trade union representatives. In companies open during the whole year the dates are determined by an individual agreement between the employer and employee.

At the time of their principal holiday employees receive one month's normal salary. On top of this, they receive holiday pay, which corresponds to the salary of three weeks and three days. White-collar employees receive this amount directly from their employer. Blue-collar workers receive it through the holiday fund through which their employer is affiliated.

Maternity provisions

From 1 January 1991 maternity leave is granted for a period of 15 weeks. Maternity leave may begin seven weeks before the date of child birth and must start one week before the date of child birth. During the eight weeks following the birth the mother may not perform any type of work. This period may be extended with the time off the mother has not taken before the delivery.

The employer may not unilaterally terminate the contract of a pregnant employee, from the moment when the employer is notified of the pregnancy until one month after the end of maternity leave. The penalty for doing so is three months' gross wages, to be added to the severance pay, if the employer cannot prove that the dismissal is not related to the pregnancy or motherhood.

Time off

An employee is entitled to paid time off in the case of a number of special events, such as marriage, birth, adoption or death of a member of the family. An employee is also entitled to unpaid time off in the case of urgent familial circumstances (ten days a year maximum).

Time off also exists for educational purposes. An employee serving on a jury or carrying out civic political duties is also entitled to time off.

A specific set of regulations exists for employees who wish to interrupt their professional career, for example, for family reasons.

Trial periods

Statutory trial periods differ for blue-collar workers and white-collar employees. For workers, the trial period cannot be less than seven days or more than 14 days. For employees earning less than Bfrs

1 037 000 the trial period can range from one month up to a maximum of six months. Where an employee earns more than Bfrs 1 037 000, the trial period can extend up to 12 months. When the contract does not specify the period of probation, the minimum period will apply.

During the first month of the trial period a white-collar employee's contract cannot be terminated unilaterally without a serious reason. After the first month, the contract may be terminated unilaterally by one party giving the other party seven days' notice.

Where a contract of employment is terminated after the first month of the trial period without a serious reason or without the requisite period of notice, the terminating party shall pay the other party compensation equivalent to the notice period. Where the contract is terminated during the first month, the compensation shall be equal to the remaining fraction of the month together with the period of notice.

For blue-collar workers, neither party may unilaterally terminate the contract of employment during the seven day trial period without a grave misdemeanour. Where the trial period lasts for more than seven days, the contract may be terminated unilaterally at any time after the expiry of the seven days.

Termination of employment

An employee's contract can be terminated for reasons of ability or conduct or for technical or economic factors. In all cases the employer must have a reason for the termination, whether it relates to the individual person or to the operation of the company.

Period of notice

There are statutory minimum periods of notice for both blue-collar workers and white-collar employees laid down in the Law on Contracts of Employment. These notice periods can be improved upon by collective or individual agreements.

For blue-collar workers, the term of the notice begins on the Monday following the week in which notice has been served. As illustrated in Table 1, the period of the notice takes into account the seniority of the person.

Table 1

Notice period	Service period
28 days	Less than 20 years
56 days	More than 20 years

For white-collar employees, the notice period runs from the first day of the month after the month in which the notice has been served. For those employees earning less than Bfrs 864 000, the employer must give the employee three months notice for every five years of service, as illustrated in Table 2.

Table 2

Notice period	Service period
3 months	Up to 5 years
6 months	5 to 9 years
9 months	10 to 14 years and so on

Where an employee's salary exceeds Bfrs 864 000 per annum the duration of the notice period is not specifically provided for by the law. The law only states that when determining the duration of notice, the employer must take into consideration the employee's length of service, using the statutory notice periods for less than Bfrs 864 000 as a minimum.

The notice period for employees earning between Bfrs 864 000 and Bfrs 1 728 000 can only be determined at the time of termination. For employees earning more than Bfrs 1 728 000, the notice period may be agreed upon at the moment of the start of his or her employment.

The notice period agreed upon cannot be less than the minimum period of notice for employees earning less than Bfrs 864 000. Where there is no such agreement, the notice period will be determined at the time of termination.

In determining the duration of the notice period, the parties may wish to refer to previous case law as a means of determining what the courts have considered 'reasonable'. In this respect, the parties may wish to use several well-established arithmetic formulae, such as the Claeys' formula which has been developed on the basis of case law. Claeys' formula takes into consideration such factors as the employee's seniority, length of service, salary and age. Whereas the Major formula includes the statutory minimum entitlement as part of the calculation plus extra entitlements for total service and service over the age of 40. If the parties cannot agree on a period of notice, the judge will decide.

During the period of notice, the employee is entitled to take two half days' paid leave per week to look for alternative employment.

The period of notice which the employee or worker must give is half that required for employers. For white-collar employees the maximum notice period the employee must give is determined by the employee's salary as illustrated in Table 3.

Table 3

Notice period	Salary
1½ months (for employees with less than 5 years' service)	Up to Bfrs 864 000
3 months (for employees with more than 5 years' service)	Up to Bfrs 864 000
4½ months	Bfrs 864 000 to Bfrs 1 728 000
6 months	Over Bfrs 1 728 000

Termination with notice

The general principle is that each party is able to unilaterally terminate the contract of employment by observing the proper notice period or special procedures in the case of 'protected workers'.

A valid notice of termination must be in writing and must indicate the starting date of the notice and its duration. Employees can terminate the employment relationship by getting a duplicate of the letter of notice signed by the employer or by sending the letter to the employer by registered mail (which takes effect on the third working day following the mailing date) or served by a bailiff (which takes effect immediately). The employer can only send the letter of notice by registered mail or by bailiff. In the absence of these formalities, the notice of termination will be considered null and void.

As an alternative, either party may terminate the employment contract without giving the specified period of notice by making a payment in lieu thereof. For contracts with an unspecified duration, the indemnity must be equal to the employee's remuneration, calculated for the duration of the notice period, or the remaining part of that period.

The employee's remuneration includes not only the base salary, but all other benefits acquired by virtue of the contract, such as fringe benefits, end of year bonus, double holiday pay and so on. The employer must withhold the employee's social security contributions and taxes.

Termination without notice

Either party may terminate the contract of employment without notice or payment in lieu thereof if the other party commits a grave misdemeanour. A grave misdemeanour is defined as any serious misconduct which makes it immediately and finally impossible for the working relationship to continue, and includes such circumstances as unapproved absences by the employee, dishonesty, or the refusal to carry out important legitimate instructions given by the employer. Misconduct by the employer can also lead to a grave misdemeanour to be invoked by the employee.

Where one party seeks to terminate the contract for a grave misdemeanour, that party must do so within three working days of becoming aware of the conduct. If an explanation of the grave misdemeanour is not given in writing at the date of termination, it must be given within the following three working days. Notification may be served by bailiff, or sent by registered mail or the addressee (if employer) may sign a duplicate copy of the letter, as mentioned above.

Fixed term contracts

A contract of employment for a fixed term or for a specific task expires automatically upon reaching its expiry date. Either party can terminate the contract prior to its expiry date by mutual agreement or for a serious reason. Where a contract is terminated prior to its expiry date without the agreement of the other party or in the absence of a serious reason, the party terminating the contract must pay an indemnity equal to the amount of remuneration which remains payable up until the expiry date of the contract. This indemnity cannot however, exceed double the amount of remuneration which would have been due if the employee had been employed on a contract for an unspecified duration.

Indemnity for abuse of right

Employers are obliged to give reasons for the termination of an employee's contract of employment to the National Office of Employment, but are not required to give reasons to the employees themselves. However, the courts have made use of the theory of 'abuse of right' to limit the employer's discretion when terminating an employee's contract in circumstances which may appear to be malicious or provocative.

The courts have used this doctrine to look at the employer's motive behind the termination when it appears that the termination was not for economic or social reasons. Where a blue-collar worker has had his or her contract of employment terminated, the burden falls upon the employer to prove that the termination was fair and justified. In the case of white-collar employees, the employee has the onus to prove that the termination was unfair.

If the Court determines that there has been an abuse of right, the employee is entitled to a 'moral indemnity' in addition to his or her regular notice. The amount of the indemnity is determined by the judge. However, for blue-collar workers the amount of the indemnity is determined by the law and is equal to six months' remuneration.

Redundancy

There is no distinction in Belgian law between an individual termination of employment and an individual redundancy. The legal provisions relating to termination include termination for reasons connected with the employee's ability or conduct or related to the operational aspects of the company.

Only in cases where a certain number of employees are made redundant, will the employer have to apply particular procedures and possibly pay supplementary indemnities to the employees, on top of the procedures and payments applicable in cases of individual terminations.

Appeal

Where an employee has been dismissed and he or she does not agree with the (financial) conditions of the dismissal, the employee may appeal to the labour courts. The Chamber of the Court comprises a career judge and two lay judges, one of whom is a worker or employee representative and the other an employer representative.

Where an appeal is successful, the worker or employee is entitled to additional compensation (not reinstatement).

There are further rights of appeal to the Labour Court of Appeal and finally to the Supreme Court.

'Protected employees'

There are groups of employees who enjoy a 'protected status' as they benefit from special protection against termination. These include:

• *Candidates for and members of company health and safety committees or works councils*

The protection against termination begins 30 days prior to the date on which the list of candidates is published, and continues until after the expiration of four years for all candidates whether successful or not. If an unsuccessful candidate has stood as a candidate previously, then this protection period is reduced to two years instead of four years.

During the protection period, the candidates' employment can only be terminated for economic or technical reasons, which have been identified prior to the termination by the Joint Committee. The Joint Committee has two months to give an unanimous decision on the validity of the economic or technical reason. If there is no decision within the two month time period, the employer can only terminate the employee's contract if the company is closing or if a division of the company is closing. If the employer wants to make a defined group of personnel redundant, then approval must be sought from the court first.

An employer who terminates a protected employee's contract without a valid reason or in breach of these procedures must pay the employee an indemnity. This indemnity must equal the employee's remuneration for the remaining term of the 'protected period', plus an amount equal to two years' remuneration where the employee has less than ten years service; three years' remuneration where the employee has between ten and less than 20 years' service; or four years' remuneration where the worker has at least 20 years' service. If the particular employee who has been made redundant does not request reinstatement, then only the indemnity (calculated in accordance with the number of years of service) is due.

Where an employer wishes to terminate a protected employee's contract for a grave misdemeanour, initial discussions must be held with the union(s) representing the employee. The parties must then go through a conciliation procedure before presenting a case to the Labour Court.

- *Union delegates*

An employer who wishes to terminate a union delegate's contract for any reason other than a grave misdemeanour, must inform the union delegate and the union organization presenting the delegate of the proposed termination. This communication must be delivered by registered mail. The union organization has seven days to challenge the validity of the termination, which may then go to the Conciliation Bureau of the Joint Committee. If there is no response from the union organization, the employer can proceed with the termination on the basis that the reason has been accepted.

The Conciliation Bureau has thirty days to reach a unanimous decision about the validity of the reason to invoke the termination. If the Bureau is unable to reach a unanimous decision, the case will be submitted to the Labour Court.

Where an employer terminates a union delegate's contract without following the prescribed procedure, the employer is liable to pay an indemnity equal to one year's remuneration. This indemnity is also due where the validity of the reason for termination is not accepted by the Conciliation Bureau of the Joint Committee, or where the employment has been terminated for a grave misdemeanour which is later overturned by the court.

A different procedure and a higher indemnity may be provided by collective agreements concluded within the competent Joint Committee for a specified trade or industry.

- *Pregnant women*

  The 'protection period' for pregnant women runs from the time the employee informs her employer of her pregnancy until one month following the expiry of her post-natal leave (eight to a maximum of 14 weeks after confinement). The employer is only able to terminate the employee's contract for cause or for reasons which are unrelated to the pregnancy.

  Where the employer terminates the employee's contract without cause, the employer must pay an indemnity in lieu of notice plus an amount equal to three months' remuneration.

- *Employees working with toxic waste*

  Employees working with toxic waste are protected from termination, except for a serious reason or justifiable reasons, from the start of such duties until between two and four years afterwards. The total protection period depends on the employee's length of service.

- *Employees taking leave for political office*

  The protection period runs from the time the employer is informed of the employee's intention to stand for office and continues until six months after the expiration of office, or three months after their defeat in elections.

Non-competition clause

A non-competition clause prevents the employee from competing directly with the employer once having left the employer's employ. In determining whether a non-competition clause should be or should not be inserted into the employee's contract depends upon the salary of the employee. In law, the employee must earn a gross salary higher than Bfrs 1 728 000 (linked to the cost of living index). The law also requires that these clauses be in writing, that they expressly prohibit the carrying out of identical or similar activities within the employer's working territory and that they can only be valid for a maximum period of 12 months. Clauses in breach of these requirements will be null and void.

Where a non-competition clause is inserted into an employee's contract, the clause should provide for payment by the employer of a fixed compensation. The minimum amount of compensation is half the employee's gross salary for the period provided in the clause. If the employer waives his rights under the clause, which must be done within 15 days of the termination of the employment relationship, the employer will not be liable to pay compensation.

In addition to the general non-competition clause, the law enables an employer to insert a specific non-competition clause which may be applicable for longer than one year and may cover countries other than Belgium. This clause can be used where the company has an international field of activity, or an important economic, technical or financial interest. They can also be used where the employee's job enables the employee to acquire specific knowledge and information about practices in the company, which could damage the company if it were made freely available.

A particular clause for trade representatives exists.

Contracting out

A contract of employment must not be contrary to the provisions of the social legislation. Any provision in a contract which tends to reduce the rights of the employee or worker or is less advantageous to the employee or worker will be declared void at law.

Statutory limitation period

The statutory limitation period is five years during the term of the contract of employment and one year after the termination date of the contract. Where there is a penalty sanctioned, the limitation period is five years as of the end of the last violation.

Employees can waiver their rights, but such a waiver is generally speaking only valid after the termination of employment.

Collective employment regulations

Contracts

Collective labour agreements regulate the individual and collective relations between an employer and his or her employees within a company, within one industrial sector or nationally. Collective labour agreements can lay down the wages, working hours, annual leave periods, notice periods for blue-collar workers (in particular), amongst other things. These agreements are negotiated between one or more employers or employer organizations and one or more representative trade union organizations. To become a representative trade union, the trade union must have an inter-occupational character, be established at national level, be represented on the Central Economic Council and the National Labour Council and have at least 50 000 members.

A collective labour agreement can be concluded within the National Labour Council, for the whole of the industry in the country; a National Joint Committee, for one sector of industry throughout the country; a Regional Joint Committee, for a sector of industry related to a specific region; a company (between employer and one or more trade unions). A collective labour agreement concluded in a joint committee or in the National Labour Council can be declared generally binding by royal decree. A collective labour agreement declared 'generally binding' applies to all employers related to the joint body in which the collective labour agreement was concluded and all their employees. The binding nature of a 'non-generally binding' collective labour agreement is more limited.

Labour regulations

Labour regulations (*règlement de travail/arbeidsreglement*) determine the working conditions which apply to a particular company. The works council draws up and modifies the labour regulations.

When no agreement is reached within the works council, the issue will be decided by the joint committee after a procedure of negotiation. Where there is no works council, the employer draws up the labour regulations and submits them to the employees, who may comment on them. Employees who have made comments are protected against dismissal.

Collective terminations for economic reasons (redundancy)

Collective termination provisions in any collective labour agreement of a company employing at least 20 employees in the preceding 12 months is governed by the National Labour Council collective agreements No. 10 of 8 May 1973 and No. 24 of 2 October 1975 and a Royal Decree dated 24 May 1976.

A collective termination occurs where the employer intends, over a continuous period of 60 days, to terminate for technical or economic reasons the contracts of employment of at least 10 per cent of the average number of employees employed or at least six employees where the enterprise employs between 20 and 59 employees.

Procedure

Pursuant to the collective agreement No. 24 of 2 October 1975, a special procedure must be followed where the employer terminates, during a continuous period of 60 days, the following employee's contracts of employment:

- at least ten employees in a company with between (on average) 21 and 99 employees during the calendar year preceding the terminations;
- at least 10 per cent of the workforce in a company with between (on average) 100 and 299 employees during the calendar year preceding the terminations; or
- at least 30 employees in a company with (on average) 300 employees or more during the calendar year preceding the terminations.

The employer must give written notice of the redundancies to the employees and to the works council. Where there is no works council, then notice must be given to the trade union responsible for the employees.   The notice must include all useful information on the number of employees affected, the age, sex and occupation of the employees affected, the reasons for the redundancies and any other information which would assist the works council and employee representatives to suggest ways of reducing the number of redundancies or mitigating the effects thereof. A copy of this notice, together with information about the company, the sector-level committee covering and details of the consultations with employee representatives must be sent by registered mail to the Subregional Employment Office. The employer must give the works council a copy of this notice. The employees' representatives have the right to make their own remarks to the Subregional Employment Office.

The employer may not give notice or terminate the employee's contracts until 30 days have elapsed, starting with the date of notification of the terminations to the Subregional Employment Office. This office has the power to reduce this time period in certain circumstances, or extend it up to a maximum of 60 days.

Payments

In addition to the usual pay for notice periods, employees having been the subject of a collective termination are entitled to special monthly payments from the employer. Generally, these payments are equal to half the difference between the net pay up to a ceiling (Bfrs 90 575 a month) and the unemployment benefit. This indemnity is generally paid for a period of four months, but it is reduced by one month for each month's notice over three months.

In large companies where a collective termination involves a large number of employees, it is common for the employees' representatives to negotiate a social plan. The purpose of this plan is to introduce a programme of measures to offset the effects of the redundancies, which often provides for additional payments on top of those payments mentioned above.

Lay-off and guaranteed payments

There are three specific circumstances in which a blue-collar worker's contract may be suspended:

- bad weather: all obligations are suspended, but the worker may terminate the contract immediately if work is impossible for one month or more;
- technical problems in the firm: all obligations are suspended, but the worker remains entitled to receive salary for the first seven days of the suspension unless refusing to perform other similar work offered which is suited to his skills and abilities;
- lack of work for economic reasons: performance of the contract can be suspended or regulations for part-time work can be implemented.

In the case of incapacity owing to illness or accident, blue-collar workers and white-collar employee will not lose any income during the first month of their illness (except for blue-collar workers whose first day of short illness is unpaid). In general white-collar employees will continue to receive their salary during that month. Blue-collar workers, and exceptionally white-collar employees, will be paid during the first month of incapacity partly by the employer and partly by the sickness fund. After the first month of incapacity staff are only entitled to sickness fund payments.

Closure of companies

The closing down of a company with more than 20 employees in the preceding 12 months is governed by the Laws of 28 June 1966 and 30 June 1967. 'Closing down' may be voluntary or caused by insolvency, and is defined as the cessation of the principal activity of the company or a division thereof, with a reduction in its workforce to below 25 per cent of the average total workforce for the previous 12 months. Under certain conditions, employees may be granted special closing payments which amounts depend on seniority.

The closing fund is responsible for making redundancy payments when the employer fails to do so. The employer's obligations to the fund are:

- to advise the fund of a winding-up operation;
- to pay contributions to the fund.

The closing fund also guarantees all the employees legal rights which the employer does not fulfil, either at the winding-up or in any other case where a firm ceases to exist. Unlike redundancy payments, this guarantee applies to all firms, no matter what their size.

Procedure

The employer is obliged to meet with the works council to inform the council of the closure. Where there is no works council, then the meeting must be held with the employees' representatives. The employees must be notified of the proposed date of closure and such other details as necessary, by the posting of a notice in the company.

At the time of notifying the employees, the employer must send by registered mail, written notice to the Ministry of Labour and Employment, the Ministry of Economic Affairs, the Subregional Employment Office, the sector-level joint committee and the 'closure fund'.

The formalities and the waiting period applying to a collective termination also applies in the case of a company closure.

Payments

The closure fund is a fund financed by contributions from employers for the purpose of making special payments to the employees made redundant following closure. Any employee with 12 months' service may receive a closure payment from the company, or in the case of insolvency, from the closure fund. This payment is in addition to notice or an indemnity in lieu of notice.

The basic indemnity is currently fixed at Bfrs 4 344 (last indexed figure) per year of service with a ceiling of Bfrs 86 800. A supplementary indemnity of Bfrs 4 344 is payable to employees over the age of 45, for each year of work performed for the company over this age. The ceiling again is Bfrs 86 800.

A transitional payment may also be payable where a bankrupt company is taken over by a new employer. This payment is made from the date employment ceased with the former employer until the date employment commenced with the new employer. The payment is equivalent to the employee's former gross monthly pay up to a ceiling, with a maximum of Bfrs 75 000 per employee per month, and a total of Bfrs 900 000 per employee.

An employee may not receive both collective termination payments and a 'closure payment'.

Language of employment contracts

In Belgium an employment contract, and all related official documents, must always be drawn up in one of the two national languages, at least if the company has an operating office in the Belgian territory where the employee is located. In the Brussels region (the capital), contracts must be drawn up in the usual language of communication of the employee concerned. If the enterprise is situated in the Flemish or Walloon region, the Dutch, or French language, respectively must be used.

In the case of documentation directed to employees the company may add a translation into one or more other languages, depending on the languages used by its staff.

Employee participation

Works councils and health and safety councils must be elected in enterprises employing at least 100 or 50 employees respectively. The main role of these bodies is to receive information from the employer and to be consulted by him or her. These bodies have decision making power only in a few specific areas and are composed of elected employees' delegates and employers' representatives.

Apart from these bodies, a union delegation can exist in the enterprise.

Collective bodies

Table 4 displays levels and sectors of collective bodies in Belgium.

Table 4

Level	Economic sector	Social sector
National inter-professional	Central Council for Industry (CCI)	National Labour Council (NLC)
Professional	Works Council	National Joint Committee National Joint Sub-Committee
Regional professional		Regional Joint Committee Regional Joint Sub-Committee
Individual enterprise		Works Council Health & Safety Committee Union Delegates

Pensions, tax and insurance

Description of the social security system

Belgium has an extensive compulsory social security system, which broadly includes:

- sickness and disability insurance (*assurance maladie-invalidité/ziekte-en invaliditeitsverzekering*) (including health costs);
- unemployment benefits (*allocations de chomage/werkloosheid-suitkeringen*);
- old-age and widow's pension (*pension de retraite et de survie/rust-en overlevingspensioen*);
- family allowances (*allocations familiales/kinderbijslag*);
- holiday pay (*pécule de vacances/vakantiegeld*);
- industrial injuries (accidents on the way to and from work included), occupational diseases (*accidents de travail, maladies professionnelles/arbeidsongevallen, beroepsziekten*);
- maternity insurance (since 9 January 1990) (*assurance maternité/ moederschapverzekering*).

It is generally considered that regulations relating to welfare compensation and social benefit to handicapped persons also form part of the social security system.

Contributions paid by employers and employees are collected by one central institution - the *Office National de Sécurité Sociale (ONSS)* or *Rijksdienst voor Sociale Zekerheid (RSZ)* - which then distributes the contributions between the organizations responsible for the payment of allowances and benefits.

All Belgian employers must be registered with the ONSS/RSZ. In case of a new enterprise, the new employer must inform this institution, which will send him a questionnaire to be completed. On that basis the employer will be issued with a registration number. Later he must complete some declarations stating the identification of his staff members and the remunerations paid. The documents are automatically provided by the administration. The employer must also inform the administration with regard to newly hired staff and provide identification data in each case.

The other main formalities for employers are affiliation to a child benefits fund and a holiday pay fund, a medical service and contracting industrial insurance. The employer should also maintain a certain number of registers.   A social secretariat can arrange for these formalities for an administrative fee. All employees should affiliate to a Belgian mutualité (for health care).

Social security contributions

Standard social security contributions for calendar year 1994 are shown in Table 5. The percentages are calculated on the gross remuneration of the employee, without any ceiling (it is interesting to note that most benefits are calculated according to a remuneration with a specific ceiling). Social security contributions are fully deductible for personal income tax purposes.

Table 5

	Manual workers		Employees	
To be paid by	Employer	Worker	Employer	Employee
	(on 108 per cent of salary)		(per cent)	
1 - 9 persons employed in Belgium	38.89	13.07	32.89	13.07
10 - 19 persons employed in Belgium	40.58	13.07	34.58	13.07
More than 19 persons employed in Belgium	40.68	13.07	34.68	13.07

There are other specific social contributions whose payment depends on the situation of the employee and the employer concerned. For instance, all employees are liable to make a monthly contribution of which the amount will depend upon the family income of the employee concerned; with respect to the employer, if the activity is performed in the construction industry sector the employer will be liable to payment of an 11 per cent contribution of the wages for inclement weather stamps and fidelity stamps, together with a small additional charge to cover various administrative costs. Other special contributions exist depending on the industrial sector of the company.

Benefits

The system provides for the following benefits in 1994:

Child benefits - The right to allowances and the amount payable will depend, among other things, on the situation of the parent to whom the payment is due and the status of the child concerned. Basically, the standard allowances are as follows: first child: Bfrs 3 848 per month; second child: Bfrs 5 523 per month; third and following children: Bfrs 7 185 per month. These amounts rise as the child passes the ages of 6, 12 and 16 (respectively Bfrs 886, 1 353, 1 655).

Child benefits are tax-exempt. Additional benefits can be granted at the time of birth, and for handicapped children, orphans, welfare and so on.

Professional compensation for disability or maternity - Professional compensation is paid in respect of disability or maternity. Compensation generally amounts to 60 per cent of the lost remuneration with a maximum of Bfrs 2 091 per day for bodily injuries. It may be reduced in accordance with the family status of the employee and the duration of the disability.

Maternity insurance - Since 9 January 1990, a new maternity insurance has been introduced into Belgium. A guaranteed salary will be paid by the INAMI or RIZIV (National Illness & Disability Institute). The employee is entitled to 15 weeks off (seven weeks before birth and eight weeks after). For the first 30 days the employee who has an employment contract will benefit from compensation equivalent to 82 per cent of the remuneration. The rest of the period is covered by a reduced compensation. Such payments are generally taxable for the employee.

Sickness and health care costs - The employee and his dependents are entitled to a refund of their health care costs. This right to a refund can be extended to other persons, such as foreign individuals residing in Belgium and registered with a municipality for at least six months. The person must be affiliated to a private organization called a *Mutuelle* or *Mutualiteit* or its state equivalent. Specific personal contributions may be required by these organizations. Refunds at different levels and limits are then available, depending on the type of costs. Such refunds are generally non-taxable for the employee.

Old age pension - The amount of the legal state pension is determined on the basis of the situation of the individual concerned, and also depends on his professional career and the gross remunerations paid. Hypothetical or estimated remunerations may also be considered for this purpose. For the head of a family, the pension entitlement is calculated at a rate of 75 per cent of the remunerations earned during his career. For other persons the rate is 60 per cent. The maximum remuneration to be taken into account is Bfrs 1 314 288 (provisional amount for 1993). The maximum pension for a full career (currently 45 years for a man, 40 years for a woman) may be estimated at a family rate of Bfrs 675 550 per year. Men and women can choose their pension age between 60 and 65.

It is important to note that, from the date on which the employee retires, only limited work can be performed, with strict levels of remuneration.

Pensions are fully taxable in Belgium but the taxpayer is in principle entitled to a reduction in his basic personal income tax.

Unemployment benefits - The employee must have been employed for a specific period of time and must comply with certain formalities (such as registration with the competent administration, no performance of any remunerated activity and so on).

Unemployment benefit varies depending on the status of the unemployed person, the length of unemployment, and possibly his or her previous work experience. Unemployment benefits are fully taxable but the taxpayer is entitled to a tax reduction of his or her basic personal income tax, as shown in Table 6.

Table 6

Beneficiary	Max/day	Min/day
Head of household (60%)	1 264	1 079
Single person		
1st year: 60%	1 264	785
after the 1st year: 40%	885	785
Cohabiting couples		
1st year 55%	1 159	634
between the 12th and 18th	737	634
month after the 18th month,		
with exceptions for persons		
with long professional careers,		
standard amount	473	

Industrial injuries and occupational diseases - In case of industrial injury or occupational disease, the benefits are in principle higher than in the case of accidents or diseases not due to occupational activities. If an employee is killed in an accident during work or on the way between his home and his work, his heirs will receive an allowance covering the costs of the funeral (lump sum) and a subsistence allowance. If the employee is only injured, he will receive an allowance depending on his income and, if the injury is permanent, the allowance will also depend on the degree of disability. The victim of an accident is also entitled to the refund of medical costs arising from the accident.

Occupational diseases are less of a factor for white-collar employees: the list of occupational diseases focuses on diseases caused by manual work.

Other schemes

Companies generally set up specific medical coverage plans in order to compensate staff wholly or partly for the part of major medical and hospitalization costs not refunded under the state system.

Application of the national legislation

Individuals are subject to the Belgian social security system if the two following conditions are met:

- the individual is employed in Belgium;
- the individual is working for an employer who is established in Belgium or for an operation established in Belgium.

A person on a foreign payroll is in principle not employed by a Belgian employer if he remains under the authority of his foreign employer. A person seconded to an operating office established in Belgium is considered to be attached to that office if he is under the control of that office, which means that he receives orders and instructions from that office, that he has to report to the office and has his salary paid by the office. A person temporarily seconded to the office in order to organize, reorganize or control its activities is not considered to be attached to this office.

It is thus possible, in theory, to be employed in Belgium without being under the compulsory social security system. However it is good practice to obtain written confirmation of the exemption from the social security authorities in each particular case in order to avoid problems afterwards. Persons exempted from payments are not covered against any social risk whatever which might occur in Belgium (for example, health costs). It is generally accepted that this is superseded by the provisions of the European regulations and by the social security treaties when they oblige Belgium, de facto and de jure, to apply the Belgian system to migrant workers, or vice versa.

Voluntary payments to social security

Within certain limits and conditions, it is possible for an employee to maintain his coverage under the Belgian social security system for a period of six months which can be extended for another six months. This exception applies to persons working abroad in a non-EU country with which Belgium has not concluded any social security treaty. The person can join the overseas social security scheme (OSSOM). The advantages of this optional affiliation to OSSOM are rather limited. Both employees and self-employed persons can join the system.

If a Belgian citizen joins, he has to participate in the old age and widow's insurance, medical insurance and the health care insurance. The insurance for health care is 'postponed' because benefits are only granted after 16 years of insurance and on condition that the employee has reached the age of 50 years. The insured pays a contribution freely chosen between a minimum of Bfrs 4 608 and a maximum of Bfrs 18 434 per month.

The insured or his widow and children are entitled by virtue of the old age and widow's insurance to a subsistence allowance calculated on the basis of individual contributions. In case of illness or accident, the insured will receive a monthly allowance depending on the amount of his contributions (he should pay at least a monthly contribution of Bfrs 6 913).

The 'postponed' insurance for health care costs also provides the insurance taker with a limited refund of health costs.

It is also possible to participate in a supplementary insurance scheme for medical care, industrial injuries and accidents in general. The terms and conditions of the insurance policy are determined by mutual agreement between the insured and the OSSOM/DOSZ.

Social security treaties

Besides the European multilateral agreements, Belgium has signed social security treaties with Algeria, Austria, Canada, United States of America, Israel, Morocco, Poland, San Marino, Switzerland, Tunisia,

Turkey, Yugoslavia, and Zaire. The principles generally provided for in these treaties consist in applying the local social security on the (part of the) activities performed in the country concerned. This may possibly lead to the payment of contributions to several state schemes. Exceptions to the rule mainly concern activities performed by a temporarily seconded employee or a person working simultaneously in two states, or a possible mutual agreement between the relevant state authorities in the interests of the employees.

Article 14 (1) (a) and (b) of EU Regulation 1408/71

In principle the conditions required by the Belgian social security authorities for application of article 14 (1) of the EU Regulation will be that the individual still remains an employee of the undertaking in the home country and that he or she does not enter the service of a firm located in the other country. If the employee enters fully into the activity of the foreign place of business which gives work instructions and pays his or her salary, the employee should normally be considered as employed in that place of business and is hence subject to the local social security system. In practice this situation may be assumed if the individual is put on the local payroll and registered in the personnel registers of the local company.

Article 17 of EU Regulation 1408/71

For individuals posted to Belgium, the Belgian authorities generally agree to grant an extension of the coverage period under the home country scheme for a maximum term of posting of five years. They would not normally agree to go beyond this limit.

Additional pension schemes

Pension plans are generally private optional plans. They can be drawn up for all qualifying employees (group insurance plans, pension plans) or restricted to some high level executives. They can be financed either by both the employer and the employees, or by the employer only. Employees' contributions are deductible for personal tax purposes if the plan is established in Belgium.

Depending on the kind of plans, employers' contributions are not always fully deductible for corporate tax purposes. Benefits from the plans can be tax-exempt or taxed at a favourable rate.

Foreign executives can participate in these plans if the conditions of the statues of the plans are met. The benefit these executives would obtain may eventually be tax-exempt in Belgium, for instance, if they no longer reside in Belgium when the benefit is paid.

Premiums paid to a foreign scheme are generally not deductible for the employee or employer. Depending on whether the employee has acquired vested rights in the plan which can be clearly assessed, employers' contributions can constitute a taxable salary for the employee.

Health and safety

Every firm must be affiliated to an inter-company medical service. This service works preventively; in other words, it carries out examinations to seek possible sources of illness or danger.

Regulatory bodies

All disputes relating to employment and social security law fall under the jurisdiction of the Labour Tribunals.

There is one labour tribunal per district. Each labour tribunal is composed of judges and of representatives from employers, employees and the self-employed. The representatives are nominated by the King for a fixed period. The Chair is always a judge. Appeals against a judgment given by the labour tribunal may be brought before the Labour Court. There are Labour Courts in Brussels, Antwerp, Mons, Ghent and Liege.

Recruitment and training

Recruitment

The collective agreement No. 38 of 6 December 1983 stipulates some rules concerning recruitment and selection.

The employer is obliged to bear the costs of selection, to keep the documents that the candidate sent the employer at his or her disposition for a reasonable period of time after the candidate has been unsuccessful, and to give the candidate some evidence affirming the candidate's application, for unemployment control purposes. The employer cannot ask the candidate to hand over 'legalized' transcripts of diploma's, certificates or other documents during the procedure of selection.

The collective agreement also contains a number of provisions which do not have the force of law, but merely constitute a gentlemen's agreement. These provisions concern the information the employer has to provide when he or she offers a place of employment, the equal treatment of candidates, respect for the candidate's privacy, the duties of the candidate, the reasonable duration of the recruitment procedure and so on.

Training

The National Employment Office organizes courses for those wishing to improve their skills or retrain for a new career.

An employee can participate in certain courses during working hours. In that respect, the employee is able, in accordance with the applicable legislation to leave work (education leave) during the hours of the course. During the periods of educational leave, the employee is entitled to his or her normal salary. On request, the remuneration paid by the employer for these hours will however be reimbursed by the Ministry of Labour.

Only the hours that the employee is present at the courses can be taken into consideration in order to determine the period of paid educational leave. Furthermore, the law provides how many hours a year the employee may follow courses in order to benefit from these regulations.

This chapter was written by Véronique Pertry, Coopers & Lybrand, Belgium.

Cyprus

Introduction

Employment relations in respect of rights and duties of employers and employees are regulated partly by statute and partly by voluntary agreements and procedures. There are either individual contracts or collective agreements. Collective labour agreements are concluded in individual companies by sectors and even at company level. The social security law secures employees against social risks.

Individual employment regulations

Contracts

Contracts of employment can be concluded orally between the employer and employee. There are no legal requirements for contracts to be evidenced in writing either by contract documents or by statement of terms and conditions. However contracts which, on demand by either party, are evidenced in writing usually specify the terms of employment, including remuneration, working hours, holidays, fringe benefits, duties and so on. In cases where the contract is of a non-permanent nature it will also specify the period of employment. For employees at management level individual agreements are in practice expressed in writing.

Wages and salaries

Minimum wage provision - Minimum wages are fixed by law (Minimum Wages Law of 1979) for shop assistants, clerks, nurses and nursery assistants. As a rule the actual wages paid are higher than the minimum. The law does not provide for fringe benefits but it is customary in most businesses to pay an extra month's salary at Christmas. Minimum wages are also specified in collective agreements and an individual agreement can effectively only specify more, not less pay.

Method of payment - Usually payments are made at the place of establishment but payments may also be agreed and arranged to be made by bank transfer to the employee's account.

Deductions from pay - The only deductions from pay which an employer can make without the express agreement of the employee concerned are those in respect of income tax, social insurance contributions and defence tax.   An exception is deductions in pursuance of a court order.

Itemized pay statement - Every employee has a right to an itemized pay statement, at or before the time payment is made, showing in writing the gross and the net amounts, amounts and purposes of any deductions and the amounts of payment where different parts of the net amount are paid by different methods.

Hours of work/shift work/overtime

Cyprus has ratified the International Labour Organisation (ILO) convention providing for the eight hour working day. The average working hours in the private, public and banking sectors vary between 36 and 42 hours a week. Currently both the five and six day week are used. Working hours are mainly regulated by collective agreements. Sunday work is prohibited by law unless expressly permitted.   It is generally accepted that overtime work counts as time and a half while overtime worked on public holidays and weekends counts as double time. Employees are not obliged to work overtime.

Holidays

Minimum annual holiday entitlement according to the Annual Holidays with Pay Law of 1967 is 15 working days for employees with a five day working week and 18 days for a six day working week, provided that at least 50 weeks of service have been completed. An employee is entitled to a proportion of this leave on completion of 13 weeks of service. Employees obtain their holiday entitlement out of an employee sponsored central holiday fund, except where the employer provides better holiday terms than the ones required by law, in which case entitlements are obtained directly from the employer.

Maternity provisions

Maternity leave according to the law extends to 14 weeks. At least two weeks must be taken before the expected date of birth and at least nine weeks must be taken after. During maternity leave the employee is entitled to a maternity allowance under the Social Security Scheme. Usually the employee on maternity leave is entitled to a supplementary allowance from the employer. From the time that pregnancy is acknowledged by the employer on receipt of a doctor's certificate until three months after the lapse of the 14 week maternity leave, the employer is prohibited from terminating the employment of the employee. For a period of six months after the birth the employee is also entitled to one working hour off per day.

The law also provides for the safety of pregnant employees from professions considered dangerous.

Time off

There is no legislation providing for employees' entitlement to other leave of absence. It is a matter of agreement between the employer and employee. An entitlement to sick leave is provided by the Social Security Insurance Law, which provides for both sickness and accident.

Disciplinary and grievance procedures

If an employer is dissatisfied with an employee the employee can be dismissed, provided the legal notices as prescribed by the Termination of Employment Law are observed. The law also prescribes those grounds justifiable for dismissal. Procedures for the settlement of disputes in relation to collective agreements are provided in the procedural part of the Industrial Relations Code, which is a purely voluntary agreement; no legal sanctions can be imposed on those not complying with its provisions.

Lay-off and guaranteed payments

If the employer fails to provide work, salary must still be paid. In case of termination of employment by reason of redundancy the employee is entitled to compensation from the government's Redundancy Fund.

Period of notice

The Termination of Employment Law provides for minimum periods of notice before dismissals. These range from one to eight weeks, depending on the length of service, both in cases of redundancy and dismissal. Payments in lieu of notice are also allowed.

Dismissal

The legislation sets out the grounds which justify a summary dismissal and which give no rise to compensation. Such grounds are misconduct, theft, embezzlement, violent behaviour, unsatisfactory performance of duties and so on. Dismissal on grounds other than those specified constitutes an unfair dismissal, which confers rights upon the employee for complaint and compensation computed according to the provisions of the law.

The law also sets out specific grounds which do not constitute justifiable reason for dismissals; these include pregnancy, religion, colour, culture, membership of unions and so on.

Redundancy

Any employee who is declared redundant within the terms of the statutory definition is entitled to a redundancy payment out of the Redundancy Fund which is exclusively financed by employers' contributions.

Collective employment regulations

Trade unions

The right to organize freely and to belong to organizations of one's choice is recognized by the Cyprus Constitution, which guarantees the freedom to form or join a trade union. Unions may stipulate collective labour agreements binding on all those who belong to the category of workers to which the agreement refers. Such agreements are terminal and renegotiable and in cases where agreement cannot be reached the Ministry of Labour and Social Insurance acts as mediator. Collective bargaining is carried out through procedures stated in the Industrial Relations Code agreed upon by employers, trade unions and the government.

Trade disputes

Essentially the Industrial Relations Code contains an undertaking to promote collective bargaining in good faith and also a commitment by both sides of industry to try and limit the incidence of unofficial and unconstitutional strikes.

Where disputes arise in negotiations of new collective agreements or the renewal of existing ones failing direct negotiations, the Ministry of Labour and Social Insurance acts as a mediator to resolve the dispute. If despite the Ministry's mediation services the dispute is still unresolved a deadlock is declared and either party is free to take any lawful measures after a ten day cooling off period in support of its claim.

Disputes arising during the interpretation or implementation of an existing collective agreement first go through domestic grievance procedures and then to mediation or binding arbitration. Violation of collective agreements gives immediate right to lawful actions including strikes or lockout.

Employee participation

There is no legal right conferred upon employee unions to be represented on the board of management of an enterprise and neither is the employer obliged to give employees' representatives information on the financial state of the enterprise or consult them on any decision making process.

Pensions, tax and insurance

Income tax and national insurance

Employers have a statutory obligation to deduct income tax, defence tax and national insurance contributions. The income tax rates are progressive from zero to 40 per cent, whereas defence tax and national insurance contributions are based on fixed rates of 2 per cent for defence tax and 6.3 per cent for national insurance contributions on earnings. (National insurance contributions apply only up to a maximum amount of earnings beyond which no contributions are deducted.) Employers must account monthly to the Inland Revenue for such deductions.

Sickness benefit

Every person between 16 and 63 years of age, subject to satisfying certain qualifying conditions, is entitled to sickness benefit. The period of entitlement is up to a maximum of 312 days, depending on the contributions made.

Retirement pensions

The retirement age is 65. Under certain conditions state retirement pensions become payable at the age of 63 and this can be extended up to the age of 68. In the case of miners who have worked for at least a period of five years the retirement age is reduced by one month for every five months of service up to a maximum of five years. The entitlement period extends up to the date of death and the contribution is paid at the end of each month. Employers often provide their own pension schemes in addition to that of the government.

Health and safety

The government, through a number of protective statutes such as the Factories Law and Shop Assistants Law, recognizes its responsibility to protect its citizens against the risks of sickness and accidents.

Regulations in respect of accident prevention and working conditions which include, amongst others, fire prevention systems, protection devices for machinery and equipment, lighting and so on are enforced through regular inspections by duly qualified inspectors. Advice and information on state methods of operation are offered by the general inspectorate and prior approval by the chief inspector of the building plan is required before the granting of a business permit to set up a factory.

There is a legal obligation for employers to take out insurance against liability.

Anti-discrimination regulations

There are no specific anti-discrimination laws. The constitution guarantees the right to establish trade unions and precludes any discrimination with regard to religion. The Termination of Employment Law provides that any dismissal made on the grounds of race, colour, sex, religion, ethnic or cultural origin is considered as unfair dismissal. Recently legislation providing equal payment between men and women for work of equal value has been enacted.

Foreign employees

Foreign employees cannot take employment in Cyprus without a valid residence employment permit. Such permits are granted only if there are no Cypriots available who are qualified for the position in question. Such permits may be refused or cancelled for reasons of public interest.

This chapter was written by Panikos N Tsiailis, Coopers & Lybrand, Ioannou, Zampelas & Co, Cyprus.

Czech Republic

Introduction

The main employment legislation in the Czech Republic consists of the Labour Code (Act No. 65/1965, including the latest amendment - Act No. 74/1994), the Employment Act No. 1/1991, the Act on Wages, Remuneration for Working Readiness and Average Earnings (Act No. 1/1992 Coll.), the Act on Incomes and Rewards for Working Readiness in Budgetary Organizations (Act No. 143/1992 Coll.) and Government Order No. 43/1992 Coll. Collective labour law is governed by the Act on Collective Bargaining.

This chapter summarizes the fundamental principles of labour law and the employment relationship between employer and employee.

Individual employment regulations

Contracts

An employment relationship commences upon the signing of a contract between the employer and employee. The employment contract is required to contain information on the following matters:

- the type of work in which the employee will be engaged;
- the place where the work will be performed (town, organizational unit, or other specified place);
- the date of the commencement of employment.

In addition, the employment contract may include other relevant details. The contract can only be amended if both parties agree to the changes. Where the contract was concluded in writing, the subsequent amendments must also be concluded in writing.

The normal trial period for an employee is three months, during which period either party may terminate the employment contract for any reason, or without stating a reason. A shorter trial period may be agreed to in writing, but cannot be subsequently extended.

The employer must provide the employee with a copy of the contract.

The employment relationship can be established for an indefinite period or for a fixed period of time. There are however, some restrictions upon making fixed term contracts.

There are two types of agreements for work performed outside the employment relationship. The first type of agreement is where the employer employs a person specifically for an individual project, where the expected duration of the project is no longer than 100 hours. Such agreements may be concluded in writing or orally.

The second type of agreement is similar, except for the fact that the expected duration of 100 hours may be worked over a longer period. The person cannot work more than half of the prescribed normal weekly working hours for the duration of the project. These agreements must also be concluded in writing.

Employees under the age of 18 can only be employed with the approval of their lawful guardians. Adolescents aged between 15 and 18 years cannot be employed on night shifts and cannot work overtime. In addition, adolescents and women cannot be employed to work underground.

Wages and salaries

Minimum wage provision - The minimum wage varies in accordance with a government schedule, which recognizes 12 grades of work. The lowest minimum wage is 12Kč per hour and 2 200 Kč per month.

Deductions from pay - In accordance with the General Health Contribution (Act No. 550/1991 Coll.), employers are required to pay

9 per cent of employees' gross salaries to a General Contribution fund. Employees must pay an additional 4.5 per cent of their gross salaries to the same fund.

Employers and employees must also contribute to the social security, pension and unemployment funds established by the State Employment Policy Act of November 1992. Employers and employees contribute 26.25 per cent and 8.75 per cent, respectively, of the employees' gross salaries. In total, employers are required to pay 35.25 per cent and employees 13.25 per cent of the employees' gross salaries.

Hours of work/shift work/overtime

The normal working hours are from 8.00 am to 4.15 pm, with a maximum of 43 hours per week. Employees younger than 16 years of age may not work more than 33 hours per week. Employment contracts should include a 30 minute meal break and a rest after five hours of uninterrupted work.

The employer can employ persons for less than the normal number of weekly hours.

Any time worked over and above the hours stipulated in the weekly schedule or worked outside the work shift schedule is considered to be overtime, and may only be worked in exceptional cases. Overtime must be limited to eight hours per week and 150 hours per calendar year.

The Labour Code breaks organizations into categories, for instance budgetary, contributory, private businesses and manufacturing organizations. Employees of private businesses and manufacturing organizations are entitled to be paid a premium payment for overtime, of at least 25 per cent of the employee's average earnings or time off in lieu, regardless of whether the work is done on weekdays or weekends. The premium payment for holiday work is at least 50 per cent of the employee's average earnings or time off in lieu. The employer is able to increase these premiums payments, if desired.

Holidays

The minimum holiday entitlement for an employee with at least one year's service is three weeks annual leave. Employees who have worked for more than 60 days but less than one year are entitled to one-twelfth of their leave entitlement for each month of service. Employees with more than 15 years' service are entitled to four weeks annual leave.

Even those employees who do not have 60 days' service with the same employer in a given calendar year, are entitled to annual leave. These employees should receive one-twelfth of their annual leave entitlement for every 22 days of work completed.

The public holidays observed in the Czech Republic are as follows:

1 January	New Year's Day
April	East Monday
1 May	Labour Day
8 May	Liberation Day
5 July	Cyril and Metodius Day
6 July	Jan Hus Day
28 October	Declaration of Independence Day
24 December	Christmas Eve
25 December	Christmas Day
26 December	Boxing Day

Maternity provisions

A pregnant woman is entitled to 28 weeks maternity leave, in connection with the birth of her child and its post-natal care. If a woman gives birth to two or more children at the same time, or if she is a single parent without another income, the maternity leave period is increased to 37 weeks. The employer must grant additional maternity leave to mothers who request it, for periods up to the child reaches three years of age.

There are special working conditions for pregnant women and women who are caring for young children. Pregnant women and women who are within nine months of giving birth are prohibited from working in certain positions, designated by the Ministry of Health as being 'disadvantageous to their health'. If the woman occupies an unsuitable position, the employer is required to reassign her to another position. Pregnant women who work night shifts may request a transfer to day shifts.

In addition, the employer cannot require a pregnant woman or a woman caring for a child under the age of one to work overtime; or for a pregnant woman or a woman caring for a child under the age of eight years to be sent on business trips without her consent.

Time off

All employers are entitled to paid time off in the following cases:

- to take care of a sick member in the family;
- maternity leave;
- a doctors or dentists appointment;
- to accompany a family member to a doctor's examination;
- the death of a family member;
- in the case of marriage or marriage of children;
- looking for a new job when the employee has already given notice.

Supplemental employment

Secondary or supplemental employment is defined as any employment relationship other than the one in which the employee works the stipulated weekly working time. Supplemental employment may only be agreed upon for work hours shorter than the prescribed weekly work time. Supplemental employment taken during the employee's annual leave period is not considered to be supplemental employment.

Either party may terminate the supplemental employment relationship for any reason, although no reasons need to be stated, by giving the other party at least 15 days notice.

Period of notice

Both parties may terminate the employment relationship by giving notice. The notice must be in writing and delivered to the other party in order to be valid. The standard notice period is two months for both employer and employee. Notice commences on the first day of the calendar month following the date on which the notice is delivered, and expires on the last day of the next calendar month.

The employee may give notice to the employer for any reason (although there is no requirement to specify that reason) and at any time. The employer is more restricted, as he or she can only give the employee notice in specified circumstances. Those circumstances are as follows:

- if the company or part of the company is dissolved or relocates;
- if the company ceases to exist, or if part of it is transferred to another company, which cannot employ the employee in accordance with his or her employment contract;
- if the employee is not willing to be transferred to a suitable alternate position, in an agreed location;
- if the employee becomes redundant as a result of production or organizational changes;

- if the employee has lost his or her capacity to perform work as a result of long-standing health problems, verified by a medical doctor's certificate or a decision of a public health board or social security board;
- where the employee does not perform his or her work satisfactorily, after having received a written warning from the employer within the last 12 months;
- where the employee has seriously breached work discipline, or has consistently committed infringements against it; provided that the employer warned the employee in writing, within the previous six months, that notice of termination was possible.

The employer cannot give the employee notice during a protected period, namely, when the employee is:

- temporarily unable to work due to an illness or injury that has been certified by a medical doctor; provided that the employee did not cause the incapacity through his or her own wilful acts, or in a drunken state;
- called up for military service; the protection period commences on the day the employee receives the call-up order or when the ordinance containing a general call-up order is published, and continues for two weeks after the employee is released from such service;
- a pregnant woman or a single female or male employee who has no other income besides his or her wage, and who must care for at least one child under the age of three;
- given long-term unpaid leave in order to serve in a public office.

Dismissal

The employment relationship may be terminated in any of the following ways:

- by mutual agreement;
- by one party giving notice of termination to the other party;

- by immediate dismissal;
- by termination of employment during the employee's trial period;
- upon the expiry of a fixed term contract.

If the employer and employee mutually agree to sever the employment relationship, such agreement should be in writing. The employment relationship will terminate upon the agreed date.

Immediate termination

The employer may dismiss an employee immediately only if the reason(s) for the dismissal are expressed in writing and one of the following situations has occurred:

- the employee is sentenced to a prison term exceeding six months for committing a wilful criminal act related to his work activity;
- the employee is sentenced to a prison term exceeding one year for committing a wilful criminal act not related to his work activity;
- the employee breaches work discipline in a particularly gross manner.

The employee may immediately terminate his or her employment relationship with the company:

- where, in accordance with a medical doctor's certificate, the employee cannot continue working for the employer without seriously impairing his or her health and the employer has failed to transfer the employee to an alternative and suitable position within 15 days of the submission of the doctor's certificate;
- where the employer has not paid the employee his or her wage or compensation within 15 days after its maturity.

Redundancy

An employee made redundant because of reorganization is entitled to a redundancy payment equivalent to two months' average wages.

Collective employment regulations

Collective labour law is governed by the Act on Collective Bargaining. In the Czech Republic two types of collective agreements exist:

- collective agreements agreed between trade organizations (unions) and employers' organizations;
- a company's collective agreement agreed between a specific trade organization and employer (one firm or one branch).

Collective agreements

Collective agreements arrange:

- individual relationships between employers and employees (individual commitments);
- collective relationships between employers and employees (collective commitments); and
- the rights and duties of contracting parties.

Pensions, tax and insurance

State benefits

A person is entitled to a state dole, after the loss of his or her employment. The amount of the state dole is calculated as a percentage of the person's former salary as follows:

- one to three months after the loss of employment, the employee is entitled to 60 per cent of his or her last average salary;

- four to six months after the loss of employment, the employee is entitled to 50 per cent of his or her last average salary.

Where an employee leaves employment, whether a permanent or temporary position, to retrain or re-qualify, the employee is entitled to 70 per cent of his or her last average salary.

Retirement pensions

Men are entitled to receive a state pension at the age of 60 and women are entitled to retire between the ages of 53 and 57, depending upon their number of children.   Government and Parliament are currently discussing changes to the retirement age, for instance women should be entitled to receive a state pension from the age of 60 and men should retire from the age of 65. If this proposal is approved, it will come into effect as from 1 January 1996.

Taxation - tax code overview

Information about employee taxation in the Czech Republic is summarized below, incorporating all the main amendments up to the end of June 1993.

Tax Framework Act

On 15 April 1992 the Czechoslavok Parliament adopted the Tax Framework Act. This Act specifies all the taxes imposed in the Czech Republic as from 1 January 1993:

- Individual income and corporation taxes;
- Value added tax;
- Real property tax;
- Road tax;
- Inheritance, gift and transfer of real property ownership tax;
- Excise duties tax (fuel, alcohol, tobacco products).

These acts have already been amended since their adoption by the Government, with further amendments currently being prepared. All Czech tax residents, both local and foreign, are subject to these taxes. Where a double taxation treaty exists, the foreign national may receive some tax reliefs.

Individual Income and Corporation Taxes Act

This Act (No. 586/1992 Collection of Laws) was adopted on 30 November 1992 by the Czech Parliament and came into force on 1 January 1993. Apart from certain exceptions, this Act does not differentiate between the income received by expatriates and income received by local staff as far as taxation is concerned. As a result of the latest amendment the tax rate has increased from 15 per cent up to 44 per cent of annual taxable income.

Under domestic law, tax residents are individuals whose domicile or residence is in the Czech Republic. Residence is determined on the basis that the person must be present in the Czech Republic for a period or periods exceeding in aggregate 183 days in the fiscal year concerned. The period of residence in the Czech or Slovak Republics includes the person's arrival and departure dates. The fiscal year is the calendar year.

Tax residents are taxed on their worldwide income, whereas other individuals are only taxed on their income, the source of which is located in the Czech Republic.

Taxable income

Taxable income includes income from dependent personal services (for example wages, salaries and directors' fees), income from small businesses, rental income, dividends, interest, annuities and other income.

If a company car is used for private travel, the employee's wage tax base will be increased by 1 per cent of the car's purchase price every calendar month. The company will also pay for all private expenses. This will apply regardless of the employee's proportionate use between business use and private purposes. The employee is taxed on the increased wage tax base.

A company charges depreciation and the cost of petrol consumed for business travel as costs. Petrol consumption for business purposes is established in two ways:

- mileage book; or
- company lump sum.

The local authorities require the calculation of the lump sum to be based on the three to six months aggregate of all employees' business mileage as stated in their mileage books.

If an entrepreneur uses his flat or house for business purposes, it is possible to charge part of the rental payments, phone fees and so on as costs. If a flat or house is used by an employee for business purposes and it is agreed in the employment contract, a proportional part of these costs may be charged to the employer. The exact proportion of allowable deductible costs should be agreed with the tax authorities.

Annuities, rent, interest and dividends are subject to withholding tax at various rates, if the source of that income is located in the Czech Republic. If the source of income is derived from outside the Czech Republic, this income will be included in the employee's normal taxable income.

The Act also defines non-taxable income, for example insurance premiums, prize income up to a limited level, social security receipts, and so on.

The tax base comprises the amount of taxable income less expenses and allowances permitted by this Act.

Expatriates

Expatriates who work in the Czech Republic are subject to tax on their salary if:

- they are employed by a Czech person (either an individual or a legal entity);
- the cost of their salaries is borne by a permanent establishment of a foreign company; or
- they are employed by a foreign company but stay in the Czech Republic more than 183 days in aggregate.

Expatriates who are either tax non-residents under local law or covered by a double taxation treaty are subject only to tax on their local source income. Those expatriates who are tax residents of the Czech Republic are subject to tax on their worldwide income.

If an expatriate has a permanent 'home' outside the Czech Republic and has been sent to the Czech Republic as an expert, to work exclusively for a Czech company, Czech branch (permanent establishment) or a foreign company and is resident in the Czech Republic only in order to provide those expert services, then:

- the expatriate will be taxed only on income derived from the Czech Republic; and
- will be entitled to claim an exemption from tax of 30 per cent of his or her income.

Expatriates from countries without a double taxation treaty may avoid taxation for a period of one year if they arrive in the middle of one year and leave the Czech Republic before the following year, provided they are not 'domicile' in the Czech Republic.

Under the Individual Income and Corporation Taxes Act, a foreign company will have a permanent establishment in the Czech Republic after six months of carrying out certain activities within the Czech Republic. This applies to technical or other advisory activities, management or middleman services and similar activities if carried out by either employees or persons working for the foreign company. The six month period is calculated on the basis of calendar days. Any interruption longer than 12 consecutive months will not be included in the six month period.

Given the above, every employee who works for a foreign company providing these activities for a period longer than six months may be liable to income tax immediately, instead of being exempt for 183 days.

Double taxation

The Czech Republic has a double taxation treaty with the following countries: Belgium, Brazil, China, Denmark, Finland, France, India, Italy, Japan, Yugoslavia, Cyprus, Nigeria, the Netherlands, Norway, Austria, Greece, Sweden, Great Britain, Canada, Germany, USA, Slovakia and former Comecon countries except Hungary.

Tax rates

Net income is taxed at the following rates:

From Kč	To Kč	Tax payable
-	60 000	15%
60 000	120 000	9 000 Kč plus 20% of tax base above 60 000 Kč
120 000	180 000	21 000 Kč plus 25% of tax base above 120 000 Kč
180 000	540 000	36 000 Kč plus 32% of tax base above 180 000 Kč
540 000	1 080 000	151 200 Kč plus 40% of tax base above 540 000 Kč
1 080 000	and above	367 200 Kč plus 44% of tax base above 1 080 000 Kč

Social security

Under the current interpretation of the policies of the Health and Social Affairs Ministries, every foreign company which has a permanent establishment registered in the Commercial Register is liable to social security and health contribution payments. The employer (permanent establishment) is liable to withhold 13.25 per cent of the employees' gross salaries as social security and health insurance contributions. In addition, 35.25 per cent of the total amount of gross salaries will be payable by the employer. These contributions are to be withheld and paid monthly.

Expatriates who have an employment contract directly with a foreign company and who work in the Czech Republic either in a branch or any other permanent establishment need not pay the Czech social security and health insurance contribution.

Health and safety

Employers are obliged to provide safe working conditions which are not disadvantageous to the employees' health. Employers must establish, maintain and improve the necessary protective facilities and must implement technical and organizational precautions with legislative acts and regulations for ensuring safety.

Employers are also required to provide the necessary personal protective work aides for their employees' use. Trade union bodies have the right to supervise the state of safety and health protection in individual organizations.

Foreign employees

The conditions for entry and residence of foreigners in the Czech Republic are set out in the Act on the Stay (Residence) of Foreigners on the Territory of the Czech Republic (No. 123/1992 Coll.).

The Act describes the following types of stay:

- *Short term* - A foreigner may stay in the Czech Republic for a maximum of 180 days either as specified in his or her visa, or as stipulated by the government or by an international agreement (in cases where a visa is not required).

- *Long term* - Long term residency may be granted for the period of time necessary to complete the purpose of the journey, but for no longer than one year. Long term residency may be extended upon the foreigner's request for at least one year.

- *Permanent* - Permanent residence may be granted to a foreigner for the purpose of family unification or other humanitarian reasons or if it is in the political interest of the state.

The Employment Act stipulates that foreigners and persons without any state citizenship employed under Czech legal regulations shall enjoy the same legal position as Czech citizens. They may be employed only if they are granted a residence permit and a work permit.

The Labour office will issue a work permit once a stay permit has already been issued.

A work permit is not required in the following cases:

- a foreigner who has been granted refugee status and
  - has been living on the territory of the Czech Republic for a period of at least three years; or
  - is married to a Czech citizen and the marriage still exists; or
  - who has at least one child who is a Czech citizen.
- a foreigner who has been granted a permanent residence permit;
- a foreigner who is a family member of an employee of a diplomatic mission or consulate, or a family member of an employee of an international governmental organization whose headquarters is in the Czech Republic, provided an international treaty signed by the government allows reciprocity.

A work permit is required by a foreigner who is an employee of a foreign employer, but who will work in the Czech Republic on the basis of a contract concluded between his or her employer and a Czech legal person.

This chapter was written by Blanka Votavová and Danielle Hruby (MCS), and Monika Svobodová and Henk Goossen (Tax Department), Coopers & Lybrand, Czech Republic.

Denmark

Introduction

The legislation on employment and labour relations is diverse and is to a great extent supplemented by collective agreements. It can be divided into two main groups: one deals with working conditions in general for only certain types of employees; the other covers nearly all employees on special matters relating to their employment.

All the laws covered by the first group can be described as social protection laws. The most important laws in this category are the Employees Act (*Funkionaerloven*) and the Vocational Training Act (*lov om erhvervsuddannelser*). Examples of the second group of laws include the Holidays with Pay Act (*Ferieloven*), the Work Environment Act (*Arbejdsmiljoeloven*), the Supplementary Old Age Pension Act (*ATP-loven*) and various laws on compensation for loss of earnings due to industrial injury and unemployment as well as various laws on equal rights.

The collective agreements are agreements about general wage increases, working hours and holidays which are entered into by the Federation of Danish Employers (DA) and the trade unions.

The Main Agreement (*Hovedaftalen*) of 1973 that was entered into by the Federation of Danish Employers and the Danish Council of Trade Unions (LO) constitutes the basis of collective labour bargaining in Denmark and has in fact acted as a substitute for legislation in this field. This main agreement was amended by the Agreement of 1 January 1993.

In some areas no legislation or agreements apply. In these cases employment is based on the individual employment contract. Employment of general managers, for instance, is not covered by legislation but is based on an individual contract. In practice the contract often refers to the provisions of the Employees Act.

Individual employment regulations

Contracts

The fundamental principle of law is that contracts of employment can be concluded informally. Thus, in practice, some are concluded orally. However in some specific cases employment is only valid if a written contract is drawn up, for instance in the case of articles of apprenticeship (Vocational Training Act). Where a contract has a term of notice longer than that stated in the Employees Act, and the employee is covered by these provisions, it must be agreed in writing. Certain covenants in restraint of trade must also be agreed in writing.

Wages and salaries

Minimum wage provision - There are no minimum wage provisions fixed by law, but several minimum wage provisions are incorporated in the collective agreement. The levels of pay are adjusted by individual negotiations (for non-members of trade unions) or by collective bargaining. Collective agreements on wage increases are normally negotiated every two years. The agreements are normally based either on standard wages or on a minimum rate system.

Method of payment - There are no legal requirements restricting the method of payment. In practice most employees are paid by transfer to their bank accounts. Manual workers are normally paid every fortnight; salaried employees are paid monthly. Public servants are paid in advance; employees in the private sector are paid in arrears.

Deductions from pay - A Danish employer may only deduct from the employee's salary those deductions that are required by law. The employer must withhold tax on any payment of salaries and wages,

Labour Market Contribution, the employee's contribution to the Supplementary Old Age Pension Fund and, on request from the public authorities, certain debts owned to them by the employee. Any other deductions may only be made by agreement with the employee.

Itemized pay statement - Every employee has a right to an itemized pay statement from the employer at the time payment is made, showing in writing the gross and net amounts, as well as the nature and amounts of any deductions.

Hours of work/shift work/overtime

Denmark has no legislation on maximum hours of work or required pay for overtime, shift working, night work and so on. These matters are regulated by collective agreements. The rates of such payments range from 125 per cent to 150 per cent for weekdays to 200 per cent for Sundays. There are however, statutory rules on consecutive periods of rest, weekly days of rest and limits on the working days of children and young persons.

The principal rules are as follows:

- 11 consecutive hours' rest for every 24 hour period;
- one day off for every seven day period.

Exemptions to these rules may be granted under certain circumstances. Among others they do not apply to farmers and market gardeners, or employees engaged in offshore drilling. The rules are more restrictive with regard to juveniles.

Most wage earners have a five day, 37 hour week. With effect from October 1990, the contractual working week was reduced to 37 hours for all employees.

Holidays

All employees have a statutory right to a holiday of not less than five weeks a year. Entitlement to holiday accrues during each calendar year and may be taken in the holiday year following the year of accrual. Holiday years run from 2 May in one calendar year to 1 May in the following calendar year. A full year's work, whether or not it has been with the same employer, entitles the employee to full holiday entitlement in the following holiday year.

The employer must pay the employee during holidays. The employer's obligation to make payments in respect of holidays is calculated pro rata to the employee's service with that employer in the year of accrual. However the employer is always free to pay more than the amount stated in the Act.

The holiday payments are as follows:

- Salaried employees will normally be paid full salary during the holiday period plus 1 per cent of their salary in the year of accrual.

- Wage earning employees (for instance employees who are not paid on a monthly basis) receive holiday pay from the national Holiday Giro, but not directly from their employer. Holiday pay is calculated at 12.5 per cent of wages in the year of accrual. The Holiday Giro is funded by employers who make quarterly payments at the rate of 12.5 per cent (net of tax) of the current wages.

- For both wage earners and salaried staff the employer must pay holiday allowances to the Holiday Giro upon termination of employment. Holiday allowances are calculated at 12.5 per cent of wages or salary in the year of accrual. These payments are also calculated after tax has been deducted.

Maternity provisions

Women are entitled to paid maternity leave for at least four weeks before and 24 weeks after delivery. The father can opt for paid leave for the last ten weeks of the mother's 24 week period, but only as a reduction of the mother's maternity leave. Furthermore, fathers are entitled to two weeks paid paternity leave. Both benefits are calculated on the same basis as sickness or unemployment benefit.

Woman have a legal right to return to work after their maternity leave as the employer may not dismiss her on the grounds of maternity. If the employer does dismiss her, she is entitled to compensation.

Special provisions apply to salaried employees. The salaried employee shall inform her employer of the expected date of the commencement of her maternity leave, which shall not be later than three months before the expected date of birth.

New employees are required to inform their employer if they are pregnant at the time employment commences.

Time off

Danish legislation contains many provisions which directly or indirectly entitle employees to paid time off which include those on compulsory national service (whether civil or military), elected workers' representatives, members of the Board of Directors and representatives of safety committees of the employer company.

Disciplinary and grievance procedures

There are no disciplinary or grievances procedures prescribed by law. However, if an employer is dissatisfied with an employee, the employee can be dismissed, provided that the legal or agreed notices are observed.

In the case of gross breach of contract, the employer is entitled to summarily dismiss the employee; whether such dismissal is justified is often decided by the courts. In case of dismissal the employee must be informed in writing, and the message must be delivered to the employee in person.

In cases where an employee is dissatisfied with their conditions at work, the matter can be referred to the employees' trade union representative, who can discuss the case with the employer. Where the matter cannot be agreed, the case may be taken to the Labour Relations Court.

Lay-off and guaranteed payments

Where work cannot be carried out by the employees because of lack of work, weather or supply difficulties or for some other similar reason, different provisions will apply. During a lay-off, a salaried employee is entitled to normal benefits of employment. The same rule may apply to circumstances provided for in certain collective agreements.

In other cases workers are considered unemployed. This means that workers are entitled to unemployment benefits, if they are members of an unemployment fund. The unemployment benefits can amount up to 90 per cent of the most recent wage earned (up to a specified maximum amount) and are payable from the first day of unemployment.

Period of notice

Wage earners - Neither the length of notice which wage earners must give their employer nor the length of notice which employers must give wage earners is stipulated by law. However provisions about the length of notice are in general laid down in collective agreements and often differ.

For example, the lengths of notice applying to wage earners who are members of the Danish Metal Workers' Federation are displayed in Table 1.

Table 1

Length of employment	Required notice
Less than 9 months	No notice
9 months - 3 years	21 days
3 - 6 years	49 days
Over 6 years	70 days

Special rules apply for workers over 50 years of age as illustrated in Table 2.

Table 2

Length of employment	Required notice
Over 9 years	90 days
Over 12 years	120 days

The length of notice which wage earners must give their employer is shown in Table 3.

Table 3

Length of employment	Required notice
Less than 9 months	No notice
9 months - 3 years	7 days
3 - 6 years	14 days
6 - 9 years	21 days
Over 9 years	28 days

Large-scale dismissals - Since 1 April 1978 all enterprises who employ more than 20 employees shall give at least 30 days' notice, if the number of employees dismissed exceeds 10 per cent of the staff. Legislation to this effect was enacted to comply with European Union regulations.

Salaried employees - Provisions regarding termination of employment of salaried employees are laid down in the Employees Act. The term 'salaried employees' means:

- shop and office assistants employed in buying and selling, in office work or equivalent stockroom duties;
- persons whose work consists of furnishing technical or clinical assistance (not being in the nature of handicraft or factory work) and other assistants who carry out comparable work;

- persons whose work consists wholly or mainly in directing or supervising the work of other persons on behalf of the employer;
- persons whose work is mainly of the type referred to above.

Legally, any termination on the part of a salaried employee shall be made by one month's notice to expire at the end of a calendar month.

The term of notice to be given by an employer is determined by the salaried employee's length of service (with that employer), according to the scale shown in Table 4.

Table 4

Period of service (including notice)	Notice entitlement
Less than 9 months	No notice
9 months - 3 years	7 days
3 - 6 years	14 days
6 - 9 years	21 days
Over 9 years	28 days

Where employees have 12, 15 or 18 years service with the same employer, they are entitled to an additional allowance of one, two or three months' salary, respectively. Salary may be paid in lieu of notice.

If an employee has agreed to give more than one month's notice to the employer (which is the minimum legal requirement), then the employer must make a similar increase in the period of notice given to the employee.

In the case of a gross breach of contract on the part of the employee, the employer is entitled to terminate the contract of employment immediately without having to pay any salary in lieu of notice.

Dismissal

The principal rule of Danish law is that employers are entitled to dismiss employees according to their own judgement, provided that the legal or agreed notice periods are observed. However the Employees Act, special laws and collective agreements contain provisions about unfair dismissal:

- If the employer refuses to accept the services of the salaried employee, terminates the employee's contract of employment without good cause, or terminates the employee's contract by reason of the employer's gross breach of contract, the employer shall be liable to pay the employee compensation. This compensation shall, at least, be equivalent to the amount of notice that the employee should have received upon termination of employment.
- It should be noted that there is no provision for reinstatement of the dismissed employee.
- If the dismissal is not deemed reasonably justified by the conduct of the employee or the circumstances of the enterprise, the employer shall pay compensation.
- Pregnancy, maternity leave or adoption may not be used as grounds for dismissal. Where an employee is dismissed for any of these reasons, the employer shall pay the employee compensation. The amount of compensation is determined in accordance with the employee's period of service and any other relevant circumstances, but is limited to a maximum of 78 weeks' salary.
- If the reason for the dismissal is the employee's membership or non-membership of a particular trade union, the compensation paid by the employer shall not exceed 78 weeks' salary.
- As a general rule employees elected as representatives or spokesmen cannot be dismissed for these reasons. Similar provisions apply to employees who are members of Boards of Directors and safety committees. Protection of employment in such cases is based on collective agreements. Such representatives are also normally entitled to longer periods of notice than other employees.

Redundancy

Employers are entitled to dismiss employees for reason of redundancy provided that the legal or agreed notices are observed. Since 1 April 1978, all enterprises employing more than 20 employees must give at least 30 days' notice in the case of large-scale dismissals. Large-scale dismissals are defined as dismissals of more than 10 per cent of the employer's workforce. Other conditions apply for large co-operations.

The employer is obliged to negotiate with the employees or their representatives to avoid or limit the number of dismissals.

In the case of disposal of an enterprise, the disposal in itself must not constitute a reason for dismissal. However a dismissal may be effected if it is based on economic, technical or administrative reasons.

Whether the employee is entitled to compensation in addition to his or her normal salary depends upon the employee's length of employment. This entitlement stems from the general provisions stated in the Employment Act or in the collective agreement concerned.

An Employees' Guarantee Fund has been established by law for the purpose of ensuring that employees do not lose their claim to salary if the employer goes into bankruptcy or becomes insolvent. The Fund refunds salary immediately if this situation arises. The refund cannot exceed Dkr 75 000 per employee after tax, exclusive of holiday allowance. After payment is made to the employees, the Fund enters the employees' claim for salary on the list of claims against the employer.

The employer contribution to the Fund is referred to in the section on 'Pensions, Tax and Insurance'.

Collective employment regulations

There are 26 different trade unions affiliated to the Danish Council of Trade Unions (LO). The Danish LO has approximately 1.5 million members. Some national unions are not affiliated to the LO. The

Federation of Danish Employers (DA) has over 23 000 members, representing 37 trading and industrial organisations. The largest organization affiliated to the DA is the Confederation of Danish Industries (*Dansk Industri*), which has half the members of the DA.

The status of the two parties is based on the September Agreement of 1899. The so called Main Agreements of 1960, 1973 and 1981 that were concluded by the LO and DA are the fundamental basis of the collective labour laws and as such they work as a substitute for legislation.

- The Main Agreement establishes formally that employees have a right to be members of trade unions. On the other hand, if an employee does not want to be a member of a particular trade union, the employer cannot dismiss the employee for non-membership.
- Collective agreements on general wage increases, working hours, holidays and other working conditions are negotiated every two years, but usually run for a four year period. The agreements are mutually binding on the parties and their members. If the parties fail to reach an agreement, there is recourse to the Official Mediator. If the parties are still unable to reach an agreement, Parliament is entitled to enact legislation to adjust wages and working conditions for the next two year period.
- If the parties cannot reach agreement, employees can resort to strikes and blockades while employers can resort to lockouts and boycotts. The steps mentioned are directly justified in the Main Agreement.

Neither party may take industrial action during the negotiation of the collective agreements. When the representatives of LO and DA have succeeded in reaching a collective agreement, it is only binding on the employees and the employers if a majority of LO and DA members vote in favour of the agreement. If there is a majority of votes against the agreement, legal strikes and lockouts may take place.

Employee participation

Trade unions have no legal right to be represented on the Board of Management of an enterprise. However, the Danish Companies Act and an Act relating to business related funds provide that, in all Danish companies having more than 35 employees, and in which the average number of employees in the preceding three years exceeded 35, the employees have a right to elect among them a representative to be a member of the Board of Directors. The number of members elected by the employees can be equivalent to half the number elected to the Board of Directors by the shareholders, but not less than two.

Danish registered companies which constitute a group are covered by similar provisions, which means that the group's employees shall also be entitled to elect among them representatives and substitutes for such representatives to the Board of Directors of the parent company.

Pensions, tax and insurance

Income tax and national insurance

All Danish employers are required to withhold income tax ('A-tax') on any payment or credit entry of salaries, wages and similar income ('A-income'). The employer shall pay the tax withheld to the tax authorities on behalf of the employee. Under certain circumstances the employer's payment of driving and travelling allowance is exempted from tax.

The amount of tax withheld is calculated separately for each employee on the basis of a tax certificate issued by the tax authorities which the employee must give to his employer. If such a certificate is not given to the employer, 60 per cent of the salary must be withheld. At the beginning of each calendar month (not later than the tenth day) the employer is required to pay to the tax authorities the 'A-tax' withheld during the previous month.

The PAYE system is administered by the Employers' Control Department, which has an office in each department of the local Tax and Customs authorities. In addition, the employer has to withhold the so called Labour Market Contribution and the employee's contribution to the Supplementary Old Age Pension Fund (the ATP Fund). Contrary to tax and Labour Market Contributions, the contribution to the ATP Fund must be paid to the authorities on a quarterly basis.

The financing of the social security system has been reorganized with effect from 1 January 1994. Prior to this, social security was primarily financed through the taxes. Under the new system both employer and employee must, in principle, contribute to the three new Labour Market Funds. However, only employees must contribute to the funds during the period 1994 - 1996.

The employer must withhold the employee's Labour Market Contribution (in 1994, it was 5 per cent of the employee's gross salary including some fringe benefits). Employers do not have to contribute to the Labour Market Funds before 1997. In 1997 the employer's contributions will amount to 0.8 per cent of the salary (inclusive of some fringe benefits) per employee.

Besides the Labour Market Contribution, employers pay a contribution per employee to the Supplementary Old Age Pension Fund (ATP) amounting to approximately DKK 2 340, of which approximately DKK 1 170 per annum per full-time employee is refunded by the state. Employees are required to pay DKK 778 per year to the ATP Fund which is withheld by the employer.

Certain employers are not liable to VAT but must, in accordance with specific rules, pay a payroll tax (*lønsumsafgift*). The amount of the payroll tax varies depending upon the occupational group. For example doctors, dentists and travel agencies pay 2.5 per cent and banks, insurance companies, and stockbrokers pay 4.5 per cent of the total remunerations plus 90 per cent of the wage costs, or the company's loss/profit.

Industrial injuries insurance - Premium rates are assessed on a per capita basis varying according to the type of work being done. The employer must insure his employees against industrial injuries with a recognised insurance company. However, with effect from 1 January 1988, a grant amounting to Dkr 1 800 per employee is given by the state towards the employer's premium for industrial injuries insurance.

According to the enabling legislation the insurance must cover:

- medical treatment;
- compensation for loss of working capacity;
- compensation for disablement;
- compensation for death.

The annual amount of compensation given to an injured employee is stipulated on the basis of the employee's annual salary. Disabled people would generally receive, in addition to this amount, a state disablement pension.

Sickness benefit

From 2 April 1990 wage earners are entitled to receive from their employer up to five weeks' sick pay, at the rate of 90 per cent of their current wage (up to a maximum amount). After one week of sickness, sick pay is refunded to the employer by the state. Under certain circumstances the employer may be excused from payments. For example, small companies can avoid making sickness payments if they pay a contribution equal to 0.8 - 1.6 per cent of the wage costs to the Sickness Payments Fund (*Dagpengefonden*). Payments are suspended regarding temporary employees and in cases of fraudulent information regarding health.

Salaried employees are entitled to receive normal salary for up to 120 days' sickness. The employer may from 1 April 1990 recover from the state any payments (up to a maximum amount) made in respect of sickness for a period of more than two weeks.

In certain circumstances a female employee is entitled to half her salary, provided her absence is due to unfitness for work as defined in the Employees Act. When a female employee also receives a maternity benefit during this period, the employer takes over her right to that benefit. However the employer will only be refunded 90 per cent of the salary paid.

As stated above, maternity leave covers the period from four weeks before delivery to 24 weeks after delivery. However, if the employee is still unable to work as a result of her pregnancy, she is entitled to receive sickness payment, provided a proper medical certificate is submitted to her employer.

Retirement pensions

The social security system also provides for old age pensions (from age 67 for men and 62 for single women) and supplementary early retirement pensions (from age 60 for both men and women, on application). In general, occupational pension schemes (established with banks or insurance companies) are made available only to salaried employees. There are no legal requirements in this respect, or in respect of other fringe benefits.

Health and safety

Health and safety at work is governed primarily by the Work Environment Act, which came into force on 1 July 1977 and covers both trade and industry. The purpose of the Act is to ensure that enterprises have a safe and healthy working environment.

The Act applies to all people at work: public servants as well as employees in the private sector. Implementation of the Act is the responsibility of the Ministry of Labour, but this responsibility is delegated to a central Work Environment Council and local safety committees on which employees and trade unions are represented.

The more important parts of the Act concern:

- hours of work;
- safety committees: most enterprises must establish safety committees which represents employees; the employer is obliged to ensure that the members of the safety committee have sufficient knowledge of safety and health;

- industrial health service: the health service acts in a consultative capacity; its main objective is to supply preventive medicine.

Anti-discrimination regulations

Since 1978 anti-discrimination legislation has been in force. The legislation provides for equal treatment of men and women in employment, transfer or promotion. In addition, men and women at the same place of work must be treated equally with regard to working conditions, dismissal, training and so on. The Act prohibits dismissal due to pregnancy.

According to recent legislation, an employer cannot dismiss an employee because the employee is a member of a trade union. In addition, an employer cannot dismiss an employee as a result of the employee's non-membership of a trade union, unless the employee was aware that membership of a particular trade union was a prerequisite condition of the employee's employment.

Regulatory bodies

The Labour Relations Court

If conflicts arise between two parties governed by a collective agreement, both parties normally endeavour to settle them through the Labour Relations Court. The Court also deals with disputes about the interpretation of collective agreements, infringements of them and individual cases regarding collective agreements of salary and working conditions. The Court may impose fines in cases of collective infringement. Fines are in principle stipulated on the basis of economic losses and as a sanction. At present fines imposed in connection with strikes which are contrary to the collective agreements are normally fixed at Dkr 27 per man hour of strike for unskilled workers and Dkr 32 for skilled workers. The fines are raised Dkr 20 per man hour after one week of strike.

If the trade union concerned supports a strike which is contrary to a collective agreement, the Labour Relations Court can impose a fine upon the trade union.

Foreign employees

Work and residence permits

Individuals arriving in Denmark to work must first obtain a work and residence permit before arrival.   The permit is obtainable on application to the official Danish representative at the place of departure.   Work and residence permits are usually granted to specialised managerial staff of Danish subsidiaries or branches of foreign companies.

Citizens of the Nordic countries (for instance Denmark, Finland, Iceland, Norway and Sweden) may enter Denmark freely without any work and residence permit. Citizens of the European Union countries must apply for a residence permit, but do not need a work permit according to the provisions of the European Union law.   The application must be filed with the local Chief of Police in Denmark.

People taking up residence in Denmark must register with the National Register in the municipality in which they settle not later than five days after arrival. The registration is automatically reported to the tax authorities.

Recruitment and training

Recruitment

The State Employment Service offers free services and provides contact between those seeking employment and employers. It also gives assistance regarding choice of business and education. Private recruitment bureaux need a special licence.

Training

There is free and equal access to education, which is financed almost entirely out of public funds. Most education incudes vocational elements in the last stages of schooling.

The proportion of school leavers who receive little or no further education is falling. Even unskilled workers may receive vocational training. Employers contribute to the cost of such training programmes under collective agreements.

In recent years the educational system as a whole has given increasing weight to a longer education with a technical or commercial content.

This chapter was written by Böje Nansen, Elizabeth Brandt and Mette Müller, Coopers & Lybrand, Denmark.

Finland

Introduction

In Finland regulation of employment and labour relations is effected partly by statutes and partly by voluntary agreements and procedures. The key concept of labour law is the employment relationship. It is defined as a legal relationship in which one party, the employee, under a contract and for remuneration performs work for the other party, the employer, under the latter's direction and supervision. The concept of the employment relationship is used to define the scope of application of the various items of legislation in the field of labour law.

Collective agreements regulate in a very detailed manner the terms of employment relationships.

Individual employment regulations

The Employment Contracts Act (1970) regulates the employment contracts concluded individually between employers and employees. The employer and employee are in principle free to agree on the terms of their relationship: the provisions of the Employment Contracts Act are to a large extent optional. They are applicable only as far as the parties have not agreed otherwise. The Act also contains a number of mandatory provisions over which the parties have no power.

Contracts

The contract can be concluded orally but it must be evidenced in writing if either party demands it. A contract of employment may be concluded permanently or for a fixed term. If the contract is for a fixed term it cannot last for more than five years. A contract for a fixed term must be for a special reason, such as work of a stand in nature, traineeship or work of a similar nature.

Wages and salaries

Minimum wage provision - There is no minimum wage or salary provision. However there are minimum wage or salary provisions in some collective agreements. Collective agreements on wage increases are normally negotiated yearly or every two years.

Method of payment - There are no legal requirements restricting the method of payment. By far the most common is by transfer to the employee's bank account.

Deductions from pay - An employer is entitled to make only those deductions required by law, tax withholdings and deductions ordered by court decisions. The employer and employee can agree on other deductions, such as trade union membership fees.

Itemized pay statement - The employer is obliged to inform the employee about deductions related to taxes withheld by means of a pay-slip or similar arrangement. Otherwise the details of the wage and salary slips may be specified in the collective agreements or follow local custom. As a general rule all deductions from gross pay are specified on the slip.

Hours of work/shift work/overtime

In accordance with the general act on hours of work the normal hours of work are eight hours a day and 40 hours a week. Weekly hours can be averaged over a certain period. Many collective agreements allow for hours varying between 36 and 40 hours.

Holidays

The statutory minimum holiday is four weeks. Employees who have been working for over one year for the same employer are entitled to five weeks during each holiday year. An employer is obliged to negotiate with the employees regarding the arrangement of holidays.

Maternity provisions

The birth of a child entitles the parent to 11 months' leave without pay. This leave will be compensated through the social security system. The parents may themselves decide to some extent which one takes the leave to care for the child. A parent is allowed to return to his or her job after the leave.

Time off

Collective agreements have several provisions for employees to take time off, for example for union activities, education and care of a minor or children.

By law employment cannot be terminated in connection with compulsory or voluntary military service.

Disciplinary and grievance procedures

Summary termination of employment is possible but must be based on serious and intentional offences such as prolonged absence without permit, refusal to carry out duties, violence and certain crimes.

Employees have the right to terminate employment immediately if the employer has seriously neglected duties, for instance by allowing prolonged delays in paying wages.

Lay-off and guaranteed payments

The right of an employer to lay-off employees is regulated by law and collective agreements. The lay-off can as a general rule be carried out at 14 days' notice. Maximum lay-off period is 90 days if not otherwise agreed in the relevant collective agreement. During lay-offs an employee is entitled to normal benefits of employment such as holiday and sick pay, but the employer is not obliged to pay wages or salaries.

Period of notice

Employers are entitled to a minimum of one month's notice from the employee if the latter has been employed for a period not exceeding ten years and to a minimum of two months' notice in other cases. Employees are entitled to a minimum of two months' notice. The period of notice is gradually increased to six months when the employee has been employed for a period exceeding 15 years.

Dismissal

An employment contract can be terminated by the employer only if sufficient reason exists. Dismissal may be connected either with the capacity or conduct of the employee or with the operational needs of the employer. A merely temporary reason such as an illness not causing permanent disability or provisional reduction of the work to be done is not sufficient.

The dismissal must be effected within a reasonable time after the ground for the dismissal has been established. The law contains detailed provisions about the procedures for settling the disputes. A dismissal effected without appropriate grounds entitles the employee to remuneration which varies between an amount corresponding to the salary between three and 20 months.

Redundancy

In general employers are entitled to dismiss personnel according to their own judgement, if the legal notices are obeyed. Information about large-scale dismissals has to be given to employees' representatives before such a decision is finally made, if there are more than 30 employees working in a firm.

There are different rules in collective agreements for compensation beyond normal salary.

Collective employment regulations

Collective law

A collective agreement according to the Collective Agreements Act concerns employment terms and conditions concluded by one or more employers or employer associations on the one hand, and by one or more employee associations on the other. A collective agreement is concluded either for a definite period not exceeding four years or until further notice. In practice most collective agreements are concluded for one or two years.

About 80 per cent of the labour force in Finland is unionized and the degree of employer's organization is equally high. A collective agreement is binding not only on the parties to the agreement but also on associations, employers and employees that are, directly or through one or more intermediate associations, members of the associations which are parties to it. If an industry-wide or craft-wide collective agreement exists its terms shall be applied (in addition) as minimum conditions by all employers in that field irrespective of whether they belong to the employers' association which has concluded the agreement.

Trade disputes

As long as a collective agreement is in force any strike, go slow, lock-out or any other industrial action relating to the agreement as a whole or part of it is prohibited. The parties to the collective agreement and their subordinate bodies are obliged to avoid industrial action and to take active steps to preserve peace on the labour front. This does not apply to individual employees. After a collective agreement expires employees can pressure employers by means of strikes, go slows and similar means. Employers may similarly apply lockouts.

Employee participation

Cooperation within enterprises

The purpose of the Co-operation within Enterprises Act (1979) is to give employees a say in decisions affecting their work. The Act applies to all enterprises employing 30 persons or more.

Keeping employees informed

The employer is obliged to give employees' representatives access to a full statement of accounts, inform them of the financial state of the enterprise, and show them the personnel plan for at least one year prior to enforcement of such. The employer must also reveal pay statistics to the categories of employees concerned.

Negotiating with employees

The employer must consult the employees involved before making any decision on the following matters:

- major acquisitions;
- major changes to job descriptions or methods of work organization;
- the number of employees assigned to each operation;
- transfers of employees from one job to another;
- timing of rest periods and meal breaks;
- timing the start and end of regular working hours;
- organization of working premises;
- changes to the product mix or services offered to customers;
- major enlargement or retrenchment of the enterprise;
- transfer of operations from one locality to another;
- utilization of outside labour.

Co-determination

The employer and employee representatives must agree on shop rules and training in cooperation before these can be put into effect.

Employees' authority

Social matters such as the allotment of company residences, provision of canteen and child care services, the use of staff premises and leisure activities for employees are for the staff to decide unless otherwise agreed.

Pensions, tax and insurance

Income tax and national insurance

Social security employee contributions are around 3 - 4 per cent of gross salaries, while employers pay 5 - 6 per cent of payroll. Pension contributions by employees are 3 per cent and by employers approximately 15 per cent of the gross salary.

Employers have a statutory obligation to withhold taxes and other charges from the pay of the employees. The withholded amount also covers the employee's contribution to social security. Employers must remit these to the state within ten days of the end of the tax month. The employer is liable for any deductions which are omitted.

Sickness benefit

Every person is insured against the costs incurred in illness. The insurance covers a portion of physician's fees, test and treatment, travel costs and medicines. Some medicines are entirely free. In addition many collective agreements oblige employers to continue to pay salaries while the employee is on sick leave.

Retirement pensions

People without income receive only the national pension. Employers are required by law to arrange pension security for their employees. The aim is to provide a pension on the level of 60 per cent of the employee's earnings by the end of this century.

Health and safety

Health and safety at work is regulated by the working environment legislation. It covers almost every type of work. The working environment must be satisfactory with regard to the nature of the work carried out.

All employers must take out insurance against liability for personal injury and disease suffered by their employees in the course of or arising from their employment. The insurance premium varies with the degree of danger of the work and it may represent a large part of the employer's social charges.

Anti-discrimination regulations

Anti-discrimination at work is regulated in the Act on Equality between Women and Men adopted in 1986. The Act is applicable to all employers irrespective of size and to employees and applicants. The provisions therein are compulsory and may not as a general rule, be superseded by way of collective or other agreement.

An unequal treatment, or any measure having a similar effect, of women and men based on their sex is prohibited. Discrimination is prohibited inter alia when employing, promoting and selecting people for training.

Where an employer discriminates against an employee or applicant, that person will be able to bring legal action against the employer. Where the legal action is successful, the employer will be liable to pay damages of between FIM 10 000 and FIM 30 000, depending upon the seriousness of the breach.

The Equality Commissioner and the Equality Board are responsible for supervising and enforcing the anti-discrimination provisions. The Board may issue statements upon request, and prohibit any action which is considered to be discriminatory.

In addition, the Criminal Code provides penalties for other types of discrimination.   Any person carrying out business activities who discriminates against any other person by not applying the same conditions to that person as applied to others, on the grounds of race, nationality, ethnic origin or religion, will be liable to fines or imprisonment.

Regulatory bodies

Finland has a permanent National Conciliator's office to deal with disputes that arise in the course of collective bargaining. Conciliation, as such, is binding on the parties to the dispute. They are, however, entirely free to accept or reject the conciliator's proposals.

The Labour Court deals with disputes arising out of the interpretation of collective agreements and fixes damages to be paid for breaking such agreements. Its decisions are final.

The Finnish Employers' Confederation (TT) deals with industrial construction and transport business. The Employers' Confederation of Service Industries in Finland (LTK) deals with service industries.

The main employees' central unions are:

- the Central Organisation of Finnish Trade Unions (SAK), which represents mainly blue-collar and low grade salaried employees;
- the Confederation of Salaried Employees (TVK), which represents white-collar employees;
- the Confederation of Technically Skilled Employees (STTK), which represents technically skilled employees and supervisors mainly on a professional basis;
- AKAVA, which represents academically skilled and others with higher education.

Foreign employees

A foreign employee, if not a national of a state member of the European Economic Area (EEA), must acquire a work and a residence permit. The permits may normally be acquired through Finland's representative abroad before arriving in Finland. The employer must therefore contact the Finnish Embassy abroad before the permission can be granted. In general, the permission request is handled by the Ministry of Interior in cooperation with the Ministry of Labour. The time for the residence permit normally corresponds to the durance of the employment relationship although the initial residence permit is generally granted for six months after which it may be extended.

An EEA national may enter Finland simply with a valid travel document. An EEA national may stay in Finland for a period not exceeding three months without a permit after which a residence permit must be acquired. The residence permit is normally granted automatically if the applicant is employed.

Recruitment and training

There are very few provisions relating to employee recruitment and training in law. All vacant jobs are notified to the local labour offices which operate under the Ministry of Labour. This does not, however, prevent each employer from recruiting personnel in the most suitable way. So in practice recruitment is done through newspapers or head-hunting firms when executives are sought.

Employee training is mostly voluntary. There are provisions in some collective agreements which state that before dismissing employees the employer must try to arrange training for them which would enable them to take up new jobs within the firm.

This chapter was written by KHT-yhteisö Coopers & Lybrand Oy, Finland. For information on this chapter, please contact Merja Raunio and Kai Wist.

France

Introduction

Labour legislation in France is intended to offer overall protection to employees. Such legislation, whether it is included in the Labour Code (*Code du Travail*) or not, is considered to represent the minimum protection available. Collective agreements (*conventions collectives*) prevail only if they grant significantly improved benefits than those required by law. Similarly clauses in individual employment contracts are only enforceable if they are more advantageous to the employee than the terms of existing legislation and the collective agreements.

Recent legislation, in particular the 'Auroux Laws' of 1982, reflects a trend towards giving employees and the government a greater say in the running of the company and has tended to complicate the mechanics of labour relations. Legislation introduced in 1986 also removed some restrictions on employers, particularly by removing the requirement to obtain the approval of the labour authorities before introducing dismissals on economic grounds. There has also been a trend towards employee profit-sharing in their enterprises.

The information contained in this chapter reflects the general employment law situation in France, and in that respect is non-exhaustive.

Individual employment regulations

Contracts

There is a legal distinction between an employee and a mandataire social. Persons in a relationship of legal subordination to the company are employees and are regulated by the labour legislation. Persons who manage or run the company are treated as non-employees and are not covered by this legislation.

Although the labour legislation does not define a 'contract of employment', there is a large consensus as to its definition.   A 'contract of employment' is an agreement under which a person undertakes to perform work in the service of, and to act under the authority of another person in return for remuneration.

Since 1 July 1993, it is mandatory for employers to give employees a written contract of employment, including the employment of part-time employees, and employees on fixed term, temporary, or intermittent contracts of employment. A written contract is required for foreign nationals who wish to obtain a residency or work permit in France.

Where there is an applicable collective agreement in force, the employment relationship will be governed by that agreement and the terms and conditions of that agreement will become incorporated into the individual's contract of employment. Many collective agreements require the employer to give the new employee some form of written contract which details the employee's entitlement to remuneration, hours of work, holidays, fringe benefits, duties and so on.

Employees can only be employed under fixed term contracts where the jobs are not linked to the company's normal activities. Fixed term contracts may only be used for specific purposes or tasks, which would include such instances as replacement of an employee on maternity leave, temporary increases in the business or temporary contracts entered into under government regulations. Fixed term contracts can only be renewed once and the total duration of the contract should generally not exceed 18 months.

Wages and salaries

Minimum wage provision - The national minimum wage in France is currently Frs 6 009.64 (gross) per month (1 July 1994). Salaries are fixed by reference to legally enforceable collective agreements, which are negotiated annually. Such collective agreements are concluded either between employees' representative bodies and employers' professional organizations (in which case all employer members of the professional organization are bound by the agreement) or in respect of sectors for which an agreement already exists and has, by government decision, been extended to cover all employers in that sector. However all employers are required to pay their employees at least the minimum wage (SMIC) laid down by law, unless the collective agreement specifies a higher minimum wage, which must be paid.

Method of payment - In certain cases wages can be paid in cash; however salaries in excess of Frs 10 000 must be paid by cheque or bank transfer and the majority of employers use one of these methods. Salaries must be paid monthly at the place of work.

Deductions from pay - Social security contributions are deducted at source from the employee's wages. This is not the case for income tax, which is payable directly by the employee.

Itemized pay statement - A detailed pay-slip must be provided with each payment, indicating the number of working hours used to calculate the salary, the gross salary, details of all deductions (employer and employee deductions) and an accurate description of any payments in addition to the basic salary.

Hours of work/shift work/overtime

By a law dated 1 February 1982, the working week was reduced to 39 hours. The number of hours worked in a single day cannot exceed ten without authorization of the labour authorities.

Women and children under the age of 18 are prohibited from working at night, with certain exceptions for women and by derogation granted by the labour authorities for children. The rate of pay for night work is higher than for an equivalent job performed during the day and is fixed in the collective agreement or by negotiation.

Overtime is also paid at a higher rate and employees are entitled to claim time off in addition; collective agreements may provide for a higher rate of remuneration in lieu of time off. The number of hours of overtime worked in a given year may not exceed 130, unless authorization is obtained from the labour authorities.

Holidays

All employees are entitled by law to two and a half days' annual holiday pay per month worked. Bank holidays are additional, although a total of five Saturdays is included in the annual amount. Employees are entitled to full pay for bank holidays. The period of reference for the accrual of rights to holiday pay is 1 June to 31 May and holidays are normally taken between 1 June and 31 October. Paid holidays not taken during the year following the one in which the entitlement is accrued is forfeited.

At the time of termination of the contract of employment, the employee is entitled to the holiday pay accruing at that date unless dismissed for having committed a serious offence.

Maternity provisions

Female employees are entitled to a total of 16 weeks' maternity leave paid from social security unless the collective agreement provides for such payment by the employer: six weeks prior to birth and ten weeks after. This leave is extended for the birth of the third and any subsequent child to a total of 26 weeks. The employer may not terminate the contract of employment while the employee is pregnant or for one month following the period of maternity leave. However, the employee is free to resign during her pregnancy without notice being served. Fathers are entitled to three days' paid leave following the birth or adoption of a child.

At the end of the paid maternity leave, employees who have at least one year's service are entitled to claim an additional 12 months' leave, in principle without pay unless provision is made to the contrary in the collective agreement. Alternatively the employee can elect to work part-time during this period. It is also possible to claim two further years' leave (in which case the contract of employment is terminated but the employee must be re-hired on a priority basis to fill any position for which she is qualified) or part-time work. Recent legislation has extended to the father of the child the possibility of taking parental leave.

While in theory an employee whose contract of employment is terminated during her pregnancy or absence on maternity leave must be reinstated, in practice the employer can simply be required to pay the salary due up to the end of the period of maternity leave, plus any damages awarded to the employee as a result of civil or penal sanctions.

Time off

All employees who act as representatives of the workforce are entitled to a certain number of paid hours in which to perform their duties. These hours are remunerated in the same way as the hours actually worked. Overtime pay is due for attendance at meetings which extend beyond normal working hours.

Employees under notice are entitled to paid time off to seek new employment.

Disciplinary and grievance procedures

All companies with more than 20 employees must draw up internal rules setting out, in particular, the disciplinary measures to be taken in the event of a breach of the rules, particularly those relating to health and safety. In order to protect employees, the law lays down the procedure to be followed by employers in applying such measures. In the first instance, employees must be informed of the reasons for the sanctions and be allowed to state their case. The employee must then be officially notified of the measures to be taken. This procedure must also be followed when an employee is given an official warning.

The law lays down no minimum standards, leaving employers free to formulate their own rules and procedures according to their business circumstances. However the courts will intervene if any penalties imposed by the employer are considered unfair.

Trial periods

Trial periods are not compulsory for contracts of employment for an indefinite period, except if provided otherwise in the collective agreements. If the contract of employment or letter of appointment does not specify a trial period, then the appointment will be permanent from the commencement of employment. If the collective agreement applicable to the employee contains the possibility of a trial period, then that trial period will apply unless the individual contract of employment contains a provision to the contrary.

When determining the duration of the trial period, consideration needs to be given to the applicable collective agreement or to custom and practice in the particular trade or profession.

The duration of the trial period should never exceed the maximum period specified in the collective agreement. It may be extended or renewed with the employee's express approval if it is provided for in the collective agreement, and in circumstances which are not abusive.

For fixed term contracts up to six months duration, the trial period should be calculated on the basis of one day per week up to a maximum of two weeks. In all other cases, the trial period should not be more than one month.

Unless otherwise specified, either party may terminate the employment contract during the trial period without notice or payment in lieu. At the end of the trial period, the employee's appointment will be considered permanent and the employment contract may not be terminated except through the resignation of the employee or by dismissal by the employer.

Termination of employment

There are two types of termination of employment by the employer: the first is dismissal based on a reason related to the employee, the second is dismissal for economic reasons. In either case, the employer must have a genuine reason or serious grounds for the termination which must be specified in a written letter of dismissal to the employee. Termination without these grounds or in breach of the specified procedures constitutes unfair dismissal.

Period of notice

Statutory periods of notice are laid down in Articles L.122-6 and L.122-7 of the Labour Code, and may be improved upon in the collective agreement. The statutory periods of notice are specified in Table 1.

Table 1

Notice period	Period of service
One month	Between six months and two years
Two months	Over two years

The contract of employment remains in force during the notice period and the employee is entitled to two hours' paid absence per day to find new employment. Where the employer does not require the employee to work out the notice period, the employee should receive compensation equal to the salary and other benefits that would have been received if the employee had worked out this period.

If the employee does not give the requisite notice upon resigning, the employee should pay the employer compensation equal to the salary which would have been due during the notice period.

The parties are not required to comply with these notice periods if the contract can be terminated without notice, or if the termination takes place during the trial period, or upon the expiry of a fixed term contract.

Termination with notice

The general principle is that the employer can terminate the employee's contract on grounds related directly to the employee, at any time, by giving the employee the requisite period of notice.

The employee is entitled to notice of termination, severance pay and holiday pay in the following cases:

- general misconduct (*faute simple*) and breach of discipline, for example repeated unjustified absences from work;
- proficiency and incompetence;
- breakdown of the working relationship and a loss of confidence in the employee;
- illness and physical incapacity, which creates serious difficulties in relation to the continued operation of the company.

Termination without notice (summary dismissal)

The employer may summarily dismiss an employee where the gravity of the breach is of such seriousness that it is impossible for the parties to continue the employment relationship. These categories have been identified as follows:

- flagrant misconduct (*faute lourde*) for example violence;
- gross misconduct (*faute grave*) for example insubordination.

Where an employee is summarily dismissed, the employee loses any rights to notice and severance pay. In cases of flagrant misconduct, the employee also loses any entitlement to holiday pay.

The employee may terminate the employment contract without notice where there has been a real and serious breach of the employment relationship by the employer. For example a failure to pay the employee, unilateral variation of the employment contract, abusive vexatious instructions and so on.

Fixed term contracts

Where a fixed term contract has been terminated before its expiry date (except in cases of flagrant or gross misconduct), the terminating party must pay the other party an indemnity equal to the salary and other benefits which would have been payable up to the expiry date of the contract. In some circumstances, the terminating party may be liable for damages for any additional loss suffered as a result of the early termination.

Termination by the employer

Where an employer wishes to terminate an employee's contract for reasons other than economic reasons, the employer must follow a specified procedure. The employer must ask the employee to attend a meeting to discuss the envisaged termination. The employee must be notified of the meeting by registered letter. The letter must inform the employee that he or she may be accompanied by another member of staff, or if there is no staff representative, by a person outside the company chosen from a list produced by the prefect (*Commissaire de la République*). The employer must state in the letter that this list may be examined at the Town Hall or at the Labour Inspectorate (*Inspection du travail*).

The employer must explain the reasons for the termination at the meeting and give the employee an opportunity to make any explanations.

After the meeting, the employer must then confirm the termination of employment by means of another registered letter, which cannot be sent less than one full day after the meeting. Where the employee does not attend the meeting with the employer, the employer is entitled to continue with the termination procedure.

The notice period will commence as from the date the employee receives the second registered letter.

Termination by the employee

An employee may terminate the contract of employment either verbally or in writing, as there is no specified form of termination. Where the contract is terminated verbally, the circumstances must show that there has been a clear and final decision on the part of the employee to do so. The employer cannot infer that the employee has terminated the contract of employment where the circumstances indicate that the employee is looking for new employment or where the employee has been unjustifiably absence.

Appeal

An employee can appeal against the termination of his or her employment contract, to the Industrial Tribunal (*Conseil des Prud'hommes*). Before being heard by the *Conseil des Prud'hommes*, all cases are referred to conciliation. If successful in conciliation, the process terminates there. The *Conseil des Prud'hommes* will uphold the employee's claim where the employee has been unfairly dismissed or where the employer has breached the necessary procedures. However, in accordance with the law of 13 July 1973, only those employees with at least two years' service and who work in companies employing 11 or more employees are entitled to compensation. Those employees not covered by this law have the right to take civil action.

Where an employee fulfilling the above criteria has been unfairly dismissed, the tribunal may propose that the employee be reinstated. Where reinstatement is not practicable, the employer must pay the employee compensation equal to six months' remuneration. The employer is also liable for repaying the ASSEDIC unemployment insurance fund all or part of the unemployment benefit claimed by the employee from the date of termination up to the date of the tribunal's decision, up to a maximum of six months.

Where an employee has been fairly dismissed, but the employer failed to follow the proper procedure, the employer will be liable for one month's earnings in compensation, but will not be liable for repaying the unemployment benefit.

There is no time limit for the presentation of unfair dismissal claims to the *Conseil des Prud'hommes*.

Redundancy

Termination for economic reasons (*licenciement pour motif èconomique*) is defined as 'termination for reasons which are not related to the proficiency or conduct of the employee, but resulting from a reduction or transformation of employment levels or from a substantial technological change'.

Although not required by law, the employer usually consults with the works council, or in the works council's absence, with the employee's representatives, when an employee is to be made redundant. The employer must send the employee a letter by registered mail inviting them to attend a meeting. The employee should be told that they may be accompanied by another member of staff. At the meeting the employer is obliged to offer the employee a retraining contract, which is an agreement entered into and financed by the unemployment authorities, the employer and the employees. The employee has 21 days to either accept or refuse this offer. Where the employee accepts the retraining contract, the contract of employment is terminated by mutual agreement.

The employer must wait for a certain period of time, depending on the number of employees laid off, before sending a registered letter to the employee confirming the redundancy. This letter should state the reason for the redundancy, the time period for accepting the retraining contract, and the fact that the employee has the right to priority in terms of re-employment by the employer. The letter should specify how the employee could apply for this priority. If the employee requests, the employer should include a list of the criteria used in selecting him or her for redundancy.

The employer must then notify the redundancy to the Labour Inspectorate.

Appeal

As in the case of termination for non-economic reasons, the employee may take action in Court to challenge the 'real and serious' reason for the redundancy. If the termination is found to be without cause, abusive, or procedurally incorrect, the employee has the same rights as for ordinary termination.

If the employer fails to consult the works council or the staff representatives before carrying out the redundancy, it may constitute a further criminal offence and be taken into consideration when determining if the dismissal was abusive.

'Protected employees'

The following groups of employees enjoy a 'protected status' against termination, except in cases of misconduct or for economic reasons. These include:

• *Candidates for and members of safety, hygiene and work conditions committee or works council*

Candidates campaigning to be members or deputy members of a works council will be protected from termination of employment for the period of three months from the date of notice of candidacy. Current or former members of a works council, and a safety, hygiene and work conditions committee will receive protection throughout the term of their duties and for a further period of six months after the expiry of their duties.

Where the employer wishes to terminate an employee's contract during the protection period, the employer must consult with the works council and then obtain the consent of the Labour Inspector. The Labour Inspector has the ability to either grant or refuse consent, after making an inquiry into the redundancies. If there is no response after a period of 15 days, this equates to rejection of the redundancies. Either party may appeal against the decision of the Labour Inspector to the Minister of Labour, or to the administrative courts. The Minister of Labour's decision can be appealed to the administrative court.

Where the employer terminates a protected employee's contract in breach of these procedures, or where the decision is reversed on appeal, the employee is entitled to reinstatement and to compensation for the period between the termination and reinstatement, if the reinstatement is requested within two months of the final decision. If reinstatement is not requested, then the employee is entitled to compensation for the period between the date of termination and the two months' delay.

The employer's failure to comply with the procedure or to reinstate the employee constitutes a criminal offence which is punishable by imprisonment for a period of between two months and one year and/or a fine.

- *Union delegates*

Where an employee's candidacy or appointment to a union is known by the employer, the employee is protected from termination until such time as the candidacy becomes official.

For union delegates and former union delegates, the protection period commences as from the date the employer is notified of their appointment and continues for a period of 12 months after the expiry of their duties.

Where an employer wishes to terminate a union delegate's employment, the employer must obtain the consent of the Labour Inspector. The parties have the same rights of appeal as mentioned above.

- *Pregnant women*

An employer may not dismiss an employee from the beginning of her pregnancy until four weeks after the expiry of her maternity leave entitlement. However, the employee is free to resign during her pregnancy without notice being served.

In the case of adoption, termination is prohibited during the term of the adoption leave and for four weeks after the end of such leave. The employee's contract can only be terminated for misconduct or for reasons unconnected with the pregnancy or adoption.

Where the employer terminates the employment without cause during the period of protection, the termination will be null and void and the employer will be liable to pay the employee for any salary due during this period. In most cases the employee will be reinstated, but where reinstatement is inappropriate, the employee will receive damages in lieu thereof.

- *Candidates and members of the industrial courts*

  Candidates campaigning for membership of the industrial courts are entitled to a three month protection period. Members and former members of the industrial courts are protected from termination of employment throughout the term of their appointment and for six months after the expiry of their term. The Labour Inspector's consent is required to terminate the employee's contract during the protection period, and the same appeal rights are available as above.

- *Candidates and administrators of social security institutions and employee representatives in agricultural boards*

  Employees who are either candidates, members or former members of these institutions have the same protection period as specified for candidates, members and former members of the industrial courts. The Labour Inspector's consent is required to terminate the contracts of employment in these circumstances also.

Non-competition clause

Where the employer wishes to prevent an employee from competing directly with the company, the employer may insert a non-competition clause into the employee's contract of employment. This clause prevents the employee from participating in or competing with the company during the employee's employment, and from joining a competing business or setting up a competing business after the employment has ended.

The French Courts have held that there should be a legitimate business interest to protect before inserting a non-competition clause into an employee's contract, and that such clauses should not prevent the employee from earning a living with an occupation consistent with the employee's professional training and skills.

Non-competition clauses should be of a specified duration, restricted to a particular geographical area and limited to the employee's profession or trade. The employee is able to challenge the validity or reasonableness of a non-competition clause by taking legal action. The courts will assess the non-competition clause on a case by case basis, and may deem the clause only partially enforceable if it is too restrictive.

Most collective agreements stipulate that the employer should pay the employee compensation in consideration of the observance of the non-competition clause.   Where the amount of the compensation is specified in the collective agreement, the amount cannot be challenged by the parties in court.

Contracting out

The laws regarding termination of employment, rights to compensation or indemnity upon termination are mandatory and cannot be contracted out of. The parties are able, however, to enter into an agreement after the termination, which renounces their statutory rights in favour of an amicable settlement.

Collective employment regulations

Trade unions

There are five recognised trade unions in France: the CFDT, the CFTC, the CGC, the CGT and the FO. None of these represents a specific profession or industry and they can set up a branch in any company (without necessarily appointing a representative). Several unions can therefore be represented within a given enterprise.

These recognised national trade unions have a great deal of influence and they must be consulted in particular concerning the negotiation of all professional and interprofessional agreements. All employees are entitled to belong to a trade union and to participate in union activities. The trade unions represented in the company have certain rights to enable them to fulfil their role: a notice board, offices, free time for representatives and so on.

Only recognised trade unions can present candidates in the first round of the elections for staff delegates and representatives on the works council. Likewise only recognised trade unions can set up a union branch within a company and appoint union representatives. To be recognised by a company, a trade union must meet certain criteria, relating principally to size, independence, financial viability, experience, activities and tangible influence.

Employee representatives (Delegues du Personnel)

Companies with more than 11 employees are required to organize elections of representatives. These are elected by the staff for a period of two years and their main function is to submit to management individual or collective complaints relating to labour laws, hygiene and safety and collective agreements. They are also responsible for presenting complaints relating to labour laws to the labour authorities and they inform the works council of any observations or suggestions made by the staff. In companies which do not have a works council, representatives are consulted on economic and social matters.

Employee representatives are entitled to a certain number of paid hours to carry out their duties and they are also provided with a private notice board and office space. Company management must meet them at least once a month to discuss any problems or complaints which may arise.

Union representatives (délégués syndicaux)

The recognised trade unions represented within the company appoint representatives from among their members on the company's payroll. Trade unions' representatives can be designated only in companies where there are more than 50 employees.

Union representatives represent the trade union with company management and inform members of trade union activities. They are entitled to a certain number of paid hours to carry out their duties and are allowed free access to all employees.

Other individuals can be appointed by the trade union to represent it on the works council in a consultative role.   Such individuals are entitled to the same protection as members of the works council; however, they can be relieved of their duties at any time by simple decision of the trade union.

Works councils (comités d'entreprise)

All companies with more than 50 employees are required by law to have a works council.   The members are elected by the staff and the trade unions can appoint a representative to sit on the council in a consultative role.

Works councils act as an intermediary between the company and its employees for all matters relating to the improvement of conditions of employment and of work, and they must be consulted concerning the company's economic problems and overall policy.   They are also responsible for managing welfare and social funds within the company.

The company must provide the works council with office space and the necessary equipment, and members are entitled to a certain number of paid hours to carry out their duties.

Meetings of the works council must be convened at least once a month by company management.   Where the company has less than 150 employees, meetings must be held once every two months.

Collective terminations for economic reasons (redundancies)

There is a collective termination for economic reasons when the employer terminates two or more employees' contracts of employment for reasons unrelated to the individual.   There are different procedures depending upon the number of employees made redundant.

Procedure

Where an employer wishes to terminate less than ten employees' contracts over a period of 30 days, the employer must first meet and consult with the works council, or in their absence, the staff delegates

(*Delègues du Personnel*). The letter convening the meeting must be sent at least three days in advance and must specify the reasons for the redundancies, the number of employees involved and the proposed time schedules.

The employer must follow any criteria specified in the collective agreements when determining which employees are to be made redundant. In the absence of such criteria, the employer must consult with the works council or the staff delegates to determine which criteria will be used.

Each employee affected by the redundancy must be invited to an interview with the employer and offered a retraining contract. The employee then has 21 days to either accept or refuse this agreement.

The employer must confirm the redundancy in writing not earlier than seven days after the day of the meeting. Each redundancy letter must mention the possibility of priority re-engagement by the employer. The employer must also inform the labour authorities within eight days.

Where an employer wishes to terminate more than ten employees' contracts of employment over a period of 30 days, the employer must also consult with the works council or the staff delegates over the proposed redundancies. The letter of consultation must contain the same information as for redundancies of less than ten employees. Where the company employs more than 50 employees, the employer must also submit a social plan to the works council or staff delegates. The social plan should state how it proposes to prevent or limit the redundancies (such as a reduction in overtime, part-time employees, early retirement) and how it proposes to redeploy redundant employees (for example, retraining programmes).

There is no requirement for the employer to have individual meetings with the employees affected by the redundancy, unless there are no employee representatives. The employer is not obliged to offer employees in companies with more than 50 employees a retraining contract, as they will be covered by a social plan.

The employer must inform the labour authorities of the proposed redundancies as soon as possible after the meeting with the works council or staff delegates. The labour authorities must be informed about the reasons for the redundancies and the employees affected, as specified above. They must also receive a copy of the employer's social plan.

The labour authorities have a specified time period within which to respond to the employer if the consultation requirements have not been compiled with. A copy of this letter must also be sent to the employee representatives. The employer must then respond to the observations made by the labour authorities and send a copy of that response to the employee representatives. The affected employees must not be informed of the proposed redundancies until after this letter has been sent.

After notifying the labour authorities, the employer must wait 30 days (if between ten and 99 employees are affected), 45 days (if between 100 and 249 employees are affected) or 60 days (if over 250 employees are affected) before issuing the notices of redundancy. During this period, the employer should hold a second meeting with the works council or staff representatives. The maximum time that may elapse between the two meetings is 14 days (ten to 99 employees), 21 days (100 to 249 employees) or 28 days (over 250 employees). If the works council calls in the assistance of an accountant, the procedure will be delayed for another two to three weeks. The accountants fees are to be borne by the employer.

Special payments

Where an employee has at least two years' service under an open ended or permanent contract of employment, the employee will have certain statutory rights to severance pay, provided they have not been summarily dismissed.

For monthly paid employees, the employee must receive one-tenth of the employee's monthly salary for each year of service. For hourly paid employees 20 hours' salary per year of service. These payments are paid in the form of a tax free lump sum. These employees will also have statutory rights to holiday pay, which is paid as compensation for the holiday lost through the termination.

Collective agreements may improve upon these statutory entitlements.

Lay-off and guaranteed payments

Employees have a statutory right to a salary. In the event that an employer is in financial difficulties, employees have a general claim on the employer's assets (movable goods and real estate) up to the amount of the salaries due in respect of work actually performed plus any amounts accruing to them. They have a preferential claim over the general body of creditors.

When a contract of employment is terminated, the employee is entitled to receive the salary payable at the date of termination plus any compensation due. The amount of such compensation depends on the circumstances of the termination and the seniority of the employee. The legal indemnity is one-tenth of one month's salary per year of service; however many collective agreements provide more generous benefits for employees with more than two years' service. No period of notice and no compensation are due if the employee has committed a serious offence (*faute lourde*).

Closure of companies

The procedure for redundancies in the case of closure or insolvency of a company is almost identical to the procedure in the case of the collective dismissal of ten or more employees over 30 days. Instead of giving the employees 21 days to accept or refuse a retraining contract, the employees only have 15 days. The essential difference is that the employer is not obliged to meet twice with the works council.

Payments

Employees are guaranteed payment of their salaries through the French unemployment funds up until the announcement of the liquidation.

Employee participation

Consultation concerning the relocation of the company

The employer must consult the works council concerning the proposed relocation of the company. If such relocation implies a substantial modification of an employee's contract of employment, the employee in question can refuse to accept relocation, in which case all the indemnities due in the case of breach of contract by the employer are due.

If, on the other hand, the relocation does not entail any substantial modification of the contract of employment, any employee who does not accept the relocation will be deemed to have resigned.

Consultation concerning health, safety and working conditions

Certain measures concerning health and safety at work must be included in the internal rules of the company. Staff delegates and the works council participate in the taking of measures to prevent accidents.

Under the 1982 'Auroux Laws', all companies with more than 50 employees are required to set up a single independent body responsible for improving conditions of work and safety. This committee plays an important consultative role and also carries out studies and tests within the company, as well as conducting investigations in the event of industrial accidents or disease.

There may be exceptions in certain sectors of activity where a health and safety committee is only mandatory in companies with a headcount of more than 300 employees (in the construction industry in particular).

Employee's right of expression

The law of 4 August 1982 gives employees a free and direct right of expression within the company. This free right of expression applies to the content and organization of individual employees' jobs as well as to the improvement of overall working conditions. Any such complaints or observations can be made directly to management, without going through the normal channels (such as staff delegates, works council), during working hours and at the place of work.

Once the employees' right of expression is recognised within a company, it must be exercised on a continuous basis by means of regular meetings. This concept has applied on an experimental basis for two years and a law was passed in January 1986 laying down the method of exercising the right.

Trade disputes

The right to strike is recognised in the French Constitution. However certain restrictions are laid down concerning strike action by civil servants and improper use of this right.

Strike action must be taken on a collective basis and notice must be given for public service strikes or if the collective agreement provides for a period of notice. During a strike the contracts of the employees involved are suspended but not terminated, except where a serious offence is committed. The employees must be reinstated upon their return to work. No salary is due to employees while they are on strike.

Profit-sharing schemes

Companies with more than 50 employees must set up a profit-sharing scheme.

Pensions, tax and insurance

Income tax and national insurance

All amounts paid to employees in consequence of work performed are subject to social security contributions covering health insurance, maternity benefits and retirement and disablement pensions. Income tax is payable directly by the employee.

Sickness benefit

All employees are covered by health insurance. The normal social security benefits are usually supplemented by the complementary insurance cover. Medical and related expenses are reimbursed indefinitely in the case of chronic illness, for example; daily sickness benefits are paid for a maximum of three years, during which time the employer may be required to pay the difference between the sickness benefit and the normal salary. At the end of this period, benefits are covered by complementary insurance if any is in force.

Retirement pensions

Pensions are funded by contributions made by both the employer and the employee. All employees who have contributed for an appropriate length of time are entitled to a retirement pension when they reach 65 years of age, or earlier if they are at least 60 and have contributed for more than 37½ years.

The amount of the state retirement pension depends on the number of years during which contributions were paid and the average annual base salary for the ten highest paid years.

Many complementary retirement plans exist and all employees who contribute to the state pension scheme must also contribute to one of these plans. Different plans exist for management and non-management employees and the amount of the pension depends on the number of years during which contributions were paid, the number of 'pension points' accrued and the value of the points. These

ension schemes involve pensions being paid directly
ntributions from people who have not yet attained
The concept is different from the capitalization
y used in voluntary plans, whereby each individual
based on the total amount of contributions.

Employees in France can therefore receive retirement pensions from
three sources:

- the normal state pension paid by the social security authorities;
- a compulsory complementary pension;
- a pension subscribed to under a voluntary scheme based on the
capital contributed by the individual.

Unemployment benefit

Unemployment benefits are payable under certain conditions to
unemployed individuals. These benefits are funded by the state and
by employer and employee contributions.

Unemployment insurance funds are managed by associations known
as 'ASSEDICs', which are coordinated by a national body, UNEDIC.

Health and safety

All companies are required to lay down special rules concerning the
prevention of industrial accidents and diseases. Since 1982 a health,
safety and working conditions committee is compulsory in all
companies with more than 50 employees. In smaller companies
employee delegates carry out the functions of these committees.

Employer's duties and obligations

Employers have a duty to ensure the safety of their employees. They
are required to establish satisfactory conditions of health and safety
within the company and to ensure that these conditions are met, for
example by actively checking that safety rules are applied.

The employer can be held responsible for industrial accidents only if personal fault can be proved. The provisions of the law seek to avoid the employer being generally and automatically held responsible for industrial accidents.

Accident rates must be calculated by companies each year, with an analysis of the degree of seriousness, and transmitted to the labour authorities. Since 1982 all employees have the right to leave their post if they consider that their safety is at risk, even if a committee on health, safety and working conditions exists within the company.

Health, safety and working conditions committee (CHSCT)

These committees were introduced in 1982. They are composed of company employees and chaired by the managing director of the company. Their role consists mainly of contributing to efforts to improve the conditions of health and safety within the company and ensuring that health and safety laws and rules are respected. They are also consulted concerning proposed changes within the company which could have an impact on health and safety conditions (for example, the transformation of a work station).

The committee can call in an expert, in which case the related cost must be born by the company. Company management must provide the committee with all information and documents necessary for the exercise of its functions. The members of the committee are required to treat as confidential all information transmitted to them concerning manufacturing processes.

Anti-discrimination regulations

Race and sex discrimination

According to Article 416 of the Penal Code, an employer may not refuse to hire or dismiss a person on the grounds of gender, origins, marital status, ethnic group and so on. It is also prohibited by law to specify in job advertisements conditions relating to the gender or marital status of potential candidates.

However an employee's gender can be determined by decree to constitute an essential condition for certain positions and activities and in such cases the provisions of the law are waived.

Article 222-33 of the New Penal Code (1992) makes it a penal offence to sexually harass an employee.

Equal pay

Employers are required to give equal pay for the same or comparable jobs, and to men and women performing the same work.

Discrimination against union members

Discrimination on the grounds of union membership or union activities is also prohibited by law.

Regulatory bodies

Labour inspectors

Labour inspectors can contact companies directly to perform checks, give advice or ensure that labour laws and regulations are enforced. They have extensive powers for the performance of tests. They can enter the premises of enterprises subject to labour laws and can consult all documents and registers which are compulsory in accordance with labour regulations. Random, surprise visits can be made and the labour inspector can also visit the company's premises following an industrial accident or in cases of industrial disease.

Industrial tribunals

In the event of a dispute, an effort towards conciliation must be made before the case is put before the courts. If conciliation efforts fail, the parties present their case to the 'Bureau de Jugement du Conseil des Prud'hommes' which is the sole competent authority to rule on industrial disputes concerning employment contracts in the first instance. These tribunals are a bipartite body comprising equal numbers of employer and employee representatives. Appeals against decisions of the *Conseil des Prud'hommes* can be made to the Court or Appeal and, as last resort, to the Supreme Court (*Cour de Cassation*).

Magistrates courts (tribunaux d'instance)

Magistrates Courts are competent to rule only on certain types of industrial dispute (for example, disputes concerning elections) specified by law. Appeals against the decisions of the magistrates court can be made to the Court of Appeal and the Supreme Court.

Supreme Court (Cour de Cassation)

The Supreme Court rules only on matters of law but it has issued many useful rulings and judgments. Appeals can only be made to the Supreme Court if they are submitted within two months of the judgment by the Court of Appeal.

Foreign employees

Apart from nationals of the European Union, all foreigners need a work permit. The work permit is granted by the International Migrations Office (OMI). Before issuing a work permit, the OMI will consider the employment situation in the applicant's field. Because of the present unemployment situation, a work permit may not be granted as long as French nationals with the same experience and qualification are at OMI's disposal.

This chapter was written by Anne-Elisabeth Combes, Coopers & Lybrand, CLC Juridique et Fiscal, France.

Germany

Introduction

Originally German labour law dealt with individual service contract law as codified in the German Civil Code. It has gradually developed into a more specialized field of law with an increasing number of Acts and regulations governing the employment relationship, for example the Civil Code, Commercial Code, Dismissals Protection Law, Vacation Law, Working Time Regulations and the Corporate Pension Act. In addition, judgments of the Federal Labour Court and the European Court of Justice have become very important. There are also collective agreements negotiated between the trade unions and employers' associations.

The draft of an Employment Law Act does exist but its enactment is uncertain.

Distinct labour law principles are applied. One such principle states that where the terms of an individual contract of employment conflict with the terms of a binding collective agreement, the one which is more advantageous to the employee is applicable.

Individual employment regulations

Contracts

There are various references to employees in German labour law. Although there is no statutory definition of an 'employee', there is a definition of 'self-employed'. A self-employed person is a person who is essentially free to organize his or her own work and determine his or her own working time. As a consequence, an employee is held to be a person who is obliged to work for somebody else on the basis of a private contract in a relationship of personal subordination.

The Federal Labour Court has complicated the notion of personal subordination by introducing a number of factors to help determine the employment status of the 'employee'. Those factors include:

- whether the employer expects the individual to be available at all times to accept the new tasks;
- whether the individual is unable to refuse the tasks offered by the employer;
- whether the individual is to a certain extent integrated into the structure of the employer's organization;
- what length of time is required by the individual to perform the tasks for the employer.

Labour law applies to both white-collar employees (*Angestellte*) and blue-collar employees (*Arbeiter*). As the result of a 1990 decision made by the Constitutional Court of the Federal Republic, there is no longer a sharp distinction between blue-collar workers and white-collar employees, as the Court considered such a distinction to be unconstitutional.

Persons who are considered to be 'leading employees' (*Leitende Angestellte*) generally receive the same protection under the legislation as white-collar employees, except in the case of unfair dismissal. When seeking to terminate an employment relationship for unfair dismissal, the employer does not need to state any reasons for his or her application. In these instances leading employees are limited to damages.

Generally, the law does not require contracts of employment to be in any particular form. Written contracts are required for employees of sickness institutions, social security institutions and municipalities and districts (*Öffentlicher Dienst*) where the law requires that essential terms of employment of apprentices and trainees (*Auszubildende*) be specified in writing, after the contract has been entered into.

Employees can be employed under fixed term contracts, but the term of these contracts are subject to the scrutiny of the labour courts. In this respect, it is necessary to ensure that the term is 'reasonable' in relation to the custom of the business and the nature of the employment. Fixed term contracts can be used in certain professions where it is a customary form of employment, for example artists, or where there is a temporary increase in work or to cover for absences. If no reasonable grounds exist, then the contract will be held to be indefinite.

Fixed term contracts which are repeatedly renewed are dealt with more stringently by the labour courts. Each renewal has to be 'reasonable' and justified. In most cases fixed term contracts renewed for a second time, would be interpreted as contracts of employment for an indefinite period.

Wages and salaries

Minimum wage provision - There are no statutory requirements as to minimum wages or salaries. Collective agreements have minimum salary provisions for the various categories of employees and employers.

Method of payment - Salaries of employees are paid on a monthly basis, customarily in arrears at the end of a calendar month. Wages of workers are usually paid on an hourly basis, also usually at the end of a calendar month.

Deductions from pay - The employer has to deduct income tax from earnings, and church tax if the employee is a member of the Protestant or Catholic Church or of another religious group, if it has the rights of a public law corporation, as well as social security contributions.

Itemized pay statement - Itemized pay statements are not required by law but are issued by various employers.

Hours of work/shift work/overtime

Social employment protection includes a general ban on work on Sundays and public holidays, although there are exceptions. It also establishes a fixed maximum number of working hours per week (48 hours with variations). Within this, there is no legal limit for overtime. For overtime an additional bonus is usually paid.

Certain other laws, such as the Youth Protection Law and the Trade Law, offer special rights to those persons subject to them, in particular as to working time, notice periods and vacation.

Holidays

The minimum holiday is 18 working days a year and 20 working days in the New Territories. However almost all collective and private agreements provide for longer holiday periods for different categories of employees, for instance 22 to 30 working days a year. Payment in lieu of holiday may not be permitted except where the employee is leaving.

A holiday bonus dependent from the employee's income is provided for in many collective agreements.

Maternity provisions

Without regard to marital status, expectant mothers are protected against dismissal during their pregnancy and for the first four months following the birth of their child. Expectant mothers may not continue to work beyond the seventh week before the expected date of birth, or work for the first eight weeks following the date of the birth.

Maternity leave may be extended for a period not exceeding 36 months after the birth, in which case the mother is protected against dismissal.

Maternity benefits are payable by the health insurance fund, together with a contribution from either the employer or the Federal Government. After six months, the payment of maternity benefits is dependant upon the parents' income.

There are no special provisions for the New Territories.

Time off

Employees may have a relatively short period of time off for personal reasons, such as sickness. Time off may also be granted for extraordinary events in the family such as death, the employee's own marriage, birth of child (usually one day), court hearings, visits of a doctor and other activities such as a lay judge.

Members of a works council have to be given time off work to perform their duties. In larger enterprises (for example 300 to 600 members) there are fixed hours of time off according to the size of the enterprise. Collective agreements or an agreement between the works council and the employer may specify different regulations for time off.

In several states in the Federal Republic, employed persons are entitled to educational leave.

In all these circumstances wages and salaries continue to be paid.

Disciplinary and grievance procedures

There are no formal disciplinary or grievance procedures. Disputes are settled by the labour courts.

Trial periods

There are no legal limits on the duration of the trial period, but such periods must be 'reasonable' in accordance with the criteria used for fixed term contracts. The normal duration of a trial period is three to six months.

As an alternative, the parties may enter into a fixed term contract for the duration of the trial period. In all cases the parties can agree that the contract may be terminated with the minimum period of notice. Where a fixed term contract is continued, for example by stipulating another fixed term period, the nature of the employment changes from being fixed term into an indefinite contract.

Termination of employment

There are three principal Acts governing termination of employment. They are:

- Protection Against Dismissal Act 1969 (*Kündigungsschutzgesetz*);
- Civil Code (*Bürgerliches Gesetzbuch*);
- Works Constitution Act 1972 (*Betriebsverfassungsgesetz*).

Termination of an employee's contract under the Protection Against Dismissal Act will only be socially justified if it relates to the personality or behaviour of the employee (*personenbedingte Kündigung*) or is the result of operational reasons (*betriebsbedingte Kündigung*).

Period of notice

The law does not prescribe the form of notice of termination, therefore notice may be given verbally. However, in most cases, the contract of employment will require notice to be in writing.

The statutory minimum periods of notice are specified in the German Civil Code, but can be improved upon in contracts of employment. Generally the employer can terminate the employment contract with four weeks notice to the fifteenth of the month or to the end of the month. The period of notice increases with length of service as illustrated in Table 1.

Table 1

Notice period	Service period
1 month	2 to less than 5 years
2 months	5 to less than 8 years
3 months	8 to less than 10 years
4 months	10 to less than 12 years
5 months	12 to less than 15 years
6 months	15 to less than 20 years
7 months	More than 20 years

Service with the employer prior to the employee's twenty-fifth birthday is not taken into account.

Termination with notice

The philosophy in German labour law is that no one should remain in an employment relationship longer than they wish. Pursuant to the Protection Against Dismissal Act, an employee is protected against unfair dismissal if they have been employed in a company with five or more employees, and have six months' or more continuous service. The employer can only terminate the employee's contract of employment for socially justifiable reasons. Ordinarily the employer must give the employee notice, except where the employee has been summarily dismissed.

Notwithstanding the existence of a socially justified reason, the termination of employment will still be illegal if the employee can be transferred to a comparable job in the employer's employ, with comparable working conditions, either immediately or after retraining.

The employee is entitled to notice of termination in the following circumstances:

- misconduct or unsuitability;
- violations of obligations;
- breakdown of the working relationship.

Termination without notice (summary termination)

Termination without notice is used when any fact or circumstance is of such seriousness that it is unreasonable to expect the terminating party to continue in the employment relationship until the expiry of a notice period or, in the case of a fixed term contract, the expiration date of the contract. Such situations include:

- persistent refusal to comply with the employer's lawful instructions;
- gross breach of the contract of employment;
- criminal acts to the detriment of the employer;
- serious violation of a competition restriction or secrecy clause to the detriment of the employer.

The employee may terminate the employment contract without notice where there has been a real and serious breach of the employment relationship by the employer. Such situations include the employer's failure to pay the employee, repeated breaches of the employment contract and personal insults or derogatory remarks made about the employee by the employer.

Fixed term contracts

The term of a fixed term contract can be examined by the Court to determine whether it is 'reasonable'. Where the Court holds that the term is reasonable, the contract will automatically expire upon reaching its expiry date. Where the term is held to be unreasonable, the courts can declare the contract to be for an indefinite period. Fixed term contracts initiated at the employee's request or for a trial period are usually valid. The term for trial period contracts should not generally exceed six months.

Fixed term contracts do not automatically expire or become invalid when the employee reaches retirement age, but the parties can agree upon an expiry date in the individual contract or collective agreement.

Contracts of employment which specify that they will automatically expire upon the happening of some particular event are less likely to succeed.

Termination by the employer

The employer must notify the works council in writing of every termination, before such termination takes effect. The employer must identify the employee affected, the type of termination (whether it is with or without notice), the date the termination takes effect and the reasons for the termination.

In the case of termination without notice, it can be prudent for the employer to give the employee notice of termination, in addition to summary dismissal. This is due to the fact that many terminations without notice fail because of technical or material faults. If this occurs, the employer can rely upon the valid termination with notice.

Where termination without notice is necessary the terminating party must give the other party notice of termination within a period of two weeks of the particular circumstance which results in the termination. If the terminating party fails to notify the other party of the summary termination within this period, the right to termination without notice is forfeited.

Where an employer seeks to terminate an employee's contract with notice, the employer must give the employee a clear warning about the misconduct and provide a reasonable opportunity for the employee to improve such conduct.

Once the works council has been notified, it has three days to react to a proposed summary termination, or one week to react to a proposed termination with notice. A summary termination may proceed after the three day period regardless of the works council's opinion. In the case of proposed terminations with notice, the works council can either disagree with the termination by expressing its concerns verbally to the employer or by objecting to the termination in writing. Where the works council has announced some concerns about a proposed termination, the employer must address these concerns before proceeding with the termination. Where the works council has objected in writing to the proposed termination, the employer may not proceed with the termination but must continue to employ the employee on the same terms and conditions of employment pending an appeal.

The employer can be released from the obligation of continuing to employ the employee if:

- the employee's complaint does not appear to be reasonably successful or arbitrary;
- continued employment of the employee imposes an unreasonable financial burden upon the employer;
- the works council's objection is manifestly unfounded.

Termination by the employee

Where the employee terminates the contract of employment by giving the specified period of notice, the employee is not obliged to give any reasons. After the termination, the mutual obligations between the parties continue to exist, especially in the case of secrecy obligations.

Where an employee terminates the contract without notice and without justification, the Court can declare the notice of termination to be of no effect. Although it is very difficult to compel an employee to work, the employer may take legal action to compel the employee to perform his or her employment obligations. As an alternative, the employer may seek damages.

The employee has to return all work equipment, documents and tools. Where the employee refuses to return these items, or where the employer suspects the employee has not returned them, the employer can demand information or even a declaration from the employee.

Redundancy

A redundancy occurs where the employee's contract of employment is terminated for operational reasons, such as the reorganization of the company or a reduction in work. In these circumstances the burden of proof rests with the employer to show that operational reasons exist.

Redundancy for operational reasons will not be socially justified if the employer failed to consider the social grounds in selecting the employees affected. When choosing employees in comparable positions, the employer must consider such factors as family, age, salary, length of employment and so on, and must select those employees who require the least protection.

As with terminations for personal reasons, the works council must be consulted and must be given an opportunity of either expressly or implicitly objecting to the redundancies. The consultation process, time periods and appeal rights are identical to those outlined for individual terminations, except that the parties may make specific arrangements for payment in lieu of notice.

Notice of termination pending a change of contract

The employer can give the employee notice of termination and at the same time, offer the employee a new employment contract with different conditions. The employee can accept the new contract of employment, but reserve his or her right to bring an action for socially unjustified termination. If the employee does not react within three weeks, the offer of new employment is accepted.

Appeal

Where an employee's contract of employment has been terminated with notice and the employee is covered by the Protection Against Dismissal Act, the employee has three weeks from the date on which he or she received the notice to file a complaint in the Labour Court for socially unjustified termination. No time limit applies if the employee does not rely on the termination being socially unjustified, but relies on some other grounds. Employees not covered by the Protection Against Dismissal Act are not restricted by time limits.

The employee's complaint to the Labour Court will usually be that the contract of employment has not been effectively terminated and as such, the employment relationship continues. Even if the Court holds that the termination of employment was socially unjustified, the Court may terminate the contract of employment on application of either party where it is impossible for the employment relationship to continue. In these circumstances the Court would award compensation in lieu thereof. With leading employees, the employer can request that compensation be awarded in lieu thereof without having to specify any reasons.

In determining the amount of compensation, the Court must weigh up all the circumstances including the reasons for the termination. A general guideline is that the employee will usually receive between one half to a full month's salary for each full year of employment. The statutory maximum payment is 12 months' gross salary, which includes all other remuneration. This maximum payment is increased to 15 months' salary for those aged over 50 with at least 15 years' service and 18 months' salary for employees aged over 55 with 20 years' service.

Compensation is sometimes paid out of court in the case of termination with or without notice, or where the termination is consented to by both parties. Where there is an out of court settlement, the conditions of compensation should be defined very carefully due to social security implications (for instance the unemployment benefit).

Transfer of a company

Where a company is to be transferred, the existing employment contracts will transfer to the new owner with all the rights and duties attached. The former employer will remain liable for all obligations caused before the date of the transfer (joint liability) for a period of one year after the transfer.

For a period of one year after the transfer, the new employer is not entitled to give notice to the transferred employees, if the notice is the result of the transfer. This does not affect the employers right to give notice for reasons unconnected with the transfer.

The employee is entitled to object to the transfer of his or her employment. In this situation, the employee remains with the former employer.

'Protected employees'

There are certain categories of employees who enjoy a 'protected status' as they can only have their contracts of employment terminated after special approval by the authorities or after a certain period.

- *Members of the works council or a youth assembly*

  Members of the works council or a youth assembly will be protected against termination of employment for the duration of their membership and for a period of one year afterwards. Candidates and members of the works council election committees are protected from termination of employment from the time of nomination or appointment until six months after the date of the announcement of results.

A member of a works council or a youth assembly can only have their contracts of employment terminated if the company is required to close down. Where one part of the company closes down, the 'protected' employee must be employed in another department of the company unless there are cogent business reasons why further employment is not possible.

- *Disabled persons*

Disabled persons who fall under the Statute Securing Work for the Disabled (*Schwerbehindertengesetz*) can only be given notice of termination after six months of employment with the approval of the Principal Social Security Office. Where an employer wishes to summarily terminate an employee's contract of employment, the employer must make an application to the Principal Social Security Office within two weeks of the cause being known, and the Office has two weeks to make a decision. In other cases, the Office has one month to make a decision.

The Principal Social Security Office must ask the opinion of the Labour Office, the works council and the parties involved. Where the company closes down, the Office must give its approval to the termination of employment. Where part of the company is closing down, approval will only be granted if the employee cannot be transferred elsewhere in the company.

Decisions of the Principal Social Security Office can be appealed against to the Administrative Court.

- *Pregnant women*

An employer cannot terminate the employment of a pregnant women from the time the employer becomes aware of the employee's pregnancy, and for a period of four months after the date of birth, except in the case of summary termination.

- *Employees on military service*

   Employees on leave of absence for military service effectively have their contracts of employment suspended during this period. Consequently, it is not possible for an employer to terminate the employees's contract of employment during this period. The time the employee spends in military service counts as employment service.

- *Apprentices*

   Persons employed under an apprenticeship contract cannot have their contracts of employment terminated, as they are normally employed for a fixed term period of three years. The only exception is that an apprenticeship contract may be terminated during the trial period.

Non-competition clause

Any employee may be subject to a non-competition clause in their contract of employment, which restricts the employee from actively engaging in any business which is in competition to their employer, while still employed by the employer. Commercial employees (*kaufmannische Angestellte*) and technical employees (*Technische Angestellte*) are restricted more severely than other employees as they are subject to a statutory non-competition clause which prohibits them from engaging in any work in the employer's field, except with the employer's consent. If the employee breaches this restriction, the employer can demand damages from the employee or alternatively claim ownership of the employee's work and receive or recover any consideration paid for it.

For commercial employees, the employer has three months to make a claim for breach of a non-competition restriction, which runs from the date the employer has obtained knowledge of the work or within a period of four years after the business was transacted.

It is possible that the contract will continue to restrict the employee from competing with the employer after the employment relationship has terminated, if the following criteria is satisfied:

- the non-competition restriction is specified in writing;
- the restriction is for a period no longer than two years;
- the restriction is reasonable in terms of scope and geographical extent;
- the clause provides for payment to be made to the employee, as compensation for the non-competition clause.

The employer can only waive the non-competition restriction by giving the employee written notice of the waiver prior to the end of the employee's employment. As the waiver can only take effect one year after it has been received by the employee, the employee is effectively released from the restriction immediately upon termination, while the employer remains liable for compensation until the expiry of one year from the date of notice.

Eventually the compensation for not competing can be credited against the company's pensions.

Contracting out

A clause which purports to exclude or limit the employee's rights under any labour legislation or elsewhere is invalid as the law cannot be contracted out of. This includes such provisions as minimum payments, holidays, maternity rights and rights to an indemnity or compensation. It is possible for the parties to settle an indemnity or waive an indemnity once the employment relationship has been terminated.

Collective employment regulations

Contracts

Collective agreements regulate the relationship between the employer and his or her employees, as every employee (including foreign nationals) has the right of association under German law. Collective agreements are negotiated between trade unions and employers organizations and generally only bind those companies who are members of the employers' association. However, the Federal Minister of Labour has the power to declare a collective agreement to be generally binding, in which case, all companies within a particular industry become bound by the collective agreement, regardless of whether or not they are a member of the employers' association.

In addition to collective agreements, the employer and works council may negotiate a works agreement for a particular company, which contains terms and conditions of employment not governed by the collective agreement.

Collective terminations for economic reasons (redundancy)

The Protection Against Dismissal Act defines a collective termination as the unilateral termination of the employment relationship by the employer for economic or operational reasons, within a period of 30 days, where:

- six or more employees have their contracts of employment terminated in a company employing more than 20 and less than 60 employees;
- more than 25 employees or more than 10 per cent of the regular workforce in a company employing more than 60 and less than 500 employees;
- at least 30 employees in a company employing 500 or more employees.

Procedure

Where the employer plans to collectively terminate the employment of a number of employees, the employer must first inform the works council in writing. This written notice should contain information about the reasons for the dismissals, the total number of employees employed in the company, the number of employees affected by the redundancies, the period within which the dismissals are planned to take effect and any other information required by the works council. The employer and the works council must then work together to determine whether there are any alternatives to the collective redundancy. Where the employer employs more than 100 employees, the works council has the right to be involved in identifying the technical, social and personal criteria to be applied when selecting employees for redundancy.

The employer must also notify the local office of the Labour Exchange of the proposed redundancies, together with an opinion from the works council. The employer must wait one month before proceeding with the terminations, although the Labour Exchange may extend this period to a maximum period of two months, during which time they may introduce short working hours. However, the Labour Exchange's authority is limited as it cannot prohibit the proposed redundancies altogether.

A collective termination of employment does not override the individual employee's entitlement to notice of termination under the collective agreement or individual employment contract. This may mean that the employee effectively has an extended period of notice as the notice requirement specified in the collective agreement or contract is independent of the notice period determined by the Labour Exchange.

Payments

There is no legal entitlement to a redundancy payment but the employer may make a severance payment to an employee, as a recognized way of dealing with potential claims, where the termination is effected without legitimate cause. The employer will only be obliged to pay compensation if the employee is covered by the 'law to protect employees from dismissal' (*Kündigungsschutzgesetz*) which applies to:

- companies with five or more employees;
- employees who have been working for more than six months, but does not apply to managing directors ('*Geschäftsführer*' or '*Vorstand*').

When determining the amount of compensation payable to the employee, the employer should take into consideration the employee's personal circumstances, including age, marital status, length of service and the opportunities of finding alternative employment, together with consideration of the company's economic situation and the level of the non-justified termination.

Generally the courts will use the same criteria to determine the amount of compensation as used in circumstances where the individual employee is terminated for economic reasons, namely half the employee's monthly salary for each year of service up to a ceiling of 12 months.

Notwithstanding the legal position, the employee may be entitled to severance payments by virtue of the collective agreement, or may receive special compensation where the works council has negotiated a social compensation plan with the employer to compensate for financial disadvantage.

Lay-off and guaranteed payments

Employer's insurance contributions automatically include a contribution for payment of the so-called *Konkursausfallgeld,* which is a payment of up to three months' arrears of remuneration in case of the employer's bankruptcy.

Closure of companies

Procedure

The procedure for dismissing employees in the case of closure is the same as the procedure for dismissing employees in the case of a collective termination. The employer must notify the works council in writing and consult with the works council. The employer must also notify the local office of the Labour Exchange.

Payments

Employees may receive special payments by virtue of a social compensation plan negotiated with the works council. The amount of compensation usually depends upon the employee's age, period of service and gross monthly income. In addition, employees are usually guaranteed up to three months' pay to cover any outstanding payments. Any shortfall by the employer will be compensated for by the State run fund.

Employee participation

A works council may be formed on the initiative of the employees, if the enterprise has at least five employees, to supervise the execution of existing labour legislation and to apply for improvements on behalf of the employees. The works council has co-determination rights and duties in social, personnel and economic matters. The size of the works council is determined by the number of employees in the enterprise.

Social matters include the fixing of daily working hours, remuneration policy, holiday policy and health protection. In personnel matters, the works council has rights and duties in collective and individual personnel affairs. As mentioned above, it must be informed by the employer of the recruitment and the dismissal of employees and must indicate agreement. Only in certain cases enumerated in the Works Council Law, can the works council refuse to approve new recruitment. Works councils may demand that vacant positions are advertised within the enterprise.

In economic matters the employer must, if the enterprise has more than 20 employees, inform the works council of any major operational changes. The following measures in particular are considered to be major operational changes: the reduction or closing down or relocation of plant or its substantial parts; amalgamation with other plants;   fundamental changes concerning plant organization; introduction of fundamentally new working systems.

If no consensus can be obtained between the employer and works council, a conciliation committee will decide. This committee consists of an even number of members, half of whom are appointed by the employer and half by the works council, and a neutral chair who is either elected by all other members or, in case of disagreement, appointed by the labour court. Decisions are made by a simple majority.

The conciliation committee also determines the contents of a social plan (if this is required), where major operational changes are to the disadvantage of the employees and where the employer and works council do not agree.

Senior employees and the representatives (directors) of an enterprise are not subject to the measures of the works council, and are not able to be elected as members.

Pensions, tax and insurance

Company pensions

In Germany there are four means of financing company pensions, such as old age pension, disability pension, widow's and orphan's pensions. Pensions granted by a support fund, pension fund or through direct insurance are financed externally and in this respect, indirectly obliges the employer to grant them. Direct promises are granted by the employer.

If the employee was given the promise at the date of joining the company, his or her accrued benefits will remain vested if the employee has ten years' service. If the employee was given the promise at least three years before leaving, the accrued benefits will remain vested if the employee has 12 or more years' service. Should the employer become insolvent before the employee reaches his or her retirement age, the legal insolvency protection becomes effective and the Pension Mutual Insurance Fund (PSV) will pay the pensions and keep the vested benefits.

Employees with ten or more years' service with the company are prohibited from claiming their pension entitlement when leaving the company.

State pensions

The German social security system provides for pension, unemployment insurance, health insurance and insurance for occupational accidents. Participation in such insurances is, with some exceptions (concerning health insurance) compulsory for all employed persons.

Shareholders and directors who own at least 50 per cent of the shares or have another controlling majority, are not subject to the social security system. Also a share of less than 50 per cent can cause the loss of insurance if the person is self-employed.

Contributions are borne by the employer and employee equally; the insurance for occupational accidents is borne by the employer alone. The employee's insurance contributions are deducted from salaries and wages by the employer.

Sickness benefit

Public health insurance is compulsory for all workers and employees up to a salary which is the equivalent of 75 per cent of the basic amount of pension. In 1994, the basic amount of pension is DM 5 700 per month and in the New Territories it is DM 4 425 per month. The combined contributions differ between municipalities and range between 11 per cent and 16 per cent of the employee's gross salary.

For employees earning more than DM 5 700 per month (1994), health insurance is not mandatory. Employees may choose to be insured either under the government system or under private health insurance. If certain prerequisites are fulfilled, the employer has to reimburse the employee 50 per cent of his or her contributions up to 50 per cent of the maximum contribution to the local mandatory health insurance.

Benefits under the mandatory health insurance include hospitalisation, surgery, medical and dental treatment and prescriptions for both the employee, his or her spouse and children.

Under the voluntary insurance scheme, the employee is free to determine the extent of the insurance coverage. It is customary for the employee to have supplementary private insurances, in addition to the mandatory health insurance scheme.

Employees who are sick are entitled to their normal remuneration for a period of up to six weeks. If the employee is covered by the government mandatory system, 80 per cent of their normal gross salary, but not more than 100 per cent of their net salary, is paid for a period of up to 78 weeks within three years, for the same disease. With private insurance cover the amount and duration of payment will depend upon the terms of the individual agreement.

Insurance for occupational accidents

All employers must be insured against occupational accidents relevant to their particular line of business. This insurance covers occupational accidents and diseases and accidents on the way to and from work.

Contributions are computed annually on the basis of the sum of all the employees' remunerations, with the risks of the individual job taken into consideration. The usual annual contribution amounts to between 0.5 and 2 per cent of the payroll.

The benefits provided are medical and hospital treatment, injury allowance, medical and vocational rehabilitation, disability and surviving dependants' pension.

Retirement pensions

Pension insurance comprises old age pension insurance and insurance for pensions in case of employment disability. The combined monthly contributions of both employer and employee presently amount to 19.2 per cent of the employee's gross monthly salary, up to a maximum of DM 7 600 (August 1994) and in the New Territories it will be DM 5 900. The basis for contributions, and thus the contributions themselves are raised every year.

An employee may get a pension after having paid contributions to the pension fund for:

- at least 60 months in case of the regular old age pension, disability pension or dependants' pension;
- 180 months in case of old age pension because of unemployment and pensions for women;
- 240 months for disability pension, if the waiting period for occurrence of the disability has not been fulfilled;
- 420 months in case of early old age pension and old age pension for disabled and severely handicapped persons.

In addition, persons who claim pensions have to meet further conditions, such as compulsory pension insurance and periods of paying contributions.

The employee must have reached a minimum age to be entitled to the pension. Normally this is 65 years, with the possibility of retirement at the age of 62 after at least 35 years of contributions. Up until 1992 women could retire at 60, but due to the harmonization transitional regulations (which are in force until 2012), the retirement age has been extended.

Unemployment benefit

Unemployment insurance provides for payments in the case of unemployment, short-time work and bad weather work shortage (for example in the construction industry). These contributions are also used for educational courses in the employee's own or even a different field, and for maintenance during such courses. The combined monthly contributions amount to 6.8 per cent of the employee's gross salary on the basis of DM 7 600 per month and DM 5 900 in the New Territories from August 1994.

Health and safety

Numerous regulations exist with regard to health and safety measures at work, which are mainly regulated by public law. They relate to the safety and prevention of labour accidents and to social employment protection. The regulations concerning technical matters protect employees against dangers from technical facilities and production. They also include medical protection and preventative medical examinations. There is special protection for certain groups of employees, such as women and juveniles.

The labour authorities have considerable powers to enforce these laws and regulations. Enterprises with more than 20 employees must appoint one or more safety commissioners, and the works council has to control the observance of the safety rules.

Anti-discrimination regulations

The Constitution provides that all people are equal before the law and that men and women have equal rights. For employees in the public service, there is an Equal Rights Act. Foreign workers (*Gastarbeiter*) are treated in the same way as German nationals, at least where collective agreements are concerned.

Regulatory bodies

Litigation is pursued in special labour courts, the normal labour courts, the Courts of Appeal and the Federal Supreme Labour Court. Each party has the right to file a suit against the other party in a labour court. In all labour courts both employers and employees are equally represented as members of the court.

The governmental labour offices have lost their monopoly on the recruitment of people, as private agencies also recruit personnel. Personnel are recruited through advertisements in regional or national newspapers or professional periodicals. Labour offices also provide the names and supporting documentation of people looking for work.

Foreign employees

Residence permits

Foreign nationals who wish to work in Germany must first obtain a residence permit. To obtain such a permit, they must have a valid passport and a visa. To avoid difficulties, the visa must be applied for at a German consulate in the foreign country before entering Germany.

After the visa has been received, the papers will be sent to the German aliens registration office (*Auslanderamt*) dealing with the intended place of residence in Germany. The residence permit may be granted for a limited or an unlimited period. It may be restricted to a certain area and may also be subject to certain impositions. If a person wants to work in Germany the residence permit is only granted in connection with a work permit.

Nationals of member states of the European Union just need a valid identity card. They are first given a preliminary residence permit in Germany and must find a job within a certain period of time in order not to lose their residence benefits deriving from their EU membership. Once they have found a job they are given a permanent residence permit.

Work permit

With a number of exceptions, including EU nationals, all foreign nationals working in Germany require a work permit. The work permit is granted by the local labour office (*Arbeitsamt*). It can be issued either for a certain activity at a certain enterprise or for unlimited activities within Germany. The work permit is usually valid only within the district of the local labour office. The normal work permit is granted for a maximum of two years but can be extended; certain work permits are granted for five years.

Before issuing a work permit, the labour office will consider the employment situation in the applicant's field. Because of the present unemployment situation, a work permit may not be granted if there are German nationals with the same experience and qualifications available.

No work permit is required for persons who are legally entitled to represent a company. For instance:

- directors (*Vorstand*) of a corporation (*Aktiengesellschaft*) or directors (*Geschäftsfuhrer*) of a limited liability company (*Gesellschaft mit beschränkter Haftung*);
- all partners of an unlimited partnership (*Offene Handelsgesellschaft*);
- the personally liable partner of a limited partnership (*Kommanditgesellschaft*);
- managerial employees with either a general power of attorney or a commercial power of representation (*Prokura*).

These persons only need a residence permit. If a person is appointed as managing director without intending to take up residence in Germany, no permit is required.

Generally, no work permit is required for citizens from an EU country. Instead they must hold an EU card to distinguish them.

Benefits

In general a foreign employee can only be exempted from pension and insurance contributions for up to two years if he or she is an EU citizen or a citizen of a country which has concluded a social security agreement with Germany, according to the terms of such an agreement.

A prerequisite in both cases is that the remuneration and the directives come from the home country employer.

According to the EU regulations and various social security agreements with other countries, contributions in Germany may be taken into account with regard to pensions paid outside of Germany.

Recruitment and training

Employees are recruited either through advertisements in the local newspaper or, if skilled personnel, in professional periodicals or supra-regional newspapers as well as through the local governmental labour office or private agencies.

Exceptions can be made only for a few certain groups of employees, such as artists.

There are no legal requirements for the training of employees except for members of the works council in connection with their function. Larger firms may have training courses at regular or irregular intervals.

This chapter was written by Ulrike Hill and Rita Reichenbach, Coopers & Lybrand GmbH, Treuhand-Vereinigung Deutsche Revision AG, Germany.

Greece

Introduction

Employment and labour relations in the private sector (excluding the agricultural sector) is regulated by labour legislation. In the public sector, employment and labour relations are regulated by special legislation.

Sources of employment and labour relations include statutes, case-law, collective agreements, articles of association of unions, arbitration decisions, established customs and practices and employment regulations agreed between employers and employees. In case of conflict between any of the above, the most advantageous term to the employee will always be applied.

The law distinguishes between employees who are paid on a monthly basis and those who are paid on a daily basis.

Individual employment regulations

Contracts

Individual contracts of employment may be written or verbal. There are different provisions regulating dismissal, severance pay and so on, depending upon whether the contract is for a specified period of time or for an unspecified period of time. As a minimum, the contract of employment must specify:

- the employee's obligation to provide service to the employer;
- the employer's obligation to remunerate the employee;
- the term of the contract.

The employer must notify the Organisation for the Employment of the Labour Force (OAED) within eight days of engaging an employee and must register the employee with the employee's local pension fund.

Wages and salaries

Minimum wage provision - Minimum wage provisions are found in the National General Collective Labour Agreement, which is renewed annually by the Confederation of Trade Unions and the Union of Employees. The minimum wage increases with length of service, skills, marital status and so on.

Salaries and wages are computed on a 14 month basis. The employee also receives the following bonus payments:

- Christmas bonus equal to a double month's salary (25 days' wages) is paid at Christmas if the employee has been employed from 1 May to 30 December - otherwise a portion thereof;
- Easter bonus equal to an extra half month's salary (13 days' wages) is paid at Easter if the employee has been employed from 1 January to 30 April - otherwise a portion thereof;
- Vacation bonus equal to an extra half month's salary (13 days' wages) when the employee's annual vacation is taken, after completing one year's service with the same employer, or portion thereof (two days' pay for every month worked, up to a maximum of 13 days' pay) if the employee resigns or is dismissed before completing the year.

For certain categories of employees there are additional benefits, such as bonus for unhealthy work, purchase of uniforms, preparation of the annual balance sheet, family bonus, out of town allowance and so on.

Method of payment - Wages and salaries can be paid in cash or in kind for the portion exceeding the minimum wage specified by the Labour Agreement. There are no legal requirements restricting the method of payment.

Deductions from pay - The employer is obliged to deduct and withhold, without the express agreement of the employee, income taxes, social security contributions, stamp duty and the farmers' insurance fund (OGA). Additionally the employer may deduct an amount up to one-quarter of the employee's salary without the employee's express consent, if required to by a court order for the payment of alimony.

Itemized pay statement - Every employee has a right to an itemized pay statement at the time payment is made, showing in writing the type of payment, the gross and net amounts, and amounts and purposes of any deductions.

Hours of work/shift work/overtime

A five day week of 40 hours is generally worked.

Persons under the age of 12 may not be employed. Persons between the age of 12 and 18 may not work night shift and may not perform certain types of (unhealthy and dangerous) work.

Table 1 below serves as a general guideline of overtime rates:

Table 1

Day/hours worked	Hourly rate
40 - 41 hours per week	Normal rate
42 - 48 hours per week	Plus 25%
More than 48 hours per week	Plus 25% - for the first 60 hours of overtime per annum if permission from the labour office has been obtained
More than 48 hours per week	Plus 75% - for more than 120 hours overtime per annum if permission has been obtained from the labour office
More than 48 hours per week	Plus 100% - if permission from labour office has not been obtained
Night work (10pm - 6am)	Plus 25%
Sundays and public holidays	Plus 75% if considered normal working days
Sundays and public holidays	Plus 175% if not considered normal working days

Holidays

After one year of employment employees are entitled to an annual vacation of 20 to 26 working days. The number of days depends upon the employee's period of service and whether the employee works a five or six day working week. Employees are also entitled to a vacation bonus as detailed above.

Maternity provisions

Employees are entitled to 15 weeks' maternity leave, 52 days must be taken before the birth of the child and 53 days after child's birth. Employees on maternity leave are entitled to one month's salary from the employer and a maternity allowance from the Social Security Fund. They are also entitled to one hour's paid absence per day for a period of one year from the date of the child's birth.

The employer cannot dismiss an employee on maternity leave.

Time off

There are no specific laws governing time off. It is a matter of agreement between the employer and employee.

Disciplinary and grievance procedures

Disciplinary procedures are applied only where labour regulations exist. Disciplinary procedures can be exercised by the employer or the disciplinary council, who can impose penalties after hearing the employee's plea. The penalties are:

- verbal or written reproach;
- reprimand;
- penalty forfeit of up to 25 per cent of the employee's daily earnings;
- temporary dismissal of up to ten days in each calendar year.

Labour disputes are settled either through the labour office or through the courts.

Lay-off and guaranteed payments

Employees may be temporarily suspended on half pay for a continuous period not exceeding three months. In certain industries, for example the tourist industry, lay-off without pay is permitted during the off season.

Period of notice

Employees paid on a monthly paid basis are entitled to certain statutory minimum periods of notice, determined in accordance with the employee's period of service with the employer. However, there are no statutory minimum periods of notice for daily paid employees.

The period of notice for monthly paid employees ranges from one month for up to one year's service to two years for more than 28 years' service. If the employer complies with the stipulated minimum period of notice the employee is entitled to one-half of the legal severance payment. If the minimum period is not complied with, the employee is entitled to the full severance payment.

Employees with less than two months' service can be dismissed without notice and severance pay.

All the employee's earnings normally received during the last period of employment prior to notice are included in the computation of severance pay. The employee is also entitled to holiday pay and a bonus if holidays were not taken during that year, plus a portion of the Christmas or Easter bonus.

The legal severance payment is shown in Table 2:

Table 2

Length of service	Severance pay
2 months - 1 year	5 days
1 - 2 years	7 days
2 - 5 years	13 days
5 - 10 years	26 days
10 - 15 years	52 days
15 - 20 years	65 days
20 years and over	78 days

On expiration of fixed term contracts, employees are not entitled to any severance pay. If employees, employed for a specified period of time, are dismissed prior to the expiration of the contract, they are entitled to compensation for the remaining term of the contract, unless dismissed for 'a serious cause'.

Dismissal

Dismissals are considered legal if the employer:

- gives notice in writing to the employee;
- pays the stipulated severance payment;
- has not abused the rights of dismissal.

Even if the above requirements are complied with, certain employees cannot be dismissed for varying periods of time, for example, officials of a trade union, women before and after child birth, men called up for compulsory army training and so on.

Employers are not obliged to give reasons for dismissal.

Redundancy

Employers employing more than 20 persons have to abide by the law governing collective dismissals. That law specifies a monthly limit on the number of employees made redundant:

- five employees where the company employs 20 to 50 person;
- 2 to 3 per cent of employees, with a limit of 30, where more than 50 employees are employed. This percentage is determined every six months by the Minister of Labour.

Collective employment regulations

The most significant employment organizations are the Greek Industrial Association, the General Federation of Professional and Workshops Owners of Greece, and local industry associations.

Trade unions

Any employee has a right to be or not to be a member of a trade union. The employee may legally take part in the lawful activities of the trade union formed at the place of work and the activities of the federation and confederation of trade unions of that trade union. Membership or non-membership of a trade union does not legally affect hiring, dismissal in any way.

A group of 20 employees can form a trade union which must be recognized by the courts. The courts examine the legality and not the purpose of the trade union. Once it is recognized by the courts the employer is obliged to accept the trade union.

Trade disputes

Employees have a legal right to strike and this right can be exercised by the trade union, federations and confederations of trade unions after 24 hours' notice to the employer. A strike is considered lawful in the case of trade unions, after a decision by the general meeting of members and, in the case of federations and confederations, after a decision by the board of directors.

During the strike the union is obliged to maintain a skeleton staff. The employer may not hire strike breakers, nor dismiss any strikers, and is prohibited from locking out employees.

Employee participation

Employees or unions generally do not participate in any management decisions. The employer is only obliged to consult with employee representatives in the case of decisions concerning health and safety.

Pensions, tax and insurance

Income tax and national insurance

Various insurance funds pay maternity benefits. Unemployment benefit is normally two-thirds of the daily wage for an unskilled worker but cannot exceed Drs 3 000 a day. Both the employer and employee contribute to the unemployment fund as part of their social security contributions.

Employers have a statutory obligation to withhold income tax, stamp duty, OGA on stamp duty and social security contributions from the employees' salary or wages. Employers must account to the Inland Revenue and the Social Security Fund for such deductions and make appropriate payments every three months to the Inland Revenue and every month to the Social Security Fund. The employer is liable for any deductions that are omitted.

Sickness benefit

Employees are entitled to a maximum of 15 days' sick pay in the first year of employment if they have been employed for more than 10 days and up to one year. For the second year of employment and every year thereafter, the employee is entitled to a maximum of one month's sick pay.

The employer is entitled to deduct from the sickness benefit any sums received by the employee from the Social Security Fund.

Retirement pensions

Both employer and employee are obliged to make contributions towards the employees pension based on stipulated percentages. Employees are entitled to belong to both a primary and secondary pension fund.

The retirement age stipulated by the numerous funds differs but generally for members of the main pension fund, the Social Security Fund, males retire at the age of 65 years and females retire at 60 years after completing 4 500 insured working days. In certain industries, such as mining, and unhealthy or dangerous professions, the retirement age is lower for both sexes.

Health and safety

Health and Safety legislation is of two distinct types. The general legislation lays down broad obligations and general duties while specific legislation sets out precise requirements in respect of prescribed premises and processes. The former is typified by Law 1568/85 and the latter by numerous laws and regulations relating to specific premises, operations, materials and other substances, in the explosives industry, mines and quarries, transportation, fishing industry and so on.

Where there are more than 50 employees, the employer's principal obligation is to employ a doctor and a safety officer. In addition, the employer is obliged to implement a cleanliness policy, to have adequate lighting and ventilation in the premises, ensure absence of dampness and generally to take steps to protect employees from all danger.

Premises are subject to inspection by the Labour Officer and violators can be penalised as follows, according to the seriousness of the violation:

- fines of Drs 10 000 to Drs 500 000;
- temporary shutdown of part or whole of the operation;
- imprisonment of up to one year for negligent transgressors;

- imprisonment of up to 10 years and a fine of at least Drs 100 000 for intentional transgressors.

Employers' liability insurance

Employers are not legally obliged to insure against liability for personal injury and disease suffered by their employees in the course of, or arising out of, their employment, but in practice it is quite common for employers to take out this insurance.

Anti-discrimination regulations

All persons working in Greece, both Greek and foreign nationals, irrespective of race and gender, are entitled to equal labour rights such as employment, pay, vacation, bonus and membership of unions. Enforcement of these rights is supervised by the appropriate Labour Offices.

Regulatory bodies

Labour office

The implementation of and adherence to labour law is controlled by the Labour Office and inspectors of the Labour Office who have the right to enter work premises at any time for the following reasons:

- to conduct investigations;
- to inspect books and documents required by law;
- to obtain necessary information from employers and employees;
- to accept complaints from employees.

Organizations for the Employment of the Labour Force (OAED)

This organization was formed to provide schools for training people in various trades such as plumbers, electricians and motor mechanics. The OAED also finds work for the unemployed and pays out unemployment benefit.

Legal institutions

Individual labour differences are settled with or by the Labour Office or by the Court of Law. Collective labour differences are settled by the Arbitration Courts.

Foreign employees

It is illegal and a serious criminal offence for an employer to employ a foreign national without a valid residence permit and work permit for that specific employer. EU members need only a residence permit to work in Greece, whereas non-EU members need both a work permit and a residence permit.

This chapter was written by George Samothrakis, Ioannou - Zampelas & Co OE - Coopers & Lybrand, Greece.

Hungary

Introduction

In Hungary there are three statutes primarily dealing with employment law. The Act XXII of 1992 contains the Labour Code, the other two statutes contain provisions dealing with the employment of civil servants. This chapter will only deal with provisions affecting the employment of persons outside the civil service.

In conjunction with the Labour Code there are several Governmental and Ministerial decrees governing employment. Under these decrees, the Government has the right to regulate the dismissal of large numbers of employees for economic reasons, to determine the level of minimum wages and control labour affairs. Amongst these powers, the Government can make proposals for the maximum duration of daily working hours and for annual days of rest.

Where the employee's duties are not regulated by statute, collective agreement or individual contract, the employer may issue directives.

A young person under 16 years of age cannot be employed if they are in full-time compulsory education or without the approval of their parents. A person under the age of 18 must not be employed in a job which is harmful to the employee's health or physical development, for example night work, overtime or jobs which require the employee to be on call.

The Labour Code applies to all employment relationships in Hungary, regardless of whether the parties are Hungarian nationals or not. The only exception are employees assigned to Hungary under the employment of a foreign employer.

The parties cannot contract out of these statutory provisions, but can provide the employee with more favourable terms in the collective agreement, individual contract of employment or employer directive.

Individual employment regulations

Contracts

A legal relationship between an employer and employee is regarded as an employment relationship if the following obligations exist. The employee must:

- spend the contracted working time at a location specified by the employer;
- work diligently in accordance with the employer's directions, and in person if not agreed otherwise;
- respect his or her own health and the health of others;
- respect the employer's property and material or moral benefit.

Conversely, the employer must:

- guarantee the employee continuous work;
- issue all necessary directives on work;
- pay the employees' wages and issue all contributions in due course.

The employment relationship is governed by an individual contract of employment. The employee's acceptance of employment is sufficient to create a contract of employment. Such contracts must not be contrary to the law or to any applicable collective agreements, unless such terms are more advantageous to the employee.

Such contracts must at least specify the employee's scope of activity, the amount of wages, and the employee's work location. Additional matters such as trial periods and the duration of employment may also be specified in the contract.

The employer may not release any data concerning the employee, except where the employee has given prior approval or as required by law.

The employee must obtain the approval of the employer prior to commencing secondary employment during work hours. Where the employment is conducted outside work hours, the employee only needs to inform the employer of the employment. Secondary employment is exempt from any notice requirements.

During the employment relationship, the employee must not jeopardize any rightful business interest of the employer. This obligation may be extended for up to three years after cessation of employment, in exchange for reasonable compensation which must be specified in the contract.

The documents and data relevant to the employment relationship are:

- the employee's personal data as stated in the employee's ID;
- a certificate from the employee's former employer specifying the duration of the employee's latest employment, any sick leave taken in that year, together with information about any debts to be deducted from the employee's wages;
- a certificate on advance tax payments;
- a certificate on the employee's social security;
- for any male employee aged 18 to 50, a military ID is required;
- if a foreigner is to be employed, permission is required from the local labour centre.

Typically employees are employed for an indefinite period of time. It is possible however, to employ employees for a fixed period of time, provided that the term does not exceed the statutory maximum period of five years. Where the employee works over five years, for example five years and one day, the contract will become an employment of indefinite duration.

Where an individual contract of employment is already in force, the collective agreement cannot amend that contract to the employee's detriment.

Employment of managerial staff

It is common practice to appoint persons to managerial positions for an indefinite period of time. If however, the person is employed on a fixed term basis, the employer cannot require the manager to resign without fair reasons. In all other cases the manager's appointment is free to be terminated at any time without reasons.

There are special rules on the employment of managers as follows:

- collective agreements do not apply to managerial staff;
- managers may be employed on a fixed term basis which exceeds five years;
- a manager may determine his or her own work schedule and vacation, in accordance with his or her individual contract of employment;
- the manager's compensation liability as well as his or her ordinary or extraordinary notice is subject to special regulations.

Unless the parties have contracted to the contrary, it is common practice for the following restrictions to apply to the manager's employment:

- secondary employment is not permitted;
- managers are not permitted to get involved in activities or businesses similar to that of his or her employer;
- the manager's employment will be terminated if a close relative becomes a shareholder or part of the management at a company with similar activities;
- compensation cannot be claimed for overtime.

Wages and salaries

Minimum wage provision - Generally wages are determined on a time based system, but may be combined with a performance based system to calculate the final wage. Notwithstanding the method of calculating such wages, the total wage must not be less than the amount of the minimum wage, regularly determined by the Government.

Method of payment - Wages must be paid in cash and in Hungarian currency. Wages should be paid on a monthly basis, usually before the tenth of each month. Such payment should take place during working hours and on the working premises.

Deductions from pay - The employer is obliged to pay a social insurance contribution. This contribution is calculated as 44 per cent of the employee's remuneration, comprising 24.5 per cent for pension and 19.5 per cent for health insurance.

The employee must also make a contribution towards social insurance. The employee's costs are 6 per cent and 4 per cent respectively, with a maximum daily cap of HUF 2 500. This contribution must be deducted from the employees wages along with the income tax advance.

The employer must transfer the social insurance contributions and the income tax advance to the relevant authorities at the beginning of each month.

In addition, the employer and employee must pay a contribution to the Unemployment Fund. The rates are 5 per cent and 1.5 per cent respectively. The base of this contribution is the gross salary payable in Hungary.

Employers other than representative offices of foreign companies are required to make a payment of 0.3 per cent to the Wages Guarantee Fund.

Apart from these specific deductions, the employer cannot deduct any other monies from the employee's wages, without the employee's consent, or unless authorized by law or pursuant to a court order. The total amount of deduction must not exceed 50 per cent of the employee's wages.

Hours of work/shift work/overtime

The statutory hours of work are eight hours a day. These hours may be determined on a weekly, monthly or yearly basis provided they equal the total statutory hours of work on an eight week basis and do not exceed 12 hours a day. Employees may only work additional hours in exceptional situations.

Between consecutive days of work, the employee must be guaranteed at least 11 hours of rest, or such other amount as specified in the collective agreement.

Overtime is worked when the permissible hours of work are exceeded. Overtime is limited to four hours on two consecutive days, or a total of 144 hours in a calendar year. This may be extended to 200 hours if permitted by the collective agreement. Employees under the age of 16, pregnant women and employees in positions harmful to their health are prohibited from working overtime.

Employees are entitled to two days of rest weekly, which should include Sunday. Where the employee is required to work during these days, the employer should provide the employee with substitute days off and make an additional payment of at least 50 per cent of the employee's daily wage. Those employees who are exempt from overtime must not be engaged in work on their rest days.

The hours between ten in the evening and six in the morning are considered to be night work. The employee is not obliged to work these hours continually unless he or she so requests.

Employees must not spend more than six hours a day under conditions which are harmful to their health.

Holidays

Employees are entitled to a basic annual leave entitlement of 20 days per annum, calculated on a pro rata basis if taken before the leave year is completed. This entitlement increases with age as illustrated in Table 1.

Table 1

From the age of	Days of annual leave
25	21
28	22
31	23
33	24
35	25
37	26
39	27
41	28
43	29
45	30

The basic annual leave entitlement is also increased for the following groups of employees:

- employees up to 18 years of age are entitled to an extra five days per annum;
- parents with children aged under 16 are entitled to the following extra days per annum: two extra days for one child; four extra days for two children and seven extra days for more than two children;
- employees working in conditions harmful to their health are entitled to such extra days as may be agreed upon in the collective agreement or individual employment contract.

Employees must take their annual leave during the year of entitlement, as accumulation of leave is not possible. The employer should approve such leave on a yearly basis and inform the employee of its decision at least 30 days before the leave commences. One quarter of this leave period should be determined by the employee at his or her sole discretion.

Annual leave should not be divided into more than two leave periods, unless requested by the employee. At least two weeks of the employees annual leave must go uninterrupted.

In addition to annual leave there are nine national holidays to be observed each year:

New Year, 15 March, Easter Monday, 1 May, Pentecost Monday, 20 August, 23 October, 25 and 26 December.

Upon termination of employment the employee is entitled to payment for any unused annual leave.

Maternity provisions

A pregnant women is entitled to 24 weeks maternity leave, with four weeks taken prior to the date of birth. Social insurance guarantees the woman 65 to 100 per cent of her average wages.

Pregnant women are not allowed to enter into employment which would be harmful to their condition. Pregnant or nursing mothers must work under the best working conditions available.

From the date of discovery of her pregnancy until the child's first birthday the woman is entitled, amongst other things, to:

- work conditions in accordance with the pregnancy health requirements (a temporary relocation cannot by accompanied by a reduction in wages);
- refusal of night work;
- refusal of overtime work;
- nursing time off while at work;
- extra leave depending upon the number of children the woman has under the age of 16.

A women cannot be refused employment because of her pregnancy.

Time off

Employees are entitled to ten days sick leave per year. All absences must be reported to the employer in advance and must be terminated as soon as possible. During this period, the employer must pay the employee 75 per cent of the employee's average wages.

Employees may be absent from work with the consent of the employer for reason of illness, for appointments, for strikes and so on. Time off may be granted for nursing mothers, for part-time education, for trade union activities and works council issues.

Different kinds of educational leave are regulated in several different decrees.

Trial periods

A trial period normally lasts for a period of 30 days, but may be extended (or shortened) by the collective agreement to a period of three months. Any longer trial period is against the law.

During the trial period any of the parties may terminate the employment relationship immediately.

Cessation of employment

Employment ceases immediately:

- upon the employee's death;
- upon the expiry of a fixed term contract; or
- upon cessation of the existence of the employer without a legal successor.

In the latter case, there is an overall rule for cessation of all employments, for example statutory notice periods do not apply.

Termination of employment

Either party may terminate the employment relationship in any of the following ways:

- by mutual consent of the parties;
- by ordinary notice;
- by extraordinary notice;
- at any time during the trial period, which occurs with immediate effect.

The termination must be in writing and the parties should supply the following documents upon termination:

- a certificate specifying the period of employment, any debts owed to the employer or the lack of such debts, any sick leave taken while employed;
- a certificate on the employee's health status and social insurance;
- a certificate on the tax advance withheld by the employer; and
- a certificate for registration as unemployed.

Termination by ordinary notice

Employment on a fixed term contract cannot be terminated by ordinary notice. Where the employee is employed under an indefinite contract of employment, both the employee and the employer can terminate the employment relationship by giving ordinary notice, although the latter is required to give a clear explanation.

Notice cannot be given during or for a further 30 days after the expiry of any of the following circumstances:

- an illness resulting in the employee's inability to work, generally up to a period of one year;
- paid or unpaid leave for nursing children or relatives;
- pregnancy with an additional six months from the date of birth;
- unpaid leave allowed for child care;
- the employee's military service.

Notice given during the last five years of the employee's employment, prior to the employee's retirement, will only take effect if it is justified.

Period of notice

The parties must give at least 30 days' notice and a maximum of one years' notice in the case of termination. The 30 day notice period will be extended in accordance with the employee's length of service with the employer as illustrated in Table 2.

Table 2

Length of service	Additional period of notice
3 years	5 days
5 years	15 days
8 years	20 days
10 years	25 days
15 years	30 days
18 years	40 days
20 years	60 days

Where the employer terminates the employment relationship by giving ordinary notice, the employer must release the employee for half of the notice period.

Termination by extraordinary notice

Extraordinary notice may be given by either party where there has been an intentional violation or grievous negligence of one party's substantial obligations or where the behaviour of the other party makes termination of employment inevitable.

The circumstances warranting a termination by extraordinary notice may be determined in the contract of employment or in the collective agreement. The right to give extraordinary notice may be executed within a period of three days from the date of discovery of the reason, or within a maximum period of six months from its occurrence.

Where extraordinary notice of termination is given, the provisions regulating the giving of ordinary notice will not apply.

Severance pay

The employee is entitled to severance pay where:

- the employer terminates the employee's employment by ordinary notice;
- the employment relationship ceases because of the employer's cessation without a legal successor;

- the employee terminates the employment by extraordinary notice.

Severance pay is calculated on the number of years employment with the employer, as illustrated in Table 3.

Table 3

Duration of employment with the employer	Amount of severance pay
at least 3 years	average monthly wages x 1
at least 5 years	average monthly wages x 2
at least 10 years	average monthly wages x 3
at least 15 years	average monthly wages x 4
at least 20 years	average monthly wages x 5
at least 25 years	average monthly wages x 6

A further three months' wages will be paid to the employee if he or she becomes entitled to severance pay during the last five years of employment.

If the employee is entitled to claim an old age pension on the termination of employment there will be no entitlement to severance pay.

Unlawful termination of employment

If the employer terminates the employee's employment in an unlawful manner, the employee has the right to overall restitution. An unlawful termination by the employee may have compensation consequences.

Compensation liability of the employer

The employer is fully liable, regardless of fault, for any employment related damages caused to the employee and/or to the employee's belongings (taken to work with the employer's permission). The employee has the onus of proving that the damage occurred in connection with his or her employment.

The employer is exempt from any liability where the damage is caused by force majeure or by the unavoidable behaviour of the employee. In addition, employers with less than ten full-time employees are only liable if the damage was caused by the employer.

Compensation for employment related damages includes any lost income, material and immaterial damages, and any justified expenses. An allowance may also be established as compensation.

Compensation liability of the employee

The employee is liable for any damages caused by a violation of his or her employment obligations, which is a consequence of the employee's actions. The employee's guilt, the occurrence and amount of the damage as well as the causal correlation shall be substantiated by the employer.

Where damage is caused by the employee's negligence, the amount of compensation must not exceed half the employee's average monthly wage, unless agreed otherwise in the contract of employment or collective agreement. The maximum amount of compensation possible in the contract of employment is one and a half month's average wages and in the collective agreement up to six months' average wages. Bank checkers and supervisors may be fully liable for damages in connection with their auditing.

In the case of intentional damage, the employee is liable for full compensation.

Employees who are under an obligation to return or account for property are liable for full losses, where the items are kept constantly in the custody of, or used exclusively by the employee. The employee may be exempt from liability where the damage is caused by force majeure or by the employer's failure to provide the adequate safeguarding conditions. The Labour Code regulates some of these circumstances and it is possible for collective agreements to make provision for the regulation of cases.

Where the employee fails to admit his or her culpability, compensation may be claimed in a law suit.

Contracts in breach of the law

Where a contract is in breach of the law, the whole contract is void. Where part of the contract is in breach of the law, that part will become void. A void contract will prevent the employee from either commencing employment or where employment has already commenced, will result in the suspension of the employee. Where it is impossible to correct the breach, the employment relationship will be terminated immediately. In this case, the employee will be entitled to compensation equal to the length of ordinary notice (except during a trial period) where the employer is responsible for the breach.

Statutory limitation period

Any liability arising from employment expires after three years. If the liability arises from damage caused by a felony, the period of limitation increases to five years, unless the relevant period of limitation in criminal proceedings is longer. The period of limitation begins on the day the demand arises and is interrupted by any action to execute it.

Collective employment regulations

Collective agreements

Collective agreements are used in addition to statute and decree to regulate the rights and obligations of the parties. They are also used to identify the relationship between the parties concluding the collective agreement and to regulate any procedural issues. In essence, collective agreements are used to cover a wide range of employment issues.

Collective agreements are concluded between trade union(s) and employer(s). Where the employer is a member of an employer's association, that association will normally negotiate the collective agreement on the employer's behalf.

Where there is a dispute about employment interests (other than a legal conflict) between the employer and the works council or trade union, there shall be reconciliation negotiations. The parties may agree in advance that a mediator or an arbiter be involved and that any decision be final.

The reconciliation negotiation commences with the submission of a written proposal to the other party. A seven day moratorium on execution of the measures debated shall then take effect.

Any agreement resulting from the reconciliation/arbitration procedure has the power of a contract.

Collective termination (redundancy)

Where the employer wishes to dismiss at least 25 per cent of the workforce (or at least 50 persons) in a company employing more than 30 employees, the employer must notify the works council and the local centre of employment three months prior to giving notices of termination.

Any employee who is declared redundant is entitled to a statutory redundancy payment from the centre of labour. The essential conditions are:

- the applicant is unemployed;
- while employed, the applicant duly paid contributions to the unemployment fund;
- the applicant is not entitled to receive any kind of pension;
- the applicant is willing to work but the centre of labour is unable to offer him or her a suitable job;
- the applicant is co-operating with the centre of labour in order to find employment.

The redundancy payment is 60 to 75 per cent of the employee's average salary in the last year of employment. The actual rate depends upon the conditions specified in the Act IV of 1991.

Further relief for redundant employees, specified in the Act includes:

- the possibility of early retirement;
- support for young persons who are unemployed and are unable to get their first employment.

Employer dispositions

The employer's right to issue dispositions may be delegated to any officers at management level. The employee must have clear knowledge of who is entitled to issue such dispositions. Any order or disposition executed by an unauthorized person is void unless the employee has good reason to believe that such orders were authorized.

Generally there is no special form for an order or disposition, but the law may specify a particular form or the employee may request a written disposition on any question concerning his or her basic interests. Any disposition issued against the law or with the possibility of resulting in a loss in lives or health, must be refused. If the employer's order may cause damage, the employee ought to warn the employer but must comply with the order.

Orders assigning the employee to another work location must be given in writing. The usual time spent on assignment must not normally exceed a period of two months per year. Expenses incurred from an assignment are reimbursed.

Written dispositions are effective upon receipt. They are required to contain an explanation and to give information about any possibility of appeal.

Any agreement, contract, order or disposition that is against the law is void. Any agreement, contract, order or disposition based upon error, abuse or threat is voidable within 30 days from the date of discovery of the cause of voidness.

Employee participation

Works councils

Employee participation is assured by the works council. The number of works council members is dependant upon the number of employees, as illustrated in Table 4.

Table 4

Number of employees	Works council members
15 - 50	1 (works representative)
51 - 100	3
101 - 200	7
201 - 500	9
501 - 1 000	11
1 001 -	13

Any capable employee having a working relationship with the employer for at least six months may be elected a member of the works council. Managers exercising the employer's rights, their relatives and members of the works council election committee are excluded from council membership.

The election procedure and activity of the works council is regulated by the Labour Code.

The works council has the right to co-operate on social affairs, agree on the works health protection provisions and give its opinion on the following matters:

- any restructuring of the company if it concerns a number of employees;
- the system of the employees' data record;
- any measures to be taken concerning the employees' education, re-employment or retirement under special circumstances;
- rehabilitation of the disabled;
- yearly plan of vacation;

- new methods on organizing work or new output requirements;
- any new intra-company regulation concerning substantial interests of the employees;
- any intra-company competition promising the employees financial increases or promotion.

The works council also has the right to information on the basic state of the employer's economic status, efficiency and liquidity, supplied on a six monthly basis. It also has the right to any information on plans to substantially change the employer's range of activities or investments.

The works council has the right to forward it's opinion or proposal to the employer within 15 days upon calling for it. If the works council does not respond by this deadline, it is deemed to have agreed to the proposed measures.

Trade unions

Membership of a trade union is voluntary and any trade union can recruit members at any particular establishment. Employee's can authorize trade unions to represent them before the courts or any other authorities dealing with conditions of living or employment. Any discrimination related to the employee's membership or non-membership of a trade union is against the law.

With the employer's prior agreement, the trade union is free to release all necessary information at the working location and to use working accommodation to execute its activity.

Any measure taken by the employer directly concerning 25 per cent or more of the workforce or more than 50 persons must be discussed with the trade union representative(s) prior to its execution.

Trade union officers are entitled to paid time off, proportional to the number of trade union members. For every three trade union members employed, the trade union officers (as a whole) are granted two hours off per month. Additionally, for each ten members employed the local trade union organization (as a whole) is granted one day off per year for educational purposes.

The employer cannot dismiss an elected trade union officer or move that officer to another working location without the prior consent of the union. The employer must notify the trade union, in advance, if any officer is subject to extraordinary notice or to the consequences of any grievous breach of labour duties.

Strike

Any allegedly unlawful measure taken by the employer may be attacked by the trade union, provided that the employee concerned does not have the right to initiate separate legal proceedings. Action by the trade union shall result in a reconciliation negotiation, the failure of which is cause for a law suit.

If a reconciliation negotiation fails after seven days or is not initiated for any reason other than the union's lack of intention, the employees shall have the right to strike. During a strike employees and employers have to cooperate to prevent personal injuries and or damage to property.

A strike is against the law if:

- no negotiation preceded it;
- its aim is unconstitutional;
- its aim is subject to the jurisdiction of the court;
- it is meant to amend any term of a collective agreement still in effect.

Strikes are regulated by the Act VII of 1989.

Pensions, tax and insurance

Sickness benefit

Employees who are unable to work for a period longer than 10 days, due to illness, are entitled to receive a social insurance allowance. This allowance guarantees the employee 65 to 75 per cent of the employee's average wages for a period of up to one year.   This limitation in time does not apply to employees who are unable to work as a result of work accidents or occupational diseases. Employees who suffer a loss of at least 15 per cent in their ability to work (but are not disabled), as a result of a work accident or an occupational disease, will receive an additional allowance.

Retirement pensions

An old age pension is available to males at age 60 and to females at age 55. Males with at least 30 years' employment and females with at least 25 years' employment may retire five years earlier, provided that the employer reimburses the pension expenses to social insurance for that period. If early retirement is necessary for redundancy reasons, an exemption to this provision may apply.

Employees who are unable to work as a result of being at least 67 per cent disabled, are guaranteed a pension by social insurance. Old age pensioners and employees who have an allowance due to an accident are excluded from this pension.

Tax provisions

Any work related expenses incurred by the employee (for example using his or her private car for company purposes) must be reimbursed. This is, however, subject to sophisticated tax provisions.

Health and safety

Work places must be equipped and operated in such a manner to avoid work related accidents and illnesses. Employees are given information about safety measures when entering employment and must be informed of any existing danger. The employer must provide washing facilities, toilets, drinking water and health care to employees and protect employees against dust, chemicals, radiation, noise, electric shock, vibration and polluted air.

Any work related accident or illness (excluding accidents from drunkenness, unlicensed work or driving, or nuisances) has to be reported, investigated and registered at the National Employment and Labour Safety Authority.

Labour safety representatives must be elected where there are ten or more employees in any working unit. These representatives are free to control local provisions concerning labour safety.

The coordination of health and safety is dealt with on a national level by the Labour Safety Committee. This Committee comprises members representing the Government, employers and employees.

Detailed provisions on health and safety are found in Act XCIII of 1993 and some decrees.

Anti-discrimination regulations

In relation to employment it is forbidden to discriminate against an employee on the grounds of sex, age, nationality, race, origin, religion, political conviction, trade union membership or circumstances not related to employment. A breach of these regulations will result in the employer facing legal action.

Regulatory bodies

The Government executes its labour policy basically via the Ministry of Labour. The Ministry of Social Welfare is entitled to deal with social affairs related to labour issues.

Ministry of Labour

The Ministry of Labour runs the National Centre of Employment, an authority established to relieve unemployment. It also controls the activity of the National Employment and Labour Safety Authority (OMMF), a governmental body established to check the labour safety provisions, anti-discrimination provisions and the basic working conditions, for example the duration of working hours, minimum wages, vacation, employment of women, minors or foreigners.

The inspectors of the Authority are free to enter all premises, to execute instant measures or suspensions if anything unlawful is found, and to initiate legal proceedings against an employer who breaches the law, up to a maximum of three million HUF.

The Ministry registers collective agreements and controls the system of training in special high schools. It also participates in the International Labour Organisation on behalf of the Hungarian Government.

Interest Reconciliation Council

The Interest Reconciliation Council consists of delegates from the Government, the employers' associations and trade unions. The Council continually harmonizes different interests and arguments, and has the right to approve massive dismissals, minimum wages, labour controls and days of annual leave. It also holds negotiations on the national wage levels. The outcome of these negotiations is issued by the Ministry as a decree.

Legal institutions

A law suit on labour disputes is subject to a prior reconciliation procedure. Labour courts, consisting of a judge and two assessors, are organized on a county basis. Appeals against the decisions of labour courts can be taken to regular county courts.

Foreign employees

A foreigner must satisfy the following conditions to work in Hungary:

- a work visa obtained from a Hungarian embassy;
- a residence permit obtained from the local police;
- a work permit issued by the local centre of labour.

Persons accepting a position at management level with a Hungarian company, together with representatives of foreign companies, do not require a work visa and work permit, but must obtain an income visa and a residence permit. British citizens are in a unique position, as they are free to conduct business in Hungary with only a residence permit.

Any employer who violates these provisions may be fined.

Recruitment and training

Local government and local centres of employment encourage career counselling in schools. Employers may contract students as future employees in exchange for financial support during their study. A compulsory period of employment resulting from such a contract must not be longer than five years.

In addition, centres of employment offer a contribution towards retraining unemployed persons or persons who are at risk of losing their jobs within one year (details in Act IV of 1991).

Whenever a vacant position is filled by the employer, as a result of a competition, or according to the law, no applicants may be employed unless the requirements advertised are met and a formal application is made.

Any employment search office, registered with the Ministry of Labour can provide assistance in finding employment. Furthermore, any employer employing a person who has been officially registered as unemployed for at least six months, may generally reclaim up to 50 per cent of the wage expenses related to that person, for a period of up to one year. For this to apply, the employer must guarantee that there have been no dismissals from a position similar to the one in question during the past six months, and that there will be no dismissals from a similar position in the following three months.

If a company employs its employees on a part-time basis (with a reduction of at least one third of its regular working time) in order to alleviate a temporary overstaffing problem, the employer can reclaim 50 per cent of the wages due for the time lost, for up to one year.

Additionally, a reduction in the corporate tax base is available for companies who employ persons officially registered as unemployed. This reduction may cover up to 70 per cent of the companies paid social security expenses for those persons, for up to one year.

This chapter was written by Attila Teplàn and Paul Grocott, Coopers & Lybrand Kft, Hungary.

Ireland

Introduction

Employment law in the Republic of Ireland stems from:

- The Constitution;
- Acts of the British Parliament still applicable (pre-1922);
- Acts of the Oireachtas (post-1922);
- European Union legislation;
- International Declaration and Directives;
- Common law;
- Statutory tribunals.

In addition to statutory influences on employment, voluntary agreements, along with custom and practice, have a major influence.

Labour legislation generally lays down minimum requirements in relation to many conditions of work concerning the individual, while collective rights are generally negotiated by trade unions and employers and usually exceed the minimum legal requirements.

Individual employment regulations

Contracts

All employees work under a contract of employment which may be in writing or verbal. There is no statutory requirement to have a written contract although this is always advisable. A contract of employment will exist when the offer of employment has been accepted by the employee. Where there is a written contract, it should be signed by both parties in duplicate and one copy retained by the employer.

An employer must provide new employees with a written statement of specified particulars of employment. Existing employees are entitled to a written statement within two months of requesting such a statement. Employees recruited after 16 May 1994 are entitled to the written statement within two months of commencing employment. In the case of employees assigned to work outside Ireland for more than a month, an employer must provide the employee (prior to departure) with supplementary information relating to the period of employment outside the State, pay and benefits in cash or kind and details about repatriation.

The information provided must include:

- the full name and address of the employer and employee;
- the address of the employer in the State or its principal place of business in the State;
- the place of work;
- the job title or nature of the work;
- date of commencement;
- expected duration (if temporary) or date of expiry (fixed term);
- rate of remuneration or method of calculating remuneration;
- whether the remuneration is weekly, monthly or otherwise;
- terms or conditions relating to hours of work; (including overtime); holidays; sickness/injury; sick pay; pensions schemes;
- periods of notice to be given to and by employees;
- a reference to any collective agreements applicable;
- a trial period, if any;
- grievance and disciplinary procedures for dismissal.

Any change in the written statement must be given to employees within one month of such a change. (Terms of Employment (Information) Act 1994, Unfair Dismissals Acts 1977 to 1993 and Minimum Notice and Terms of Employment Act 1973).

Additional terms which might be included in a contract of employment are:

- confidentiality;
- competition;
- obligation to comply with a safety statement;
- mobility.

Wages and salaries

Minimum wage provision - Apart from those in certain occupations covered by Employment Regulation Orders or Registered Employment Agreements, there is no statutory minimum wage. Minimum wage agreements are established in practice by trade union negotiation.

Method of payment - The Payment of Wages Act 1991 provides all employees with the right to a readily negotiable mode of wage payment which includes cheques, bank drafts, payable orders, postal orders, money orders, credit transfers and cash. Employers are required to make alternative arrangements for payment of wages where industrial action affects banks and other financial institutions, so that cash is not readily available. In such circumstances, wages may be paid with the employee's consent, by one of the other legally acceptable modes of payment. If the employee does not agree, the employer must pay the wages in cash. Payment must be made at the frequency agreed in the contract of employment.

Employees, who before the coming into force of the Act (1 January 1992) were paid in cash, (or by any other lawful method) are entitled to continue to be paid by this method unless another mode is agreed between the employer and employee.

Deductions from pay - The Payment of Wages Act 1991 allows an employer to make the following deductions:

- any deduction required by law for example, income tax and social welfare contributions and maintenance payments under a court order;
- any deduction required by a term of the employee's contract, for example, pension scheme contributions;

- any deductions agreed to in writing in advance by the employee, for example, trade union subscriptions, medical insurance.

Special restrictions are placed in relation to certain deductions in respect of the value of goods or services provided to employees (for example provision or cleaning of uniforms) or to make disciplinary deductions (for example till shortages, breakages and so on).

Itemized pay statement - Under the Payment of Wages Act 1991, all employees are entitled to a written statement showing:

- gross amount of wages payable;
- nature and amount of each deduction.

The statement must be given to every employee with their wages or as soon as possible thereafter (in the case of credit transfer). The employer must ensure that the information contained in the statement is confidential.

Hours of work/shift work/overtime

The Conditions of Employment Acts 1936 - 1944 regulate hours for industrial workers. These Acts distinguish between day work, overtime, and shift work. The Protection of Young Persons (Employment) Act 1977 imposes restrictions on the employment of young persons. The following are the principal limitations:

- a man or woman may not continue work after 8pm on any ordinary working day;
- overtime may not exceed two hours in any day or 12 in any week, or 240 hours in any year, or 36 hours in any period of four consecutive weeks;
- a worker employed on day work must have an interval of at least half an hour after five hours' work;
- the overtime premium must be at least 25 per cent of normal rates;
- children under 14 years of age may not be employed and there are restrictions on the employment of persons under 18 years;

- except where a shiftwork licence has been obtained from the Minister for Labour, women may not be employed to do industrial work between the hours of 10pm and 8am, that is on the so-called 'third shift'.

Women may now do night work although there should be provision for a female employee to do day work if she is pregnant.

The EU Council Directive (93/104/EC) concerning certain aspects of the organization of working time must be legislated in Irish law by November 1996.

Holidays

A minimum entitlement to holidays is provided for in the Holiday (Employees) Act 1973. This Act entitles an employee to three weeks' leave per annum. In addition, the Act provides for nine public holidays. Pay in relation to holidays must be given in advance, calculated at the normal weekly rate. Holiday entitlement is calculated as follows:

- for each month where an employee works 120 hours one-twelfth of the statutory three weeks annual entitlement;
- where, in any leave year (which runs from 1 April to 31 March for the purposes of the Act) an employee works 1 400 hours, three weeks leave.

The Worker Protection (Regular Part-Time Employees) Act 1991 provides annual leave and public holiday benefits for regular part-time employees.

Annual leave shall be increased to 4 weeks by November 1996 (*EU Council Directive 93/104/EC*).

All hours worked, including overtime and time spent on annual leave, are included for the purposes of calculating annual leave entitlement.

Where an employee on annual leave is ill and supplies a medical certificate, the period covered by the certificate shall not be counted as part of annual leave. An employee with eight qualifying months is entitled to two unbroken weeks leave.

If a female employee has 14 weeks' maternity leave, it is included for the purpose of building up holiday entitlement.

Timing of leave - The employer decides when the employee can take annual leave, but the employee's opportunity for rest and relaxation must be taken into account. The employer must consult with the employee (or his or her trade union) at least one month before leave is to be given. Leave must be taken in the current leave year or within six months.

On cessation of employment, any outstanding leave entitlement must be paid. The employer must keep and retain records for three years for inspection.

Maternity provisions

The right to maternity leave is governed by the Maternity Protection of Employees Acts 1981 and 1991. These Acts grant female employees certain legal rights, which include:

• the right to take maternity leave;
• the right to return to work;
• the right to take time off for ante-natal and post-natal care;
• the right to protection of their jobs during maternity leave.

An employee is entitled to 14 consecutive weeks' maternity leave at a time of her choice but which must include four consecutive weeks immediately before the birth and not more than ten weeks after. An employee may take up to four consecutive weeks' additional leave immediately after her maternity leave, at her own expense.

There is no service qualification for any of the legal rights under the Act. However these rights are lost if the employee fails or neglects to serve the statutory notifications on her employer.

The employer is not obliged to make salary payments during maternity leave but the employee is entitled to claim a maternity allowance under the Social Welfare Acts.

The Acts cover all female employees, including regular part-timers, who are employed for at least eight hours a week and have 13 weeks continuous service. Women on probation, apprentices and trainees are covered.

The employee is entitled to unpaid time off during 'normal working' time for pre and post-natal checks, subject to the employee giving written notification of the date and time of the appointment to her employer at least two weeks in advance.

During the period of maternity leave, all statutory and contractual rights are protected, for example rights to notice of termination and disciplinary measures.

The EC Directive 92/85/EEC introduces measures to encourage improvement in safety and health for pregnant employees or those who have recently given birth or are breastfeeding. These include:

- paid time off for ante-natal care;
- adjusted working conditions;
- no nightwork.

Adoptive leave - The Adoptive Leave Act 1994, grants leave to women on a similar basis to maternity leave. It also applies to male employees in certain circumstances.

Time off

There are two situations covered by statute where employees are entitled to payment during absence from work. These are:

Jury service - An employee is entitled to be paid while required to attend jury service. All amounts which would have been earned are payable - overtime, production bonus, attendance money and so on.

Seeking alternative employment following redundancy - Where an employee is working out notice after notification of redundancy, there is an entitlement, during the last two weeks, to a reasonable amount of paid time off to look for a new job or to arrange training.

It is normal for trade union officials to be paid while engaged on union business but this is a matter for negotiation.

Disciplinary and grievance procedures

All contracts of employment should contain terms relating to disciplinary procedures. Where called for, an employer can use these procedures to suspend or dismiss an employee. There is a right of appeal. Where specific terms are not included in the contract of employment, an employer may only discipline the employee in such a way as does not interfere with the employee's statutory rights.

Lay-off and guaranteed payments

Where lay-offs are temporary and the employer fails to give proper notice to the employee, the employer renders himself liable to a claim for redundancy payment.

Period of notice

The minimum period of notice required for termination of employment is covered by the Minimum Notice and Terms of Employment Act 1973. An employer who wishes to dismiss an employee for any reason other than misconduct must give a minimum period of notice, the length being dependent on the employee's period of continuous service, as illustrated in Table 1.

Table 1

Service period	Notice period
13 weeks - 2 years	1 week
2 - 5 years	2 weeks
5 - 10 years	4 weeks
10 - 15 years	6 weeks
15 or more years	8 weeks

An employer is entitled to one week's notice from an employee who has been in continuous employment for 13 weeks or more.

Service is not broken by strikes, lockouts, lay-offs or change of ownership of the business.

The Act provides that employees are entitled to the longer of contractual or statutory minimum notice.

If the employee is dismissed for 'misconduct' the employer does not have to give any notice or pay in lieu of notice. The term 'misconduct' is not defined in the Act.

The employer or employee may waive his or her right to notice or the employee may accept payment in lieu. During the period of notice the employee is entitled to normal pay and other rights for example sick leave and so on.

Dismissal

The Unfair Dismissals Act 1977, amended and extended by the Protection of Employees (Employer's Insolvency) Act 1984 and Worker Protection (Regular Part-Time Employees) Act 1991 and Unfair Dismissal (Amendment) Act 1993, obliged employers to justify dismissals and to have proper dismissal procedures. It introduced a distinction between 'fair' and 'unfair' dismissal. The law assumes that all dismissals are unfair unless the employer can prove otherwise. Dismissals which are based on the following are always unfair:

- age;
- trade union membership or activities;
- religious or political opinions;
- race or colour;
- pregnancy;
- unfair selection for redundancy;
- legal proceedings against the employer where the employee is a party or a witness;
- employee's sexual orientation;
- membership of the travelling community.

The redress for unfair dismissal is:

- reinstatement in the position previously held, on the same terms and conditions, with effect as and from the date of dismissal; or
- re-engagement either in the job previously held or in another suitable job, with conditions attached which the adjudicating body considers reasonable; or
- financial compensation to a maximum of two years' pay; or
- if no financial loss, the employee may be awarded up to four weeks pay.

In general terms, a dismissal may be justified by the employer if it resulted wholly or mainly from:

- the capability, competence or qualifications of the employee;
- the conduct of the employee;
- the redundancy of the employee;
- other substantial grounds;
- where continuation would be unlawful (for example under age).

Also, it may be construed as dismissal if a person's conditions of work are made so difficult that he or she feels obliged to leave.

An employer who has dismissed an employee must, if asked, give reasons for the dismissal in writing within 14 days.

The Act sets up a procedure and structure for adjudicating on cases of unfair dismissal. The structure is primarily a Rights Commissioner who can issue recommendations. Unresolved disputes are brought to the Employment Appeals Tribunal and, if still disputed, can be brought by way of appeal to the Circuit Court, High Court and, on a point of law, to the Supreme Court. Employees who wish to make a claim must give formal notice in writing within six months of the date of dismissal.

The legislation covers full-time and regular part-time employees with at least one year's continuous service.

Redundancy

The Redundancy Payments Acts 1967 to 1991, amended by EU Directive 92/56/EEC provide:

- criteria for selection for redundancy;
- a method of calculating redundancy payments;
- access of workers and representatives to judicial/administrative bodies, such as the Employment Appeals Tribunal;
- that an employee (aged 16 to 66) with 104 weeks' continuous service whose employment is terminated because of redundancy is normally entitled to a redundancy lump sum payment;
- that the lump sum is payable by the employer direct to the employee and is based on the length of service and the employee's normal earnings, subject to a maximum of £300 in 1994;
- that the employer is entitled to a 60 per cent refund of the amount paid if two weeks' notice has been given to the Department of Labour, otherwise it is 40 per cent;
- that disputes are dealt with by the Employment Appeals Tribunal.

The Protection of Employment Act 1977 provides for certain procedural requirements which an employer must follow in the event of collective redundancies, the main one of which is consultation with employees' representative at least 30 days before the first dismissal takes effect and notice must be given to the Minister of Employment and Enterprise.

An employee is considered redundant when dismissed from employment for reasons such as closure of the company or the company continuing in business with a requirement for fewer employees.

Employer insolvency

The Protection of Employees (Employers' Insolvency) Acts 1984 to 1991 provide that where an employee's employment is terminated because of the employer's insolvency, certain outstanding entitlements relating to the pay of that employee may be paid from the Social Insurance Fund for example arrears of
wages, sick pay, holiday pay, pension contributions, minimum notice award and so on.

Collective employment regulations

Trade unions

The Constitution of Ireland guarantees liberty for the exercise of the following rights, 'subject to public order and morality': the right of the citizens to assemble peaceably; the right of the citizens to form associations and unions. The Constitution also provides that the laws enacted by Parliament shall contain no political, religious or class discrimination. Subject to the above, the Trade Union Acts of 1941 - 1990 regulate trade union organization in Ireland.

Employers are not bound by statute to recognize any trade union but it is the general practice to recognize and negotiate where a union has substantial representation.

Trade disputes

The Industrial Relations Act 1990 provides that it is lawful for one or more persons to attend at or near a premise for the purpose of peacefully obtaining or communicating information or of peacefully persuading any person to work or abstain from working where such 'picketing' is in furtherance of a trade dispute. If there is any unlawful activity connected with the 'picket', the protections under the Act may be lost and the 'picket' declared illegal. Generally, secondary picketing is illegal.

The new legislation does not give a positive right to strike but trade union members, officials of trade unions, trade unions themselves who take industrial action have immunity, but may be sued if:

- it is not a genuine trade dispute;
- balloting and notice procedures were not complied with;
- non-peaceful picketing occurs;
- industrial action amounts to inducement to breach a commercial contract or unlawful interference.

In the case of disputes relating to an individual worker, if procedures are not applied, he or she will not have immunity and could be sued for damages. Thus, such procedures should be specifically included in the employment contract or collective agreement.

All trade unions now have to have a rule concerning a pre-strike secret ballot. They must give employers seven days notice. There is now a Code of Practice on procedures including levels of cover during disputes in the case of essential services. The Code is admissible in evidence before a court (for example labour courts).

Employee participation

Worker participation in state enterprises

The Worker Participation (State Enterprises) Act 1988 applies to seven major state enterprises. The Act requires that one-third of all seats on the Board of Directors be set aside for elected representatives of the workforce. There are no such provisions for private sector enterprises.

Consultation on redundancies

The Protection of Employment Act 1977 requires an exchange of information and consultation between the employer, the Minister for Labour and employee representatives 30 days before the dismissal of groups of workers by reason of redundancy.

The Act applies to all employees in any firm which employs more than 20 persons and defines the size of a 'group' for the purpose of the Act.

Consultation on transfer of undertakings

The European Communities (Safeguarding of Employees' Rights on Transfer of Undertakings) Regulations 1980 gave effect to the EEC's Acquired Rights Directive 77/187. Under these regulations workers may not be dismissed simply because control of ownership of a business is to be transferred. The regulations further oblige employers to consult with their employees' representatives in the event of a transfer. The employees or their representatives must be informed in good time of:

- the reasons for the transfer;
- the legal, economic and social implications of the transfer for the employees;
- the measures envisaged in relation to the employees.

The Regulations provide that all rights and obligations of the selling company arising from contracts of employment or employment relationships (for example collective agreements) existing on the date of transfer shall be transferred to the purchaser, with no break in continuity of service.

Pensions, tax and insurance

The Social Welfare code was consolidated in 1993 and the relevant legislation is to be found in the Social Welfare (Consolidation) Act of that year. There are amending statutes in each of the subsequent years.

Income tax and social insurance

The standard rate of income tax (1994/95) is 27 per cent progressing to 48 per cent at higher levels of income. The general rates of social insurance contribution are 5.5 per cent on gross income for the employee and 12.20 per cent for the employer. The contributions payable by the employer cease when gross income exceeds £20 900 and employers' contributions cease at £25 800. Benefits available include:

- disability benefit;
- maternity allowance;
- unemployment benefit;
- unemployment assistance;
- occupational injury benefits;
- old age (contributory) pension;
- retirement pension;
- invalidity pension;
- widow's (contributory) pension;
- orphan's (contributory) allowance;
- deserted wife's benefit.

The employer must deduct the employee's contributions and is liable for payment of both the employer's and employee's share of contributions.

In addition, employees must pay a health contribution (1.25%) plus employment and training levy (1%) on all income.

Sickness benefit

The Social Welfare (Consolidation) Act 1993 as amended covers all workers who are compulsorily insured. Benefits payable under the Act are collected from the local Employment Exchange. Payments can be made under four headings:

- injury benefit;
- disablement benefit;
- medical expenses;

- survivor benefits, which may consist of:
  - widow's pension;
  - dependent widower's pension or gratuity;
  - orphan's pension;
  - dependent parent's pension;
  - funeral grant.

Retirement pensions

The Pensions Act 1990 was passed into law on 24 July 1990. The Act is in part designed to implement the requirements of EC Directive 86/378 and mainly:

- to monitor and supervise the implementation of the Act;
- to provide for the compulsory preservation of pension entitlements (for early leavers);
- to introduce a minimum funding standard;
- to ensure disclosure of information to pension scheme members;
- to clarify the duties and responsibilities of scheme trustees;
- to establish a Pensions Board with supervisory powers;
- to implement the principle of equal treatment for men and women in terms of personal pensions;
- issue guidelines on duties of Trustees of pension schemes.

There is no obligation on an employer to provide a pension scheme for employees.

Under the Minimum Notice and Terms of Employment Act 1973, where there is a pension scheme the employer must provide information to employees. This is usually done by way of a summary booklet.

Pension schemes are invariably called occupational pension schemes because the schemes have been approved (under Finance Act 1972) by the Revenue authorities. This confers certain tax advantages:

- employees contributions (up to 15% of gross salary) are tax deductible;

- employers' contributions are tax deductible;
- certain tax concessions with regard to income and gains generated by the pension fund.

A major benefit of the Act has been the preservation of benefits for those with five years' service or more in a particular scheme. If they leave employment, employees may:

- preserve entitlements in an existing scheme;
- make a transfer payment to a pension scheme of the new employer;
- trustee may purchase an approved annuity bond.

From 1 January 1996 there will also be an annual revaluation of preserved benefits.

Health and safety

Safety in the workplace

The key piece of legislation is the Safety Health and Welfare at Work Act 1989 which defines in general terms the duty and care of all employers and employees:

- every employer has a general duty to protect the safety, health and welfare of employees at work;
- the employer's duty extends to non-employees who come on site;
- every employer must prepare a written safety statement which clearly identifies all the hazards of the workplace and their associated risks;
- the employer has a duty to consult with employees on the arrangements for health and safety at work;
- employees are legally obliged to take care to avoid injury to themselves and colleagues when at work.

The employer's general duty of care includes:

- design, provisions and maintenance of the place of work in a safe condition;
- safe access and egress;
- design, provision and maintenance of plant and machinery in a safe condition;
- safe systems of work;
- provision to employees of information, instruction, training and supervision to ensure their safety;
- control or eliminate hazards as far as is reasonably practicable;
- emergency plan;
- safe use of articles and substances.

In addition, the employer must consult a competent outside expert in safety and health to solve any safety or health problems.

Employees' duty of care includes:

- employees are legally obliged to take all reasonable care to avoid injury to themselves and colleagues when at work;
- duty to report to their immediate superior any 'defects' of which they are aware which could be a risk to health and safety;
- any person who interfers with or misuses any item provided for protection is guilty of an offence;
- an obligation to use and maintain all protective clothing and equipment provided.

Safety in industry

Many of the provisions of the Factories Act 1955 and Safety in Industry Act 1980 are still law and provide for safety (such as dangers of machinery), health (for example temperature) and welfare (such as washing facilities). Regulations also apply concerning asbestos and chemicals as follows:

- an abstract of the Act must be posted in the factory;
- health provisions relate to cleanliness, ventilation, control of dust, lighting, sanitary arrangements, overcrowding and so on;
- safety provisions to deal with machinery, fire escapes, protection of eyes and so on;
- the establishment of a safety representative or safety committee is mandatory for employers.

In general employers must provide a safe environment in which to work, covering such areas as premises, machinery and equipment. In addition, reasonably competent employees must be selected.

Office premises

The Office Premises Act 1958 applies to all offices where more than five people consistently perform clerical work. Key provisions include:

- first aid box;
- 50 square feet per employee plus adequate sanitary conveniences for the numbers employed;
- sufficient ventilation and lighting must be maintained;
- safety provisions must cover structural requirements for floors, lifts and stairways;
- minimum temperature of 63°F;
- drinking water supply;
- clearly marked emergency exits.

Dangerous substances

The Dangerous Substances Acts 1972 and 1979 regulate the conditions under which explosives, petroleum and other dangerous substances may be manufactured, handled, conveyed or stored. It provides for a system of licensing for import, manufacture, storage and sale of various substances covered by the Act.

Anti-discrimination regulations

Anti-Discrimination (Pay) Act 1974

This applies to all employers and employees and introduced the principle that equal work deserves equal pay. Women and men employed on like work by the same employer in the same place are entitled to the same remuneration. Remuneration means any consideration in cash or kind, including overtime, sick pay, bonuses, redundancy payments and so on.

The Act does not prevent the employer from paying different rates of remuneration provided that the differentiation is genuinely based on grounds other than the sex of the employee. The entitlement to equal pay for like work applies also to a man in relation to his remuneration relative to that of a woman.

The Pensions Act 1990 provides for equal treatment in occupational pension schemes.

Employment Equality Act 1977

The Act applies to all employers and employees, with certain exceptions. It provides for equal treatment between men and women as regards recruitment, employment, training, promotion and working conditions. Advertisements must not discriminate between men and women, marital status, dress, mobility, overtime, safety, redundancy and disciplinary measures.

Regulatory bodies

Irish Congress of Trade Unions

The Irish Congress of Trade Unions (ICTU) is a voluntary association of most trade unions operating in Ireland. Its main function is to coordinate their individual activities. It is represented on government advisory bodies and it nominates labour representatives to a number of bodies, such as the Labour Court, Labour Relations Commission,

National Prices Commission, the Employment Appeals Tribunal, and the National Training Body. The ICTU coordinates union action on membership, picketing arrangements and industrial disputes generally.

Congress, when requested by affiliated unions, engages in negotiations on pay and conditions with employers' organizations on a collective basis. The Advisory Service of ICTU advises unions on all matters relating to work study, job evaluation and incentive schemes.

Irish Business and Employers Confederation (IBEC)

IBEC is the representative organization of industry and business (other than the construction industry) in all matters relating to industrial relations, labour and social matters. Its policy is the promotion of sound industrial relations. IBEC is financed solely by subscriptions from member companies and maintains strict political neutrality. IBEC consults and negotiates on behalf of member companies with the government and the Irish Congress of Trade Unions on matters of national concern in labour and social affairs. At international level IBEC represents employers on labour and social matters. IBEC executives are available to member companies for consultation and advice and participate on behalf of member companies in negotiations with trade unions. When required, IBEC represents member companies at the Labour Court, Labour Relations Commission the Employment Appeals Tribunal, Equality Officer Hearings, before a Rights Commissioner and other arbitration proceedings.

Construction Industry Federation (CIF)

The CIF is the management association for the construction industry and provides its members with general industrial relations services. It also represents the industry at the labour court and in negotiations with the government.

Labour Court and Labour Relations Commission

The Labour Court was established under the Industrial Relations Act 1946 to assist in the resolution of industrial disputes and to uphold good standards in industrial relations. The Labour Court may not investigate a dispute until it has received a report from the Labour Relations Commission stating that it cannot resolve the matter and that both parties request the Court to investigate it. The Court is not a court of law and its recommendations are not legally binding in most circumstances.   The Court consists of a chairperson, deputy chairpersons and six ordinary members, three employer representatives and three employee representatives.

The Court may, if requested, register employment agreements relating to the remuneration or the conditions of employment of certain workers and these agreements then become legally binding on every worker of the class, type or group to which they apply, and upon their employers.

The Labour Relations Commission was introduced under the Industrial Relations Act 1990 and established by ministerial order in January 1991. The Commission forms part of the Labour Court and its functions are:

- to offer guidance and help to resolve disputes;
- to provide conciliation and industrial relations advisory services;
- to prepare and offer guidance on codes of practice;
- to appoint equality officers;
- to select and nominate persons for appointment as Rights Commissioners;
- to assist joint labour committees and joint industrial councils;
- in general research and monitor developments in the area of industrial relations.

Employment Appeals Tribunal

The purpose of the Tribunal is to determine matters in dispute arising under the Redundancy Payments, Minimum Notice & Terms of Employment, and Maternity (Protection of Employees), Unfair Dismissals Acts, the Protection of Employees (Employer's Insolvency) Acts 1984 and 1991, Worker Protection (Regular Part-Time Employees) Act 1991, Payment of Wages Act 1991, Adoptive Leave Act 1994 and the Terms of Employment (Information) Act 1994.

The Tribunal provides a speedy, inexpensive and informal method of adjudication. Hearings are generally held in public and evidence is given on oath. A determination in writing takes approximately six to eight weeks.

Rights Commissioners

Rights Commissioners investigate employment related disputes on behalf of individuals. They do not deal with disputes related to rates of pay, hours or times of work or annual holidays of a body of workers. Claims for redress for unfair dismissal may also be referred, with the consent of the parties, to the Rights Commissioners under the Unfair Dismissals Acts 1977 to 1993. Having carried out an investigation in private, a Rights Commissioner issues a recommendation to the parties setting out an opinion on the merits of the dispute. A party to a dispute under the Industrial Relations Act may appeal against a recommendation of the Rights Commissioner to the Labour Court, whose decision on the appeal will then be binding on both parties. Under the Unfair Dismissals Acts 1977 to 1993, an employee or an employer may appeal a Rights Commissioner's recommendation to the Employment Appeals Tribunal.

A Rights Commissioner can also hear individual grievances/disputes under the Maternity Protection of Employees Acts 1981 and 1991, the Adoptive Leave Act 1994 and the Terms of Employment (Information) Act 1993.

Foreign employees

In general employees from Northern Ireland and Britain are covered by the legislation of the Republic. Work permits are not required for employees for these countries.

Citizens of EU member states are also entitled to work and reside in Ireland as provided for in European Union law, as are nationals of Austria, Finland, Iceland, Norway and Sweden (as from 1 January 1994). Residence permits are required for individuals from outside the United Kingdom.

Recruitment and training

Recruitment agencies are licensed by the government under the Employment Agency Act 1971. Employers are generally free to recruit as they see fit, subject to possible restrictions in some trades where only members of a particular union may be acceptable.

Government schemes exist to encourage training. These include a payroll levy on some industries which fund grants to those companies training workers.

The Labour Services Act of 1987 established FÁS - the Training and Employment Authority. FÁS offers all of its services nationwide through 49 Employment Services Offices and 23 Training Centres. Its services provide training, re-training and employment schemes as well as placement and guidance services. A special Co-op Development Unit provides assistance for community groups and workers' co-ops towards the creation of jobs. FÁS through a European network (called EURES) also provides assistance to people seeking employment elsewhere in the EU. On an International level FÁS International Consultancy, a subsidiary of FÁS, provides consultancy and manpower related services on a commercial basis.

Direct government grants are available towards the training costs of most manufacturing industries and eligible distribution industries. There is an elaborate infrastructure of training establishments, ranging from management training by universities and the Irish Management Institute, to the Regional Technical Colleges. Training can also be carried out by the firm internally. All training schemes are heavily supported by government grants.

This chapter was written by Mary Walsh, Anne B Murphy and Eoin Kennelly, Coopers & Lybrand, Republic of Ireland.

Italy

Introduction

Legal regulations concerning employment and labour relations are set out in the Constitution, where the basic principles of equality of treatment between workers are emphasised, and in the Bill of Rights of Workers of 20 May 1970 (law No. 300).

Ordinary statutes cannot amend or violate the provisions laid down in the Constitution. Where there is any conflict, the ordinary statutes are subject to judicial review by the Constitutional Court.

The Bill of Rights of Workers lays down the principles relating to a worker's basic rights (freedom, dignity and so on), the freedom and activity of trade unions, the placement of workers and administrative and penal provisions. Specific regulations are set out in agreements relating to various industrial, commercial and financial sectors of the economy. All such agreements, normally called collective labour agreements, are of two types, one referring to employees and the other to managers (*dirigenti*). Those relating to employees regulate different categories, attributing to each certain general job specification.

There are also other regulatory sources, such as administrative circulars and rulings, which play an important role in interpreting the law.

Individual employment regulations

Contracts

There is no precise definition of a contract of employment. The basic definition laid down in the Civil Code does not refer to a 'contract' but rather to a subordinate employee. That definition states that a subordinate employee is someone 'who engaged himself to cooperate for remuneration in an enterprise by working manually or intellectually under the direction of the entrepreneur'. The courts have given a wide interpretation to the concept of subordination, so that it covers as many employees as possible.

In addition, the law does not require any particular form of contract of employment. The law only requires that an employer communicates to an employee at the start of the employment relationship the extent of the employee's duties and responsibilities. Under the Civil Code, the parties to a collective agreement may agree that the terms and conditions of employment of individuals employed on an indefinite basis be specified in writing. Such terms would include:

- the parties to be bound by the contract;
- the commencing date of employment and the duration of the trial period, if any;
- if the contract of employment is for a fixed term (such cases are exceptions), the expiry date must be specified;
- the rate of pay; the method of calculation of pay if requested, the frequency of payment, and any particular clauses;
- the hours of work;
- the duties of the employee and the related category in the collective labour agreement;
- the place of work and the employer's right to transfer the employee;
- for any further matters, reference must be made to the specific collective labour agreement.

Generally, Italian labour law favours contracts of employment being for an indefinite period rather than having a fixed term. However, fixed term contracts may be used in certain circumstances, for example seasonal jobs, the replacement of employees on special leave (for example maternity leave), occasional or extraordinary jobs, entertainment jobs or for executive positions. The parties to a collective agreement may specify other circumstances in which fixed term contracts may be used. These collective agreements must state the percentage of the workforce employed under fixed term contracts as a percentage of the total workforce.

Fixed term contracts must be in writing and must include an expiry date. Where a contract does not include an expiry date, the contract will be deemed to be an indefinite contract. Similarly, where the employment relationship continues after the expiry of the fixed term, the contract will become an indefinite contract of employment.

Fixed term contracts can only be renewed once, and only in exceptional circumstances. When renewing a contract, the parties can only renew it for the same duration as the original contract.

Employers are prevented from hiring employees directly as they are obliged to consult the special lists of employees held at the local labour offices. Direct recruitment is only permissible in cases of urgency, for members of the employer's family, for employees performing intellectual activities and for those belonging to specialized categories. Until recently employers have been unable to name which employees they want, but due to a statutory amendment, employers can now recruit 50 per cent of their workforce by naming those employees.

Wages and salaries

Minimum wage provision - Each category in the various collective labour agreements has a statutory minimum salary. Periodically, during each calendar year, this minimum salary is automatically increased in line with the indexation system provided for by law.

Method of payment - There are no legal requirements regulating the method by which salaries must be paid. Special agreements must be made if payment is effected by a non-cash method. An employee's salary is normally paid in twelve monthly instalments; a thirteenth instalment is paid in December and certain collective labour agreements also provide for the payment of a fourteenth and fifteenth instalment at other times of the year.

Deductions from pay - The only deductions from pay which an employer must make without the express agreement of the employee concerned, are those in respect of income tax and national insurance contributions.

Itemized pay statement - Every employee has a right to an itemized pay statement at the time payment is made, showing the gross and net amounts and the amounts and purposes of any deductions.

Hours of work/shift work/overtime

Each collective labour agreement sets a limit on the maximum number of hours to be worked per week (generally 40); the number of overtime hours to be worked in a year; and also special regulations in respect of pregnant women or persons aged under 18.

Holidays

As a general rule the right to holidays is not renounceable. The holiday entitlement due to each category of employee is set out in the collective labour agreement. Generally speaking, each individual has the right to one month's holiday a year. Employers are also required to grant leave of absence (*permessi individuali*) which may involve longer periods of leave.

Maternity provisions

A pregnant employee may not be unreasonably refused time off during working hours to enable her to keep medical appointments. She is entitled to maternity leave for the following periods:

- two months before the expected week of confinement verified by a doctor;
- the days between the presumed date of birth and the actual date;
- three months after the birth;
- an optional period of six months before the child is a year old.

Upon her return to work, which cannot be refused, she is entitled to work two hours a day less than her normal working hours until her child is one year old.

Maternity pay is fully recoverable by the employer from the social security authorities (INPS).

Time off

Union representatives in a company have the right to time off with pay to carry out their trade union tasks. The amount of time a representative may take off depends upon the number of employees he or she represents.

Other types of leave include:

- *marriage leave* - an employer must grant an employee special paid leave of 15 calendar days at the time of marriage;
- *study leave* - working students who are required to sit examinations are allowed at least five days' paid leave;
- *military service* - during the period of obligatory military service for male employees, which normally lasts for 12 months, the employee is considered to be on unpaid leave with the right to return to a job;
- *civil duties* - where an employee is involved in certain electoral activities, the employee is entitled to time off with pay to fulfil his or her duties.

Disciplinary and grievance procedures

All collective labour agreements must specify the disciplinary rules and procedures which apply to the employees. In the absence of any formal disciplinary policy or procedures, the problem will be referred to the competent judicial authority for adjudication.

Any disciplinary sanctions applied, may be challenged by the employee concerned, before a court.

Trial periods

Trial periods need to be specified in writing and agreed upon before the employee commences employment. The parties can determine the duration of the trial period up to a maximum of six months. Collective agreements usually specify a shorter trial period. Either party may terminate the contract of employment during the trial period without notice or payment in lieu of notice, unless otherwise specified in the contract of employment.

Termination of employment

In Italy, either party can terminate a contract of employment (whether an indefinite contract or a fixed term contract) for just cause or for reasons connected with the productivity or organization of the company.   In situations where one party wishes to terminate the contract of employment without cause, the terminating party must give the other party notice, as specified in the collective agreement, or where there is no collective agreement governing the relationship, in accordance with custom and practice.

Period of notice

There are no statutory provisions detailing the period of notice when terminating a contract of employment, so notice periods are determined by looking at the regulatory provisions of the collective agreement or by custom and practice.

Generally collective agreements specify that the period of notice of a particular employee is dependant upon the employee's length of service and professional qualifications. In practice periods of notice range from a minimum of 15 days in the case of low seniority blue-collar workers and from a minimum of 180 days in the case of senior white-collar employees.

Employees are generally required to give a shorter period of notice to employers to terminate their contract of employment. Many collective agreements state that the employee is only required to give one-half or one-third the notice period required of employers.

Termination with notice

Generally, either party can terminate the employment relationship by giving the other party notice.

Where one party terminates the contract of employment without giving the requisite period of notice and without just cause, the terminating party must compensate the other party by paying an indemnity in lieu of notice equal to the amount of remuneration which would have been due, if the employment relationship had not been terminated.

Termination without notice (just cause)

A contract of employment can be terminated without notice for just cause or for a justified motive (*giustificato motivo*). The courts have defined 'just cause' as any grave misconduct on the part of the employee, whether intentional or negligent, that the employment relationship cannot be reasonably continued, not even on a provisional basis.

A 'justified motive' refers to either a breach of the contract of employment by the employee, or to some objective factor relating to the employer, for example, changes in the work organization or abolition of the employee's job.

Contracts of employment cannot be terminated for reasons of political or religious belief, union membership or active participation in union activities.

Moreover, the termination of the employment relationship might occur as the result of disciplinary dismissal. Where the employee does not comply with his or her work obligations as the result of unsuitable behaviour, the employer must notify the employee in writing that dismissal for disciplinary reasons might occur.

Procedure

There are different termination procedures depending upon the size of the particular office, branch, municipality or autonomous department. Notwithstanding the size of the company, all termination notices must be in writing and the reason for the dismissal must be indicated.

Individual dismissals are regulated by law No. 108 Articles 1 and 2 of 11 May 1990.

Article 1 deals with companies with:

- more than 15 employees in each plant, branch, office or independent unit;
- more than 15 employees in the same municipality, even if distributed in different offices;
- more than 60 employees anywhere.

Article 2 deals with:

- companies with up to 15 employees for each independent unit;
- companies with up to 60 employees anywhere.

Under both Articles, the employer is required to give the employee written notice of termination. The employee has 15 days from the date of the notice, to ask the employer for reasons. The employer must answer the employee's request within a period of seven days.

Where the dismissal is for disciplinary reasons, the parties must follow the procedure under Article 7 of the Statute of Labourers.

The main difference between Articles 1 and 2 is the procedure for challenging the dismissal.

Under Article 1, the employee has a 20 day time period within which he or she may use union assistance to take the matter to conciliation. If an agreement is reached in conciliation through the Provincial Labour Office (*Ufficio Provinciale del Lavoro*), a copy must be submitted to the Judge for rectification before it can become enforceable.

The parties can only use arbitration if there are arbitration procedures specified in the collective agreement. However, this does not preclude the individual employee from taking action through the courts.

To take an action through the courts, the dismissal must be challenged within a period of 60 days. If the Judge determines that the dismissal was unjustified or invalid (for discrimination reasons), the following remedies are available:

- reintegration and the payment of damages (minimum five monthly payments);
- where reintegration is not accepted by the employee, the employee may ask the employer for an indemnity equal to 15 months' pay;
- if the employer seeks to re-engage the employee, the employee must respond to the employer's request within 30 days, otherwise the employment relationship is terminated.

Under Article 2, the employee must challenge the dismissal within a period of 60 days. The appeal to the Employment Tribunal must be anticipated by the employee's request for a settlement, submitted in accordance with the procedures specified in the collective agreements or by Articles 401 and 411 of the Civil Code. If the employee does not submit a request for settlement, the appeal cannot proceed.

Where an attempt of settlement fails, each party may defer within a period of 20 days, the litigation to a board of arbitrators.

If the Employment Tribunal determines that the employee's dismissal was unjustified, the Tribunal may order the employer to re-engage the employee within a period of three days, or pay the employee an indemnity as follows:

- between two and a half and six monthly payments taking into account the number of employees, the size of the company, the length of the employee's service, the behaviour and the conditions agreed between the parties;
- ten monthly payments, if the length of service exceeds ten years and the employer has engaged more than 15 employees;
- 14 monthly payments, if the length of service exceeds 20 years and the employer has engaged more than 15 employees.

Where the dismissal is considered to be discriminatory, the provisions of Article 1 apply.

Where the employer fails to comply with any of these procedures and/or fails to provide all the reasons for terminating the employment relationship, the termination becomes ineffective and the contract of employment continues in existence.

It is important to note that notice of termination is only valid and effective when received by the employee. It is not sufficient for the employer to prove that the notice was posted.

The burden of proof for all terminations for just cause or justified motive rests with the employer.

Fixed term contracts

Where a fixed term contract is terminated prior to its expiry date without just cause, the terminating party must pay the other party an indemnity equal to the remuneration which remains payable up until the expiry date of the contract. Where one party has just cause to terminate a fixed term contract prior to its expiry date, the termination may be effected without notice.

'Protected employees'

•   *Pregnant women*

Law No. 1204 of 30 December 1971 prohibits an employer from terminating the employment of a female employee during the entire period of her pregnancy and for one year after the birth. This prohibition does not apply where there is just cause for the termination; upon the expiry of a fixed term contract; or where the termination results from closure of the business.

The Constitutional Court has extended this right to male employees who are required to look after their children as a result of their spouse being dead, ill or under some other sort of impediment.

- *Employees on sick leave*

  The employer cannot terminate the employee's employment for reason of sickness, except for just cause.

- *Employees on military service*

  The same protection as specified above applies to persons on military service.

Non-competition clause

A non-competition clause restricting the employee's activity after the contract of employment has expired is null and void, unless it is specified in writing and provides remuneration for the period of restriction. The amount of the remuneration must be decided prior to termination and must be proportionate to the employee's earnings, generally about 20 to 25 per cent of the employee's remuneration in the last year of service.

In addition, the restriction must be limited to a specified territory, must not exceed five years duration in the case of executives (three years in the case of other employees), and must sufficiently define the activity to be restricted. Both the limits upon activity and territory must not prevent the employee from using his or her professional skills.

Collective employment regulations

Contracts

The General Confederation of Italian Industry (*Confindustria*) represents the vast majority of employers in private industry. Enterprises in which the state has a majority holding are represented by INTERSIND (IRI companies and certain other state held enterprises) and by ASAP (ENI companies).

Collective Bargaining Agreements are contracts made between the Unions and the Entrepreneurs' Associations which regulate the individual terms and conditions of employment between an employee and employer. There are effectively three different types of collective bargaining agreements.

- *Corporative collective bargaining agreements*

  Corporate agreements were created and developed by the fascist regime to enhance its corporative principles. These agreements applied to employees who were registered within the signatory party guild and to all other employees who did the same type of work. Individual terms and conditions of employment could only be more favourable than the terms specified in the corporative collective bargaining agreements.

- *'Erga Omnes' collective bargaining agreements*

  Following the fall of fascism, the new Constitution provided that collective bargaining agreements could extend to non-registered employees. For political reasons, unions never made use of these provisions. In 1959 a new law was enacted which enabled the Government to adopt certain corporate collective bargaining agreements which re-established minimum working conditions for all workers, whether they were privy to the agreements or not.

- *Common law collective bargaining agreements*

  Common law collective bargaining agreements are subject to general contract rules and are binding only on those employers who are members of the Industrial and Commercial Associations. In many instances, employers who are not privy to the agreements elect to be governed by the collective bargaining agreements to ensure that their employees have the same working conditions as other employees.

These collective bargaining agreements generally remain in force for a two or three year period. In practice however, many will continue in force beyond their expiry date until a new agreement is negotiated.

Trade unions

The right to form trade unions, to join them and to carry out union activities is granted to all employees at their place of work. No agreement or action is binding if it aims to tie an employee into joining (or not joining) a trade union or ceasing to be a member. The employer cannot dismiss or discriminate against an employee, on the basis of union membership, union activity or because of the employee's participation in a strike.

Collective termination for economic reasons (redundancy)

The Law No. 223 of 23 July 1991 deals with collective terminations of employment for reason of redundancy. A collective termination occurs when an employer, with more than 15 employees, terminates the employment of at least five employees as a result of the reduction or transformation of the business. Where this occurs, the employer must follow a specified procedure in selecting the employees to be made redundant and in consulting with the union.

Procedure

In determining which employees will be made redundant, the employer must apply the following criteria, regardless of whether an agreement has been reached with the union or not. Redundancy criteria includes:

- technical, productive and organizational needs;
- length of service and seniority;
- family circumstances.

The employer must give written notice of the proposed redundancies to the union representing the employees, through the Employers' Association. Within a period of seven days from the date of receipt of the notice, the employer must meet with the union to discuss ways of avoiding or minimizing the redundancies. The parties then have 45 days to reach an agreement.   If they are unable to do so, the negotiations will continue before the Regional Labour Office or the Ministry of Labour if the company has offices (effected by the redundancies) in more than one city.

The negotiations before the Regional Labour Office or the Ministry of Labour cannot exceed 30 days starting from the date the Office or Ministry receives notice from the employer that the negotiations with the union have been unsuccessful.

Upon expiry of this time period, the employer has the right to terminate the employment of the redundant employees unless the parties have agreed otherwise.   The employees are then placed on a 'mobility list' and are given priority for re-employment within the next year by the employer.

Any termination of employment for reason of redundancy contrary to these procedures will be null and void.

Payments

Employees made redundant are entitled to a 'mobility indemnity' equal to 100 per cent of the 'conventional salary' established by the Salary Integration Fund (currently 1 500 000 lire per month).   If the employee is younger than 40 years, the mobility indemnity is paid for 12 months, this period increases to 24 months if the employee is aged between 40 and 50 years, and 36 months for employees over 50 years. For the first 12 months the indemnity is 100 per cent and from the thirteeth to the thirty-sixth month it is 80 per cent.

The employer contributes to the mobility indemnity by making a payment of six times the amount of the conventional salary to the National Social Security Institute (Istituto Nazionale della Previdenza Sociale).   This contribution is reduced by half if an agreement is reached with the union.

In addition to the 'mobility indemnity', employees are entitled to the length of service bonus as detailed above.

Lay-off and guaranteed payments

Generally, collective labour agreements preclude the lay-off of personnel, although certain specific provisions exist for industrial companies in crisis (*Cassa Integrazione Guadagni*).

Closure of companies

The laws on collective terminations do not apply in the situation where the company has to close down or where the company is insolvent. Under the Civil Code, an insolvency is not considered to be a just cause for terminating the employees' employment, but it could be argued that it is a justified motive and that the employees should be given a period of notice.

Salary Integration Fund 'S.I.F'

This fund was established to guarantee wages to employees who were laid off or required to work reduced hours. Employees have a right to 80 per cent of their monthly pay which is based upon a maximum of 40 hours per week.

The law setting up the S.I.F has established two types of intervention, ordinary and extraordinary. Ordinary intervention occurs when the company lays off employees either because of transitory events not attributable to either party, or because of fluctuations in market conditions. Extraordinary intervention occurs because of economic, local or sectoral crises or when there is a restructuring or redeployment.

Procedure

For ordinary intervention, the employer must formulate a detailed plan setting out the organization's strategy, the number of employees affected by the reduction in hours and the estimated costs. The plan is submitted to the Ministerial Committee for Industrial Policy, where the Minister of Labour and Ministers of Industry and Economics rule on the employers request by Ministerial Decree. S.I.F intervention has recently been limited by law to a maximum period of five years.

For extraordinary intervention, the employer must give notice to the union of its intention to suspend a certain number of employees, the criteria used to identify the employees and any proposals for rotation of the employees in the S.I.F. The employer and union must then go through a consultation period which must be completed within 25 days from the receipt of the notice by the union.

Upon the expiry of the consultation process, the employer may suspend the employees and file a request for extraordinary S.I.F with the Regional Labour Office. The employer must submit a plan specifying the reasons for the request at the same time as filing the request.

The Regional Labour Office has 30 days to give an opinion on the employer's request. If it is granted, the request goes to the International Committee of Industrial Policy, then to the Ministry of Labour who will grant the request by decree.

Payments

The employees remain on the employer's payroll for the duration of the extraordinary S.I.F. Most of the cost is borne by the National Social Security Institute, but the employer remains liable for 10 per cent of the cost.

Employee participation

Employees are entitled to consult representatives of recognised trade unions when they disagree with the employer's decisions.

Consultation on transfer

In the event of a transfer, employees must be assigned to tasks for which they were originally engaged, or to those corresponding to a higher category subsequently acquired, without any reduction of salary. In the case of transfer to a higher category, employees are entitled to treatment corresponding to the status of work performed. If an employee is transferred to a different category, the transfer not being attributable to the temporary absence of another employee, there is an automatic right to continue working in that category (once a certain period of time has expired). Collective labour agreements specify the period of time, which cannot exceed three months.

Trade disputes

The 'right to strike' is generally acknowledged in the Constitution, though there is no specific laws to regulate it.

Pensions, tax and insurance

Income tax and national insurance

Employers have to deduct income tax and national insurance contributions from their employees' pay on a monthly basis. The employer is liable for the omission of any deductions which should have been made. Income taxes and social security contributions should be paid over to the relevant authorities by the twentieth day of the month following that in which withholding tax has been operated, depending on the method of transmission used.

The rates are calculated on the basis of each individual's gross earnings. Percentages applicable vary between differing activities. The percentages illustrated in Table 1 are a mere indication of average levels:

Table 1

	Employer contributions	Employee contributions
Blue-collar	45%	9.69%
White-collar	45%	9.69%
Manager (commercial)	43%	9.69%

Sickness benefit

An employee is entitled to statutory sick pay in respect of days of absence due to illness, but must furnish proof of illness in the form of a doctor's certificate. In some collective contracts a part of the sick pay is recoverable by the employer at source as a deduction from the payment due to the social security authorities.

An employee is entitled to up to 180 days' sick leave per year.

Retirement pensions

All employees have to make appropriate earnings related contributions to the State Retirement Pensions Scheme. State retirement pensions become payable at age 61 for males and 56 for females, provided that the employee has contributed for at least 16 years. A maximum of 40 years of contributions is acknowledged.

Recent reformation of the pension schemes (law of 31 December 1992) has progressively increased the retirement age, as shown in the Tables 2 and 3.

Table 2 - Pension entitlement

Validity of the pension	Male (age)	Female (age)
From 1 January 1994 to 31 December 1995	61	56
From 1 January 1996 to 31 December 1997	62	57
From 1 January 1998 to 31 December 1999	63	58
From 1 January 2000 to 31 December 2001	64	59
From 1 January 2002 onwards	65	60

Table 3 - Insurance and social contribution requirements for the old age pension

Periods	Length of service
From 1 January 1993 to 31 December 1994	16
From 1 January 1995 to 31 December 1996	17
From 1 January 1997 to 31 December 1998	18
From 1 January 1999 to 31 December 2000	19
From 1 January 2001 onwards	20

The State Retirement Pension is called *pensione di vecchiaia.* Employees also receive a pension on retirement before the normal state retirement age provided they have paid contributions for at least 36 years and their employment contracts are terminated. This is referred to as *pensione di anzianita.*

Health and safety

Introduction

Workers are entitled to control, through their union representatives, the enforcement of regulations for the prevention of accidents and work related diseases, and to promote research and develop measures necessary to protect their health at work.

General duties of the employer

The employer has certain obligations towards employees, depending upon the nature of the activity carried out. Generally the employer must provide adequate materials, safe systems of working and a safe place of work.

Premises are subject to inspection by the labour inspectorate who may issue orders for improvements or ultimately institute criminal proceedings for any breach of obligations.

The employer has a civil, and in some cases criminal, liability in the case of accidents not covered by insurance or caused by lack of safety measures.

Employers' liability insurance

Once a year an employer has to pay contributions to the National Institute for Accident Insurance (INAIL), based on the number of employees and the degree of risk associated with the activity carried out. These contributions provide cover against personal injury and disease suffered by employees exposed to certain occupational risks.

Anti-discrimination regulations

Race and sex discrimination

If an employer refuses to employ a person, or provides less favourable conditions of employment to existing employees on the basis of gender, marital status, colour, race, ethnic or national origin, the affected person may complain to a tribunal.

An employee who has been discriminated against can seek the aid of the trade union or undertake legal proceedings directly.

Discrimination and trade union membership

An employee who has been discriminated against on the basis of membership (actual or proposed) of an independent trade union may also complain to a tribunal.

Equal pay

All contracts of employment have to provide for equal pay for male and female employees for work which can be shown to be equivalent and of equal value.

Regulatory bodies

The Ministry of Labour operates the following authorities:

Social Security Authority - Istituto Nazionale Previdenza Sociale (INPS)

This organization collects all contributions withheld by employers and is responsible for administering the State Pension Scheme.

National Institute for Accident Insurance - Istituto Nazionale Assicurazioni Infortuni sul Lavoro (INAIL)

This body provides insurance coverage for employees against accidents at work.

Labour Inspectorate - Ispettorato del Lavoro

The Labour Inspectorate ensures that contributions paid over by employers are correct and that employment regulations, involving the security and safeness of working conditions are enforced.

Provincial Labour Office - Ufficio Provinciale del Lavoro e della Massima Occupazione

The Provincial Labour Office is responsible for the assignment of workers and the issue of permits.

Additionally, all companies with more than 35 employees are compelled by law to hire one or more handicapped persons, depending upon the number of employees employed. The Provincial Labour Office provides for the assignment of such handicapped persons.

The following legal institutions deal with employment regulations and have the power to fine employers for incorrect payment or failure to make appropriate contributions.

Civil tribunals

Civil tribunals are empowered to hear cases relating to employment rights, generally in respect of individuals. All labour cases are entrusted to judges expert in labour law.

Criminal tribunals

In the case of accidents due to a breach of health and safety, an employer may not only be ordered to pay damages but may also risk criminal sanctions.

Arbitration Board

The Arbitration Board is made up of representatives from trade unions and employers, and is convened only when disputes arise concerning executives (*dirigenti*) and their employers, in relation to unfair dismissals.

Foreign employees

Introduction

A foreigner wishing to work in Italy is required to obtain a residence permit. Subsequently a work permit has to be obtained from the Labour Office, as for all employees in Italy.

Foreigners residing in Italy without a residence permit are liable to fines and expulsion.

Application for residence permits

Two procedures exist, one for nationals of EU member states and the other for nationals of other countries. In the first instance the procedure is a mere formality; in the second it also involves obtaining a work permit. The residence permit must be renewed annually.

Application for work permits

The procedures are the same as for Italian nationals; work permits will be issued if a residence permit exists and will normally be for an unlimited period.

For non-EU nationals there is a requirement to obtain a 'work visa' at the Italian Consulate in the prospective employee's home country. This visa will only be issued if an employment arrangement already exists. On arrival in Italy a work permit is required (which is normally a formality) and is renewable annually.

Recruitment and training

Recruitment

All recruitment must be processed through the labour office, where anyone wishing to work must register on the employment lists. All employers (with certain exceptions including managerial posts) must engage personnel through these employment offices.

Companies with more than 35 employees are required to keep the Ministry of Labour informed as to the number of employees, to enable the Ministry to monitor the requirements to employ disabled persons.

Training

Apprenticeship - Employers of an apprentice aged between 15 and 20 must provide the necessary training for him or her to qualify as a skilled worker. This training can be given through the use of special courses for which an apprentice has to be given paid leave of three hours a week, for eight months a year.

There are regulations concerning the duration of the period of apprenticeship, working hours, vacation periods and paid attendance at supplementary training courses. Social security contributions are limited to some L 15 000 per month per apprentice.

'Formation' contracts - 'Formation' contracts have been introduced lately to encourage employers to hire young people between the ages of 15 and 32. An employer may hire young people for a period not exceeding 24 months if the central labour authorities have previously approved a special 'formation' contract. Such contracts must outline in detail the training to be given to an employee and the nature of experience which may be gained. If these contracts are approved, the employer receives a reduction in social security contributions, ranging from 25 to 40 per cent, according to the number of employees employed and the location of the company.

Other matters - There are also provisions to assist unemployed workers through training and retraining courses; and to workers who during their working life wish to obtain higher education qualifications.

This chapter was written by Marco de Ruvo and Paola Mauri, Pirola Pennuto Zei & Associati, Italy.

Luxembourg

Introduction

Employment law in Luxembourg is found in a number of Grand Ducal regulations and laws, in particular in the law of 24 May 1989, and in certain sections of the 1868 Constitution of the Grand Duchy, Article 11(4) of which guarantees to every Luxembourger a formal right to work. The law of 28 October 1969 prohibits the employment of children under the age of 15, and the law of 24 December 1977, for the time being, prohibits the employment of those who are both over retiring age and in receipt of a pension above the statutory minimum wage.

Labour laws recognize two categories of employee: manual workers, and staff (that is, employees whose work does not involve manual skills), who are covered by the law of 24 May 1989 as well as the law of 5 December 1989. There is no standard definition for 'manual' skills but 'staff' are considered to be those persons who carry out a job that is principally intellectual, but still involves manual tasks. Manual skills do not include typing or secretarial work for instance.

Individual employment regulations

Contracts

The employer-employee relationship is in principle an individual relationship, although the law recognizes that certain matters may need to be covered by collective arrangements. All employees are entitled to a written contract. The laws governing the two categories establish only minimum statutory conditions - the parties to the contract can agree to be bound by conditions more favourable (but not less favourable) to the employee.

Employment contracts must be written and prepared in duplicate, and should set out the terms of the contract under the following headings:

- type of employment and the nature of the work;
- the normal hours of work;
- the starting salary and the nature and frequency of any periodic increments or other payments;
- any terms more favourable than the statutory minimum provisions;
- the length of any probationary or trial period.

Employment contracts may also include a probationary period. The worker or employee can be dismissed at any time during the period at short notice, with notice entitlement depending on the length of the probationary period. The probationary period cannot be less than two weeks or more than six months. Where the level of education is confined to primary school, probation cannot exceed three months. For those whose basic salary is Lfrs 21 622 Index 100 (for example to LUF 112 919 as at 1 August 1994) or more per month, the probationary period can be extended up to 12 months.

Wages and salaries

Minimum wage provisions apply to all employees, although higher rates may be agreed either in collective bargaining or on an individual basis. Indexation of wages is restricted, although special provisions are made for the lowest paid. Indexation is compulsory, with pro rata pay increases for each 2.5 per cent rise in the price index.

The guaranteed minimum monthly salary for all employees over 18 years of age (as at 1 February 1994) is:

- unqualified and with no family, Lfrs 41 314;
- unqualified with family, Lfrs 42 568;
- qualified without family, Lfrs 49 577;
- qualified with family, Lfrs 51 082.

On request, manual workers (*ouvriers*) must be paid at least twice a month. Otherwise, and for staff employees, there must be at least one payment per month. The employee must be able to draw on the money on the last working day of each month.

Tax efficient salary packages may include the following:

- lunch vouchers;
- company car;
- pension contributions;
- interest free mortgage or low rate loans;
- accommodation allowance.

Hours of work/shift work/overtime

As a general rule, hours of work are restricted to eight hours per day, giving a standard working week of 40 hours. Employees under 18 years of age may work overtime only in certain exceptional circumstances. For adult employees, overtime is compensated either by an equivalent number of hours off and payment for time off in lieu not taken or by payment as illustrated in Table 1.

Table 1

	Percentage of normal hourly rate
Manual workers	125
Non-manual staff	150
Adolescents	200

The employee's 'hourly rate' is obtained by dividing the monthly wage or salary by 173 hours. A standard pay month consists of 25 working days (weekdays plus Saturday). In general, working on a Sunday is prohibited, other than in certain defined circumstances. The employer must notify and receive authorization from the Ministry of Labour or the Labour and Mines Inspectorate, as appropriate. (See law of 21 August 1913.)

There is an absolute maximum of 10 hours' work allowed daily. In common with other EU countries, special provisions apply to hours of work for transport drivers.

Employees who work on a public holiday are statutorily entitled to an alternative day off plus 100 per cent of their normal rate of pay, or where no day off is granted, 200 per cent of pay.

Holidays

The law of 22 April 1966 provides a statutory entitlement of 25 days' annual leave for all employees in the private sector, in addition to ten paid public holidays. This is irrespective of the employee's age. Employees having less than three months' continuous employment with the same employer are also entitled to holidays but cannot take them in the first three months. Employees leaving during the calendar year are entitled to one-twelfth of the annual leave earned and not taken, calculated pro rata per full month worked. A month containing 15 working days or more is considered to be a whole month.

Leave must be taken such that at least 12 successive working days are taken in one period. Employers may refuse to grant leave to employees who have been absent without good cause for more than 10 per cent of the previous year. Special provisions for additional leave apply to handicapped persons, mineworkers and those who are prevented by the nature of their work from taking at least 44 uninterrupted hours' rest period in each week.

The timing of leave is at the employee's discretion. Where establishments are closed for annual leave periods, the timing of the closure must be agreed between employer and employees (or their representatives) in the first three months of the calendar year.

As well as the annual leave, all employees or workers have the right to public holidays, the dates of which are set by the law of 10 April 1976.

Maternity provisions

Pregnant employees may not be dismissed. This protection continues up to 12 weeks following childbirth. Pre-natal maternity leave consists of the eight weeks prior to the expected date of confinement (extended if necessary to the actual date). Post-natal maternity leave consists of the eight weeks following childbirth, extended to 12 weeks in specific circumstances including premature or multiple births and mothers who are breast-feeding.

Maternity leave is not dependent on marital status. All female employees are granted maternity benefit equal to normal pay, under the social security arrangements, for the statutory period of maternity leave up to a limit of Lfrs 202 681 (as at 1 August 1994).

Non-working or self-employed women are also entitled to a maternity allowance for a period of eight weeks before and 16 weeks after the expected date of confinement.

Time off

All employees are entitled to additional paid leave in the following circumstances:

- death of grandparent, grandchild, brother, sister, brother-in-law, sister-in-law - one day;
- death of spouse, parent, parent-in-law, son, daughter, son-in-law, daughter-in-law - three days;
- employee's marriage - six days;
- wife's confinement, marriage of child, house removal - two days;
- adoption of a child under six years old (eight weeks) or between six and 16 years old (two days) (law of 14 March 1988).

In the event of the employee's incapacity for work through illness, accident or injury, employers must pay wages or salary for at least the remainder of the month in which the absence began, and for three complete calendar months thereafter. Manual workers are paid by the social security organization from the first day of illness.

A person is allowed time off when carrying out trade union/employee representative duties, looking for a new job under notice, or for civic duties.

Disciplinary and grievance procedures

Fines may be imposed on salaried employees if agreed rules are not respected. Similar provisions exist for manual workers. Breaches of the rules concerning hours of work and remuneration, payment of salary and provision of references are punishable by fines between Lfrs 2 500 and Lfrs 150 000 and/or eight days to three month imprisonment.

Proceedings against an employer must have been commenced within three months (three years prescription for salary payments) years of the breach of rules. Illegal acts include dismissal while on lawful strike, dismissal without notice, dismissal while on maternity leave and dismissal as a representative for the employees. If dismissed without notice, there is an entitlement to compensation of salary equivalent to that for the period of notice not given. If the employee would lose pension rights a further indemnity is payable, up to 12 months' salary for 30 years' service.

An additional claim for damages and interest must be made within three months of the date when dismissal is notified.

Lay-off and guaranteed payments

Special rules were developed for lay-offs of building sector workers in winter conditions. These rules have been extended to include building related companies, the steel industry and other industries. After the first two days the state is responsible for payments out of an unemployment fund up to 80 per cent of the normal daily rate. The employer has to make an advance payment and reclaim it by giving notice to the appropriate authorities within a certain time.

Period of notice

Employment may be terminated at any time by either party, subject to observance of the prescribed procedures and time limits. The period of notice to be given by the worker or employee is illustrated in Table 2 and the minimum period of notice to be given by the employer is illustrated in Table 3. The grounds for notice given by the employer must be provided if requested. All notices must be given by registered letter.

Table 2

Length of service	Minimum notice period to be given by the worker/employee
Less than 5 years	1 month
5 - 10 years	2 months
More than 10 years	3 months

Table 3

Length of service	Minimum notice period to be given by the employer
Less than 5 years	2 months
5 - 10 years	4 months
More than 10 years	6 months

Notice by the employer must commence either on the fifteenth or the last day of the calendar month.

Employees absent on grounds of illness or accident may not be dismissed before the expiry of three full calendar months after the month in which the absence commenced, 26 weeks for manual workers. Female employees may not be dismissed immediately following marriage, during pregnancy or during the 12 weeks following childbirth.

Special rules apply where ten or more employees' contracts are terminated together within 30 days, or where 20 or more contracts are terminated together within 60 days. Staff and workers' representatives are protected from dismissal by additional provisions.

If either party terminates a staff contract without observing the prescribed notice periods, the other party is entitled to compensation equal to the salary that would have been payable if proper notice had been given. Similar rules apply for manual workers.

Severance payments

Employees are entitled to severance payments on termination of employment by the employer, graduated according to length of service. Severance payments for workers and staff employees are set out in Table 4.

Table 4

Years of service	Worker	White-collar employee
Less than 5	Nil	Nil
5 - 9	1	1 month
10 - 14	2	2 months
15 - 19	3	3 months
20 - 24	3	6 months
25 - 29	3	9 months
30 or more	3	12 months

In enterprises where there are less than 20 employees, the employer can elect to make the severance payment or give an extended notice period, as shown in Table 5.

Table 5

Years of service	Extended notice entitlement (months)	
	Worker	Employee
5 or more	5	5
10 - 14	8	8
15 - 19	9	9
20 - 24	9	12
25 - 29	9	15
30 or more	9	18

Dismissal for gross misconduct

In the event of gross misconduct by either party, the other party may terminate the contract without notice. This must be notified by registered letter. The innocent party is entitled to damages with interest. If the employee or worker is responsible for the termination, the right to compensation for the period of notice of dismissal and to severance payment is forfeited. Lawful strikes are not grounds for dismissal.

Employees who are unfairly dismissed (as during a lawful strike, for unlawful reasons, or where the dismissal would constitute an economically or socially abnormal act) may claim damages and interest in addition to severance payments. Lawful strikes are those declared after consultation with the National Conciliation Office. Economically or socially abnormal acts are not defined in law; they are usually acts that do not uphold the provisions of collective agreements.

Collective employment regulations

Status of collective agreements

The laws governing individual contracts apply to all employment relationships. The law of 12 June 1965 makes provision for one or more union organizations representing workers or staff, and one or more employers' organizations, enterprises or groups of enterprises to enter into collective agreements. These collective agreements are contracts governing the relationships between the parties and dealing with general conditions of service. The National Conciliation Office may decree that collective agreements are legally binding on all employers and employees in the trade, industry or sector covered by the agreement. A declaration to this effect may be made in the form of a Grand Ducal Regulation published in the Official Gazette.

Scope and validity of collective agreements

Whether a collective agreement covers groups of enterprises or only a single enterprise, there must be only one agreement covering manual workers and only one agreement covering staff employees. Joint or separate agreements for workers/staff may be concluded, and senior staff may be excluded.

Collective agreements must be valid for at least six months and at most three years, and must be lodged with the Labour and Mines Inspectorate. On expiry, agreements may be terminated, reviewed by tacit consent or revised by the parties. Collective agreements must be in writing and signed by the parties.

Compulsory negotiation

Any employer who is requested to enter into negotiations with a view to concluding a collective agreement must do so. Refusals are referred to the National Conciliation Office.

Employee participation

Employee representatives

Under the law of 18 May 1979 (and law of 13 July 1993 related to part-time staff), every private sector enterprise employing 15 or more employees must have staff representatives, elected for five year terms in secret ballots by proportional representation. Elections must be held between 15 October and 15 November every fifth year.

Staff committees

In businesses employing fewer than 100 employees, workers and staff elect a joint staff committee. In businesses employing more than 100 employees, separate workers' and staff committees are elected, provided the organization employs at least 15 workers and 15 staff employees. In businesses regularly employing five or more young workers (under 21), separate young employees' representatives must be elected.

The general role of committees is to protect the interests of employees with respect to working conditions, job security and social legislation (except where these matters fall within the competence of any works council). The staff committee is the channel through which employee demands are communicated to the employer.

Staff representatives must be given time off with pay to carry out their duties. Special provisions protect them from dismissal.

Joint works councils

Under the law of 6 May 1974 (and law of 26 February 1993 related to part-time staff), the appointment of a joint works council is obligatory in all private sector establishments employing an average of at least 150 wage and salary earners over any three year period.

Works councils must be established in the month following elections for staff representatives, and are elected by secret ballot by proportional representation of all staff representatives. The following employees may vote:

- 18 years old;
- six months' service;
- any nationality.

Only the following candidates may be elected:

- 25 years old;
- one year's service;

- Luxembourg citizens or EU nationals or employees with work permit C.

Works councils consist of equal numbers of management and employee representatives, according to the total numbers employed, on the scale shown in Table 6.

Table 6

Staff complement	Employer representatives	Employee representatives
150 - 499	3	3
500 - 1 000	4	4
1 001 - 1 500	6	6
1 501 - 5 000	7	7
More than 5 000	8	8

Management representatives are appointed by the head of the concern on any basis. Either side has to nominate a number of substitutes equal to their number of representatives on the council.

Works councils are essentially advisory and must be consulted by management before any major decisions are made relating to plant investment, manufacturing processes or working conditions. They must be informed of the financial results and the economic outlook of the company.

Employee directors

The law of 6 May 1974 also states that a *société anonyme* (company limited by shares) must provide for employee representatives on its board of directors, if one of the two following conditions is fulfilled. The first is that the organization should have employed 1 000 workers in the Grand Duchy for a period of not less than three years. The second is that the organization shall be at least 25 per cent owned by the state, or enjoying a concession from the state relating to its principal line of business.

Organizations employing over 1 000 employees must appoint employee representatives to at least one-third of the seats on the board of directors; that is, there shall be at least three employee directors, as Luxembourg company law requires a minimum of nine board members in those companies.

Organizations with state participation must appoint one employee director for every 100 employees, provided that at least three are appointed, and provided that not more than one-third of the membership of the board consists of employee directors.

Employee directors are elected in secret ballot, by proportional representation, by employee representatives. Such directors must be employees of the firm. Separate ballots must be held of workers' representatives and staff representatives.

Pensions, tax and insurance

The social security system is built around a series of independent public institutions, each insuring a particular type of risk. They are managed by elected boards of employees' and employers' representatives under the general guidance and supervision of the Ministry of Labour and Social Security.

Disputes relating to social security are decided initially by the *Conseil Arbitral,* any appeal being referred to the *Conseil Supérieur des Assurances Sociales.* One can only appeal a second time on the interpretation of the law.

The costs of sickness insurance and retirement or invalidity pensions are borne equally by employer and employee, related on a percentage basis to wages, salaries or professional earnings, subject to certain contribution ceilings.

Accident and occupational health insurance with contribution ceilings is funded by employers at fixed rates proportionate to the degree of risk inherent in the activities of the enterprise. Unemployment benefits are financed by a tax added to income tax and by contributions from local authorities.

Income tax and national insurance

Income tax is deducted at source by the employer in a pay-as-you-earn system. The employer then pays the authorities by the tenth of the next month.

Tax tables are issued and deductions are made according to the status of the employee. A tax card is issued to each individual annually stating allowable deductions and tax category. In the case of a married couple the second person (normally the wife) is taxed during the year at a special rate of 22 per cent for a person without a child, 18 per cent for anyone with a child and not taxed if more than one child. At the end of the year the two taxable incomes are aggregated and an assessment is made of two times the tax payable by a single person earning half that aggregate. The amount thus calculated exceeded the PAYE tax deducted at source is then repayable.

Income tax rates are on a scale up to a maximum of 50 per cent. In addition a surcharge of 2.5 per cent of tax payable is levied for an unemployment fund and this is also included in the table values. The top marginal rate is therefore 51.25 per cent on an annual taxable salary exceeding approximately Lfrs 1 432 800 (single).

Sickness benefit

Usually 80 per cent of medical and dental expenses is recoverable from the *Caisse de Maladie*. Employees are entitled to social security sickness benefits from the first day of sickness. For white-collar workers, employers are required to pay full salary for the month the sickness starts and the following three months. Thereafter, for the balance of 52 weeks, the *Caisse de Maladie* will pay up to a maximum of five times the minimum wage, with the employer making up the balance of normal gross pay. Sick pay is taxed as though it were salary. The amount payable for workers is the average of the three months' earnings prior to sickness. After 52 weeks' sickness, the *Caisse de Pension* pays an invalidity pension. The *Caisse de Maladie* will pay the wages of a worker from the date of sickness, which must be certified by a doctor's certificate. Wages are paid by the employer, who seeks reimbursement subsequently.

Retirement pensions

Retirement pensions begin at age 65 for men and women although provision exists for a reduced pension at age 60 (57 in exceptional cases). Pensions consist of three elements with certain minima and maxima:

- a fixed element;
- a supplement of 1.78 per cent of the total contributable remuneration of the employees, adjusted to take account of general wage increases.

The law of 24 December 1990 set pre-retirement pensions at age 57. Widows and orphans are entitled to a widow's pension calculated on the insured's pension entitlement at the date of death. In certain industries, such as steel, ages for retirement on full pension are lower.

Other benefits

Unemployment benefit covers both full unemployment and short-term working. Rates of benefit are equivalent to 80 per cent of previous gross salary with a ceiling corresponding to 2.5 times the social minimum salary; that is, the minimum salary which a Luxembourg resident must receive.

Health and safety

Accident insurance and insurance against occupational health risks is payable by all employers according to a tariff.

The law of 17 June 1994 adopted into the Luxembourg legislation the EU Directive relating to health and safety.

The Labour and Mines Inspectorate is responsible for the application of the provisions governing working conditions and safety of employees at work.

Anti-discrimination regulations

The law of 10 July 1974 contains equal pay provisions for men and women. The law of 8 December 1981 gives equality of opportunities in finding jobs and obtaining promotion in a professional business. All reference to gender in advertisements or contracts is to be avoided.

There is also equality of working conditions. However there remain certain industries, such as mining, where special provisions relate to women. There is no anti-discrimination legislation with respect to racial discrimination. EU rules govern the treatment of EU nationals.

Regulatory bodies

The *Tribunal de travail siégeant en matière d'employé et d'ouvrier* deals with all employment law disputes.

The *Cour Supérieure de Justice* is the appeal court to which disputes between employer and employee are referred. The procedure to be followed is covered by the law of 6 December 1989.

Foreign employees

Under the provisions of the Grand Ducal Regulations of 28 March 1972 and law of 20 May 1994, non-EU nationals wishing to reside and work in Luxembourg are required to obtain a residence and work permit (with some specific exceptions).

EU nationals must obtain a declaration from the employer guaranteeing that the person is to have employment in Luxembourg. This will enable the person to obtain a certificate of residence from the *Bureau des Etrangers*. Non-EU nationals must prove good health and also obtain a work permit and a permit to remain in Luxembourg for all the members of the family (Grand Ducal Decree of 12 March 1972). EU nationals living across the border in Belgium, France and Germany may work in Luxembourg without any particular authorization.

To obtain a work permit an employee must apply to the *Administration de l'emploi.* If obtained the permit allows an employee to work for a stated period of time, which can vary from one year to an indefinite period, according to the category.

This chapter was written by Philippe Vanclooster and Frank Dierckx, Coopers & Lybrand, Luxembourg.

The Netherlands

Introduction

Dutch labour legislation can be found in several statutes. The Dutch Civil Code contains the more important rules of labour law, while other statutes deal with specific or related labour issues.

These statutes apply to the employment of employees in civil service, however public servants and other employees in the public service are governed by special legislation which is not dealt with in this chapter.

At present, Dutch employment law is in the process of change. Many regulations currently contained in the Dutch Civil Code and other acts, will be combined to form a new chapter in the Dutch Civil Code. It is expected that this new legislation will come into force sometime in 1995.

Individual employment regulations

The most important laws regulating the employment relationship between employers and individual employees are:

- the Dutch Civil Code (*Burgerlijk Wetboek*) (currently being reviewed);
- the Labour Act (*Arbeidswet*) (currently being reviewed);
- the Minimum Wages and Holiday Allowance Act (*Wet Minimum Loon en Vakantiebijslag*);
- the Collective Labour Agreements Act (*Wet op de Collectieve Arbeidsovereenkomsten*);
- the Act on Workers' Councils (*Wet op de Ondernemingsraden*);

- the Equal Treatment Act (*Wet gelijke behandeling Mannen en Vrouwen*);
- the Act for Parental Leave (*Wet op het Ouderschapsverlof*); several Acts with respect to the Social Security Legislation.

As managing directors have, in many instances, a unique legal position under these laws, this chapter will only deal with those provisions affecting the employment of employees generally.

Contracts

In the Netherlands, a person can agree to provide services or to perform some kind of work during a certain period of time and at a certain price. These agreements are not considered to be employment agreements.

The Dutch Civil Code defines an employment agreement as an agreement between two parties, whereby one party agrees to perform work during a certain period of time or during an indefinite period of time for remuneration and under the supervision and guidance of the other party.

Employment agreements may be concluded orally or in writing. Competition clauses and/or penalty clauses must however, be agreed upon in writing to be valid.

It is common practice for employers to informally conclude an employment agreement by letter rather than by a formal written contract of employment. The employer does however, have a statutory obligation to provide employees, including part-time employees, with specific employment information. This information should be provided in writing within one month of the employee commencing employment, and should specify the following matters:

- the place or places where the work should be performed;
- the function of the employee or the nature of his or her work;
- the date on which the employee commenced work;

- if the agreement was concluded for a definite period of time, the duration of the agreement;
- the entitlement to a holiday or the way this entitlement can be calculated;
- the period of notice which should be observed or the way a period of notice can be calculated;
- the wage and the time of payment. Where the wage depends upon work results, the employer should specify the amount of work which will be offered to the employee per day or per week, the price per piece and the time required to perform the work;
- the usual working hours per day or per week;
- participation in a pension scheme (if applicable);
- should the employee work outside the Netherlands for a period of more than one month, the duration of the work, the housing, the applicability of Dutch social security law and specification of the organizations responsible for conducting these laws, the currency in which payment will be made, the amount of remuneration and treatment of the employee upon his or her return;
- whether a collective labour agreement or regulation of a public organization is applicable.

The employee must be notified in writing, of any changes to these conditions, within one month after the change has come into force, unless it is the result of legislation, amendments to the collective labour agreements, or regulations issued by (semi) governmental organizations.

Where the agreement concerns the employment of housekeeping personnel working less than three days a week, the employer only has to provide this information upon request.

Contracts of employment may be concluded for a definite or indefinite period of time. Contracts concluded for a definite period of time must specify the expiry date. The contract will automatically terminate upon reaching that expiry date, by virtue of law. Contracts concluded for a certain event or specific task must define that task or event, and will terminate automatically once that task or event has been completed. A definite term contract can only be terminated prior to it's expiry date in the following circumstances:

- during the trial period (if any);
- by summary dismissal;
- during bankruptcy by the official receiver;
- when parties have agreed that notice prior to the expiration date is possible;
- by mutual consent;
- by judgment of the Cantonal Court.

Where either party reserves the right or becomes entitled to influence the expiry date, the agreement will no longer be considered to be definite, and will require the approval of the Regional Director of the Labour Office (*Regionaal Directeur voor de Arbeidsvoorziening*) ("RDA") or a Cantonal Court judgment to terminate it.

Where a definite contract has been extended beyond its expiry date, the employer can only terminate the extended contract at the end of the successive contract year with the prior approval of the Regional Director of the Labour Office, or with the consent of the Cantonal Court. Where the employee has continued to work beyond the expiry date of the employment agreement, this is considered to be a tacit renewal of that agreement.

Wages and salaries

Minimum wage provision - The Minimum Wages and Holiday Allowance Act applies to all agreements concluded under civil law. The Act also applies to employment relationships with certain Dutch nationals working abroad.

The Minimum Wages and Holiday Allowance Act provides for a statutory minimum wage for all employees aged between 23 and 65. The current statutory minimum wage for a full-time employee aged 23 years is NLG 2 163.20 per month. Employees under 23 years of age are entitled to a percentage of this amount, which varies between 35 per cent for employees aged 15 years and 85 per cent for employees aged 22 years. Part-time employees are entitled to a minimum wage pro rata to their hours of work.

The Minister of Social Affairs can review the amount of the minimum wage twice a year.

Method of payment - Normally wages or salaries are paid monthly or every four weeks, unless agreed otherwise. It is normal practice for the employer to pay the employee's salary directly into the employee's bank account. In principle the employee should receive his or her salary in monetary form, but certain benefits (as specified by the law) are also a form of salary.

To assist in calculating the amount of the employee's wages, the Dutch Civil Code states that a calendar year has 260 working days, a month has 22 working days, a week has five working days and one day equals eight hours.

Deductions from pay - The employer may only deduct amounts from the employee's salary for the following reasons:

- compensation for damages to be paid to the employer;
- any penalty due to the employer as a result of a written penalty clause in the employment agreement;
- the rent of a house, building, piece of ground or instrument, used and rented by the employee in the employee's own business; providing a written rent agreement exists;
- the purchase price of some daily necessities, purchased by the employee;

- any advance on the employee's salary;
- any amounts paid to the employee in excess of the employee's salary;
- health care costs as specified by the law.

Any further deductions can only be made against the employee's final salary upon termination of employment.

Itemized pay statement - All employers are required to issue a pay statement at the time payment is made, showing the gross amount of salary, the amount and purpose of any deductions, the method of calculation of the salary and the applicable minimum wage. Where the parties have agreed that different parts of the net salary are paid by different methods, the employer must provide the above information for each part payment.

The pay statement must also specify the name of the employer and employee, the term of the payment and the agreed periods during which the employee must work.

Hours of work/shift work/overtime

The Labour Act states that the maximum working week (excluding overtime) is 48 hours. As most agreements are concluded for a maximum of 40 hours per week, the government has recently proposed an amendment to the Labour Act which would reduce the working week to a maximum of 45 hours, 9 hours per day.

Table 1 illustrates the current maximum hours of work and periods of rest for different sectors.

Table 1

Type of business (for other sectors other rules apply):	Industrial Plants	Offices	Shops
Duration of work (maximum)	8½ hours per day and 48 hours per week	8½ hours per day and 48 hours per week	9 hours per day and 48 hours per week
Limits of work time	Monday - Friday: 7.00 - 18.00 Saturday: 7.00 - 13.00	Monday - Friday: - Saturday: until 13.00	Monday - Friday: 6.00 - 19.00 Saturday:
Periods of rest	Where more than 5½ hours are worked, at least ½ hour rest after 4½ hours	After every 5½ hours of work ½ hour rest	Where more than 6½ hours are worked, at least ½ hour rest after 5½ hours; and 1½ hours rest if work starts before 13.00 and finishes after 18.00
Actual day of rest	Sunday	Sunday	Sunday
Half a day off	Saturday after 13.00	Saturday after 13.00	During one day a week after 13.00 or on Monday until 13.00.

In accordance with the Labour Act, an employer requires a permit from the Regional Labour Inspectorate (*Arbeidsinspectie*) before operating shift work. Under the proposed amendment to the Labour Act, the prior permission of the Regional Labour Inspectorate will no longer be necessary, but shift work will still be strictly regulated.

Persons below the age of 18 may not work in shifts.

In principle the employer must obtain a permit from the Regional Labour Inspectorate before requiring any of its employees to work overtime. These permits are usually granted without any investigation by the Inspectorate.

It is quite common that overtime hours do not exceed the statutory maximum number of hours per week. There are cases however, where the employer has a structural situation requiring the employees to work overtime hours exceeding the statutory maximum.

Collective labour agreements generally regulate the extent of overtime and shift work, and the amount of remuneration to be paid for such work. It is quite common for employees to receive a bonus payment and a percentage increase in their salaries.

Holidays

Employees are entitled to a minimum of 20 working days' holiday per year, provided that they have worked at least 40 hours per week. In practice, most collective labour agreements provide 25 working days' holiday per year and specify during which periods the holidays should be enjoyed. Part-time workers are entitled to a pro rata number of holidays.

Businesses and industry are normally closed on seven paid public holidays: New Year's Day, Easter Monday, Queen's Day, Ascension Day, Whit Monday, Christmas Day and Boxing Day.   Other holidays sometimes include Good Friday (March/April) and Liberation Day (5 May).   Some other religious festivals lead to public holidays in particular areas.

Under the Minimum Wages and Holiday Allowance Act, an employee is entitled to a minimum annual holiday allowance equal to eight per cent of his or her gross salary.   In principal, the holiday allowance for the preceding year is paid in June, based upon the amount of salary received in May.   The parties may however, agree to alternative methods of calculation by written agreement or as specified in the collective labour agreement.

Maternity provisions

A pregnant employee is entitled to at least 16 weeks' maternity leave, during which period the employee will receive a sickness benefit equal to 100 per cent of her daily earnings, up to a maximum of NLG 286.84 per day.   The pregnant employee must cease work at least four weeks, but generally not earlier than six weeks before the expected date of birth.

During pregnancy the employer may not give notice to terminate the employment relationship, unless it is terminated for an urgent cause or has reached the expiry date of a definite term contract.

Parental leave

As from 1 January 1991, all employees who have been employed for at least one year and who work for more than 20 hours a week are entitled to parental leave.   Employees who have or care for a child under four years of age are entitled to take part-time leave (a minimum of 20 hours) to care for that child, up to a maximum period of six months.

Employees who take parental leave are only entitled to wages for the hours actually worked. Once parental leave expires, the employee must return to his or her normal working hours.

Families with one parent can apply to the social security fund for a supplementary income benefit, if their income is below a threshold set at 80 per cent of the statutory minimum wage.

Time off

The employer must grant the employee leave without pay to participate in parliamentary sessions if the employee is a member of parliament.

Employees who start work directly after completing a period of ten years' school attendance or at the end of the school year in which they attain the age of 16, are required to follow part-time courses at educational institutes, or at apprenticeship training schools for two years. The employer has to provide paid leave to these employees on contract.

Other periods of paid leave may be regulated by the collective labour agreement. In exceptional circumstances the employee may be granted leave for special activities.

Trial periods

The parties may agree that the first two months of employment should be a trial period. Either party may terminate the employment relationship during this period without having to observe the statutory requirements for termination of employment. A trial period exceeding two months is null and void.

Where the maximum trial period of two months is considered to be too short, the employer may avoid the mandatory provisions by entering into a contract for a definite duration with the employee.

Termination of employment

In general there are four ways to terminate an employment relationship:

- by virtue of law (agreements concluded for a definite period of time and during a trial period);
- by mutual consent;
- by one party giving notice of termination, with the prior permission of the RDA or dismissal for urgent causes (summary dismissal);
- by way of judgment from the Cantonal Court.

Further, employment agreements terminate upon the death of the employee.

Termination by mutual consent

The parties can enter into a mutual agreement that the contract will terminate at a particular time. It is preferable, for the sake of certainty, that this agreement be specified in writing.

Strict rules have been developed through case law, to ensure that the termination is not too severe, particularly for the employee as he or she will encounter problems with respect to the unemployment benefit where termination has been consented to. In this respect, a termination by mutual consent will not be assumed quickly.

The employer cannot rely on the employee's consent to termination of employment where the employee acted on impulse, without reasonable time to reflect upon his or her actions. This could be the case where the termination was caused by a dispute between the employer and employee. Furthermore a termination by consent will not be effective, if it was the result of undue influence.

In practice, it is quite common for employers and employees to terminate their employment relationship by mutual agreement. The parties will usually agree on a formal procedure, to be instituted by the Cantonal Court, to terminate the contract. The Cantonal Court will normally render judgment on which date the contract of employment will be terminated without any further investigation. Such judgments usually contain an express statement stating that the employee is not to blame for the termination.

Termination by notice

To terminate an employment relationship by notice, the employer as well as the employee must obtain the prior authorization of the RDA. Where either party attempts to terminate the relationship without this prior authorization, the other party has six months from the date notice is given to invoke proceedings to nullify the termination.

In practice, employers do not usually object to employees giving notice of termination. Where the employer does object, the employee can request authorization of the RDA, which is usually granted. The RDA will not generally enforce the rules against the employee, but will against the employer.

Prior authorization of the RDA is not required for the following employment relationships:

- managing directors of legal persons (companies);
- ministers of religion;
- civil servants;
- governmental employees;
- housekeeping personnel, working three days a week or less.

The parties must follow a specified procedure, which is mostly in writing, when applying for authorization. Once an application is made, the other party gets an opportunity to respond and to defend him or herself against the statements of the applicant. It is usual for both parties to have a further opportunity to make statements. Thereafter the application and the defence are discussed by a committee (*ontslagcommissie*). In some cases, the committee will set a date for a hearing but this is the exception rather than the rule.

In all circumstances the RDA will weigh the interests of the employer against the interests of the employee and will determine whether the application complies with the rules of reasonableness and fairness. The Ministry of Social Affairs has given specific directives to the regional directors of the labour office on the examination of an application and defence. Where the application complies with these directives, RDA authorization will be given.

RDA authorization is usually given in the following circumstances:

- for economic reasons, such as a reduction in the labour force due to a decrease in business;
- where the employee is not competent to perform his or her job, and no other jobs are available for the employee in the company;
- where the relationship between the employer and employee has deteriorated in such a manner, that based upon the rules of reasonableness and fairness it is impossible for the employment relationship to continue.

Any application to terminate an employment relationship for economic reasons is subject to the seniority principle, based upon the 'last in, first out' rule. Where the work of several employees in one establishment of the company is interchangeable, the employer must apply to terminate the employment of the employees with the shortest service first, unless other reasons prevail.

The parties cannot appeal against the decision of the RDA as it is final. However, where authorization is refused, either party can institute proceedings in the Cantonal Court to have the contract of employment dissolved.

There is currently a new proposal to amend the legislation, by removing the requirement to obtain RDA authorization prior to issuing notices of termination.   Under this proposal, the parties will be able to claim compensation if the termination is considered to be irregular.

Period of notice

The employer and employee may specify a period of notice in the contract of employment or notice may be regulated by the company's employment regulations, provided that it does not exceed six months' duration and that the period to be observed by the employer is no shorter than the period to be observed by the employee. Where the employer's period of notice is shorter, the employer is obliged to give the same period of notice as required by the employee.

In the absence of a notice clause in the contract, collective labour agreement or company regulation, the minimum statutory period of notice is equal to the period between two successive salary payments, providing it is not longer than six weeks.

Furthermore, the following special provisions have to be observed:

- where the employer gives notice, the notice period is one week for every year of service subsequent to the employee's eighteenth birthday, up to a maximum of 13 weeks;
- where the employee gives notice, the notice period is one week for every two year period of service subsequent to the employee's eighteenth birthday, up to a maximum of six weeks;

- the period of notice to be given by the employer will be extended by one week for every full year of service after the employee's fourty-fifth birthday, up to a maximum of 13 weeks;
- the period of notice to be given by the employer is at least three weeks for employees aged at least 50 with at least one year's service;
- the maximum period of notice possible under the above provisions is 26 weeks.

The foregoing provisions do not apply to employees who have reached the age of 65.

Except where different regulations are specified in the collective labour agreement or public regulations, a period of notice cannot be less than the statutory minimum.

Notice may only be given on an agreed date, or such dates as may be specified in the company's employment regulations. Where there is no agreement or regulation, notice must be given on a customary date. Such dates usually occur on the last day of a salary period (for example, one week, four weeks, one month, at the end of the quarter).

It should be noted that there are currently some proposals to amend the statutory notice periods. In the present proposed amendment, the period of notice for employees will be one month and for employers it will be:

- one month if the employment relationship has lasted less than five years;
- two months for between five and ten years' service;
- three months for between ten and 15 years' service;
- four months for 15 years' or more service.

Statutory prohibition against giving notice

The Dutch Civil Code prohibits termination of employment by notice in the following circumstances:

- the marriage of the employee;
- during the employee's illness, unless such illness has lasted for at least two years;
- during the employee's pregnancy or during the period when the employee is entitled to a sickness benefit, even though the employee may be working;
- during military service.

Where the employer gives notice in contravention of these statutory provisions, the employee is entitled, within a period of two months after notice has been given, to invoke proceedings to nullify the notice. The employer can only terminate the employment agreement during these 'protected' periods, pursuant to a judgment from the Cantonal Court.

Collective labour agreements or public regulations may however, provide for different regulations than those specified in the Dutch Civil Code.

Other labour regulations provide further prohibitions. For example:

- The employer cannot give notice to terminate the employment of a member of a works council without the prior approval of the Cantonal Court, unless it is terminated for an 'urgent cause'. Approval will not be given when membership of the works council is or may be the cause for the request to terminate the employment relationship. Former members of the works council or candidates for membership of the works council enjoy a limited protection, as employment can only be terminated after obtaining permission of the Cantonal Court. The membership or former membership cannot be the cause for the request to terminate the relationship.

- The employer is prohibited from giving notice as a result of the employee evoking his or her rights under the discrimination law (the Equal Treatment Act).

Summary dismissal

The contract of employment may be terminated without notice and with immediate effect, for an urgent cause (summary dismissal), provided the other party is notified of the cause. In this respect, it is always advisable for the notification to be in writing.

Under the Dutch Civil Code, any serious act or circumstance in which it would be unreasonable to expect the employer to continue with the employment relationship would give rise to an urgent cause, for example:

- misleading or false statements by the employee in relation to certificates of competence (skills) or termination of the employee's former employment at the time of concluding the employment agreement;
- the serious lack of competence in the performance of the employee's duties;
- the commission of theft, fraud or other crime causing a breach of the employer's trust;
- serious insults or threats to the employer, the employer's family or relatives or one of the employee's colleagues;
- attempts to entice the employer, the employer's family or relatives or one of the employee's colleagues to commit improper or illegal acts;
- intentional damage to the employer's property;
- the employee exposing him or herself, or other people to serious danger either deliberately or after a warning;
- divulging secrets to third parties;
- refusing to observe reasonable directives or orders of the employer;

- gross or deliberate negligence in the performance of the employee's duties.

There must be an 'clear' urgent cause to enable one party to terminate the employment relationship immediately. Any delay, other than a brief delay to seek legal advice, may result in a judge finding that the cause was not urgent.

The employee may legally challenge the termination for an urgent cause within two months of the date of termination. During the proceedings, the employer will be required to submit evidence of the urgent cause. Where the court determines that the cause was not sufficiently serious and urgent to justify the summary dismissal, it will declare the dismissal null and void and the employer will be required to continue the employment relationship with the employee. Furthermore, the employee will be entitled to his or her salary from the date of the annulled termination until the date the employment relationship is terminated regularly.

To avoid the above situation, it is common practice for employers to institute a provisional procedure with the RDA or the Cantonal Court at the same time as terminating the employment relationship for an urgent cause. This ensures that the employer will be in a position to terminate the employment relationship legally if the cause is judged not urgent or serious.

Because of the serious consequences for the employee (for example the employee will loose his or her right to an employment benefit), the Cantonal Court will follow strict rules to determine whether the cause was serious and/or urgent.

Termination by judgment of the Cantonal Court

The Cantonal Court can terminate the employment relationship upon the request of either party. The request must result from a 'serious reason', which is defined by the Dutch Civil Code, as either an 'urgent cause' or a change of such nature in the circumstances of either party, that it would be reasonable to terminate the employment relationship immediately or after a short period of time. For example:

- when the employer no longer has work for the employee;
- when the employee is ill or disabled for a foreseeable length of time, and should be replaced;
- when the relationship between the employer and employee is seriously damaged.

The request for termination should state where the employment takes place together with the name and address of the defendant. Once a request has been submitted, the Cantonal Court will set a date for the hearing, where both parties have the right to be heard.

Where the Court grants the request, it will set the effective date of termination, which cannot be retroactive. The Court may, at its own discretion, grant the employee compensation if the termination is the result of a change in circumstances. Alternatively, the employee may claim compensation.

As there is no statutory formula available to calculate the amount of compensation, compensation amounts tend to differ on a case by case basis. The Court must however, apply some principles to ensure that the amount of compensation is fairly assessed.

Where the Court decides to grant the employee compensation, it will firstly inform the parties of this intention and will specify a period during which time the employer may withdraw his or her termination request.

The fact that compensation may be claimed or granted in the Cantonal Court, is the main reason why most employers choose to institute proceedings through the RDA. Although the RDA is not entitled to grant compensation, the employee is still entitled to request a severance payment through the Court, once notice has been given.

A judgment of the Cantonal Court for these types of proceedings cannot be appealed against.

Remedies

Severance payment

The employer may be liable to pay the employee a severance payment where the Court determines that the termination was obviously unreasonable, even though the employer complied with the requisite termination provisions. The Dutch Civil Code provides a non-exhaustive list of when an obviously unreasonable termination occurs:

* when the employment agreement is terminated without or with a pretended or false reason;
* when the consequences of the termination for the employee are more serious compared to the interests of the employer, taking into account such matters as the possibility of finding alternative work;
* during military service;
* when the seniority rule has not been observed.

The employer may also claim a severance payment on the same grounds, although the law only mentions as an example, the pretended or false reason for termination and the weighing of the respective interests. No formula exists to calculate the amount of the severance payment, although there are some guidelines, depending upon the factual situation.

Damages

Either party who terminates the employment relationship 'irregularly' is liable to pay damages. The termination will be considered 'irregular' in the following circumstances:

- when the employment relationship is terminated without notice;
- when the statutory provisions and/or the contractual and/or regulatory provisions with respect to the period of notice and the effective date of notice have not observed;
- in the absence of an urgent cause in the case of summary dismissal.

If any of these situations occurs, the terminated party may institute a claim within six months for compensation based either on fairness or on the real damage suffered. The difference between these claims are firstly the legal foundation and secondly the obligation to prove damage.

The damage which may be claimed is equal to the salary that the employee is entitled to during the time the employment relationship remains in force.

Reinstatement

As an alternative to damages or compensation, either party may, within six months after the date of termination, request the reinstatement of the employment relationship. The Cantonal Court will rarely grant this request however.

Under future legislation, it appears that it will no longer be legally possible for the employee to request reinstatement. The employer will be the only party able to request such a remedy from the Cantonal Court.

Attestation

After termination of the employment agreement the employee is entitled to an attestation, describing the nature of his or her employment and the duration of employment. If requested by the employee, the employer must include a statement detailing the manner in which the employee performed his or her duties and the reasons for termination.

Non-competition clause

A non-competition clause must be reasonable and specified in writing to be valid. The Cantonal Court has jurisdiction to cancel or converse a non-competition clause or a part thereof, if the restriction upon the employee is disproportionate to the business interests the employer seeks to protect.

Furthermore, the Cantonal Court has the power to award compensation to the employee, where the non-competition clause seriously obstructs the employee from excepting new employment. The amount of compensation will be determined on the basis of reasonableness and fairness.

Collective employment regulations

Organizations

In the Netherlands the three major workers' organizations are:

- Federation of Christian National Workers' Unions (CNV) (including the Protestant unions);
- Federation of Netherlands Trade Unions (FNV) (both non-denominational unions and Catholic Unions);
- Council for Medium and Higher Employees (Unie BLHP).

Unions are organized according to branches of industry or sectors, not individual crafts. Union membership for workers is not compulsory, except in the printing and allied industries, where a closed-shop system exists.

There are two major employers' organizations:

- Association of Federation of Netherlands Industries *(Vereniging van Nederlandse Ondernemingen or VNO)*;

- Association of Dutch Christian Employers *(Nederlands Christelijk Werkgevers Verbond or NCW)*.

These organizations represent large trade associations as well as some large Dutch multinationals who negotiate their own collective employment agreements. There are two general organizations for medium-size and small enterprises:

- Royal Dutch Employers' Federation *(Koninklijk Nederlands Ondernemers Verbond or KNOV)*;
- Dutch Christian Union for Small Industries *(Nederlands Christelijk Ondernemings Verbond or NCOV)*.

The unions are represented as members of two Government advisory bodies, namely the Social Economic Council *(Sociaal Economische Raad)* and the Foundation of Labour *(Stichting van de Arbeid)*.

Collective labour agreements

Collective labour agreements are negotiated by trade unions with either individual employers or employers' associations. The collective labour agreement governs the employment relationship of those categories of employees listed in the agreement, who are employed by the employer who concluded the agreement or employed by a member of an employers' association, which concluded the agreement.

The main Acts dealing with collective labour agreements are:

- the 1927 Act on Collective Labour Agreements *(Wet op de Collective Arbeidsovereenkomst)*;
- the 1937 Act on Compulsory Applicability of Collective Employment Agreements *(Wet op het algemeen verbindend en het onverbindend verklaren van bepalingen van collective arbeidsovereenkomsten)*.

By virtue of the 1937 Act, the Minister of Social Affairs has the power to declare a particular collective labour agreement applicable to an entire industry.

Company labour regulations

Under the Dutch Civil Code, the employer is able to regulate the parties rights and obligations by virtue of the company labour regulations. These regulations are determined by the employer, but will only bind the individual employee in the following circumstances:

- the draft regulations must be filed for inspection;
- the individual employee has to declare, in writing, that he or she will be bound by the regulations;
- the employer has to provide a copy of the regulations to the employee;
- the employer has to register a copy of the regulations with the Registrar of the Cantonal Court;
- the employer has put a copy of the regulations on a publishing board in the work place.

The employer cannot unilaterally amend these regulations, as each individual employee has to accept the amendment to be bound by it.

Collective termination for economic reasons (redundancy)

A collective redundancy is defined as the termination of at least 20 employees in the region of one Labour Office within a period of three months. If the employer makes five or more petitions to the Cantonal Court for dissolution of employment contracts for economic reasons during this same period, those petitions will count as part of the '20' in determining whether a collective redundancy exists. The employer must request prior authorization of the RDA to terminate the employees' contracts of employment for reason of redundancy.

Procedure

When applying to the RDA for authorization, the employer must file the following information:

- the number of employees the employer proposes to make redundant;
- the number of employees in the total workforce;
- the personal details of those proposed as candidates for redundancy (for example age, sex, job and length of service);
- the reasons for the proposed redundancies including details of the business and financial situation (which is made available to the employees and employees' representatives) and the efforts of the employer to avoid the contemplated measure;
- the criteria for the selection for the proposed candidates for redundancy;
- the way in which the possible redundancy payments are calculated;
- whether the company has a works council (which is compulsory for all companies with 35 or more employees) and if and when the works council was informed about the collective redundancies;
- the proposed timetable for the redundancies.

The employee must notify the RDA and the relevant trade union(s) of the proposed redundancies. Both the RDA and trade union(s) are entitled to copies of the letters the employer sends to the other.

The employer must also consult the works council on the proposed redundancies and obtain the works council's opinion before implementing the redundancies. If the employer rejects the works council's opinion, or a part of it, the employer must inform the works council of the reasons for the rejection. Under the Works Council Act, the employer is obliged to suspend the execution of its decision for a period of one month, unless the decision corresponds to the advice of the works council. The works council has one month to appeal against the employer's decision to the Company's Chamber of the Amsterdam Court of Appeal.

The RDA will wait for one month, after the date of receiving the employer's application, before authorizing the redundancies. This period is pertinent to ensure that the employer consults with the works council (if any) and that the trade unions receive all the necessary information. Where the RDA is not satisfied that the employer has complied with the statutory requirements, it can order a further delay.

Following the expiration of the one month period (or further delay), the RDA will request the trade union(s) to submit any counter arguments they may have. The RDA will also use this opportunity to enable any employees, who may be made redundant, to file their individual defences.

The employer's application together with the trade unions' counter arguments and the defence of the employees will then be submitted to the Labour Inspectorate and the Dismissals Committee for their views, before the Director of the RDA renders a decision. The parties are notified of the decision within three days. The decision is final and binding.

Redundancy payments

It is common for employers, in consultation with the trade union(s) and works council (if any) to implement a redundancy scheme to reduce the social consequences of a redundancy. Most collective labour agreements provide for specific social conditions when a collective redundancy takes place.

In the absence of such agreements, the only compensation the employee is entitled to is payment in lieu of notice, where the employee is not required to work out his or her notice period. Dutch law does not provide for any statutory redundancy compensation.

An employee may submit a claim for severance to the Cantonal Court if he or she considers the termination to be obviously unreasonable.

However, as most collective redundancies provide for measures to reduce the social consequences of redundancy, the employee's chance of success will not be high.

Transfer of business

Where a company transfers its business to another company, the rights and obligations of its employees will also transfer to the new company, who will act as the employer from the date the transfer takes place.

The liability for wages, taxes, social security premiums and so on of the former and new employer are illustrated in Table 2. The new employer will not however, be liable for the pension arrangements of the former employer or liable for the payment of pension premiums, back service obligations and so on.

Table 2

	Liabilities	
Employer	Debts originated before the transfer of the business	Debts originated after the transfer of business
Former Employer	liable during a period of one year after the transfer	not liable
New Employer	liable (several liability)	liable

Employee participation

Works councils

Pursuant to the 1979 Works Council Act *(Wet op de Ondernemingsraden)*, enterprises with 100 employees, or 35 or more employees who work at least one-third of the normal working week, must establish a works council *(Ondernemingsraad)*. It is possible for a group of companies to establish a 'group works council' in certain conditions.

Council members are chosen directly by the employees from their own ranks, the number can vary from three to 25, depending upon the size of the company. One of the members is appointed as chairman of the works council.

The company's management and the works council must meet within two weeks of one notifying the other of the wish to do so. These meetings should be held at least six times a year. The law prescribes at least one such meeting for certain major issues and for every subject on which discussion is deemed necessary by either management or the works council.

The chairmanship of these meetings can be arranged between the parties concerned. If no agreement can be reached, the meeting will be presided over alternately by a representative of management and the chairman of the works council.

Scope of authority

The company's management (or group of companies as the case may be) in which a works council is established, should seek the advice of the works council before making a decision on one of the following subjects:

- transfer of say in the company or a part thereof (inter alia the transfer of shares);

- the acquisition or the transfer of say in another company, joint ventures or the dissolution thereof, cooperations, termination of the activities of the company or a major part thereof;
- important investments in the company or in other enterprises;
- substantial new credit facilities obtained by the company;
- hiring groups of employees on a permanent or temporary basis;
- assignment of an advisory expert from outside the company;
- establishment, takeover or disposal of another enterprise.

Any decision of management which is contrary to the advice of the works council may be appealed against by the works council within one month. During this period, the management must postpone the execution of its decision.

Further, the Act requires that management obtain the consent of the works council on decisions regarding regulations for:

- pensions, insurance, profit-sharing or savings;
- working time and vacations;
- merit systems;
- safety, health or welfare connected with work;
- policies concerning hiring, discharges and promotions;
- personal training and appraisal;
- consultation on employment matters;
- handling of complaints;
- the position of young people in the company;
- labour regulations.

Where the works council refuses to give its consent, the company's management may request permission from the Cantonal Court to implement their contemplated decision. The Cantonal Court will only give permission if it considers the works council's refusal to be unreasonable, or if the decision needs to be taken as a result of very serious organizational, economic or social reasons.

Any decision taken in contravention of this procedure will be null and void. The works council has one month after the decision has been brought to its attention to invoke the nullity.

In addition, the management of the company must inform or consult the works council about a number of other issues concerning the company. For example, the works council must be presented with the company's annual accounts and be given an opportunity to discuss those accounts. The works council must also be given the opportunity to review the company's report on the company's present and future social policy and to discuss the future plans of the company, including the company's national and international investments.

The works council also has the right of appeal to the Companies' Chamber of the Court of Appeal at Amsterdam *(Ondernemingskamer van het Gerechtshof te Amsterdam)* against any important socio-economic decisions made by the employer.

Works councils in smaller enterprises

An extension of the Works Council Act of 1 September 1979 came into force on 1 May 1982. Under this Act every enterprise with 35 to 100 employees must establish a works council. In these smaller enterprises, however, the works council only has the right to advise on the decisions that must be reported to it and does not have the power to withhold its consent. The decisions on which the works council's advice must be sought are those arising from important financial and organization matters which might result in employee redundancy or in changes in the character, terms or conditions of employment of at least a quarter of the employees of the enterprise.

Direct participation in smaller enterprises

For enterprises where 10 to 35 people are employed, a simplified participation regulation has been introduced. The employer is obliged to hold a meeting with its employees at least twice a year. The employer must also convene a meeting if a minimum of one quarter of the workforce asks the employer to do so and gives the employer their reasons. The employer must discuss the general state of affairs of the business with the workforce at least once a year.

Pensions, tax and insurance

Tax and social security premiums

Employers must make statutory deductions for taxes and social security premiums from the employees' pay on a monthly basis, and are liable for any omissions. Social security contributions are compulsory and must be paid by employers and employees. They are expressed in percentages of wages and are adjusted every six months, in January and June. On 1 July 1994, the social premiums were established at 38 per cent.

Standard tax deduction rule

Individuals who are resident in the Netherlands are taxed on their worldwide income after deducting personal allowances. In the Netherlands income and social security tax are included in a single tax. The combined tax of 38.00 per cent (30.95 per cent social security tax and 7.05 per cent income tax) is levied on income up to NLG 43 267 (the first bracket). Income between NLG 43 267 and NLG 86 532 is taxed at 50 per cent (the second bracket) and income in excess of NLG 86 532 at 60 per cent (1994 figures).

The Netherlands has an extensive compulsory social security system including social security taxes and social insurance premiums. These premiums apply only to employees working in the Netherlands.

Contributions are payable up to a maximum annual assessable income of NLG 74 360 (1994). This results in maximum social insurance premiums payable of approximately NLG 10 000 (excluding sickness fund).

Non-resident individuals are only subject to Dutch income tax on specific Dutch sources of income. If the individuals are not subject to Dutch social security tax and their Dutch income is less than 90 per cent of their worldwide income, their tax rate in the first bracket is 25 per cent; if their Dutch income is greater than 90 per cent of their worldwide income, the rate is 7.05 per cent.

Illness benefit

The Illness Benefit Act *(Ziektewet or ZW)* insures employed persons under the age of 65, against loss of wages as a result of illness, accident or pregnancy. The insurance provides a benefit amounting to 70 per cent of the daily gross wage, but not exceeding 70 per cent of NLG 286.84 per day.

The first six weeks of entitlement are for the account of the employer, this period is decreased to two weeks for smaller enterprises. The employer is obliged to pay the employee 70 per cent of his or her salary, with the minimum amount being no less than the statutory minimum wage. This benefit is payable up to 52 weeks following the first day of illness.

Disability Insurance Act

The Disability Insurance Act *(Wet op de Arbeidsongeschiktheidsverzekering or WAO)* provides benefits to those persons who, after they have received benefits under the Illness Benefits Act for 52 weeks, are still at least 15 per cent incapacitated for work. The present system for calculating the benefit is rather complicated. The amount of the benefit exists as a minimum amount, this level will be increased with a certain percentage of the employee's salary, depending on the age of the employee and his or her past employment. The level of the WAO benefit depends further on the degree of incapacity. The benefit ends on the first day of the month in which the employee reaches the age of 65.

In 1993 several new Acts were adopted as a means of reducing the number of employees making use of the disability insurance. Generally these Acts oblige the employer to pay employees 70 per cent of their salaries for the first six weeks of illness. Furthermore, employers can be rewarded for employing disabled persons or punished for not employing disabled employees in jobs other than their original jobs (bonus/malus-system).

Health Insurance Act

The Health Insurance Act *(Ziekenfondswet)* provides for medical, pharmaceutical, dental and hospital care, nursing and other services. Employees earning a yearly wage of less than NLG 58 100 are statutory insured for medical expenses with the National Health insurances *(ziekenfondsen)*.

The insured person's spouse and children below the age of 16 are, as a rule, also insured free of charge (providing they are not themselves in paid employment). Students can remain insured until their twenty-seventh birthday.

Retirement pensions

The Retirement Pension Act *(Algemene Ouderdoms Wet)* provides for a maximum pension for married couples and for single persons at the age of 65. These benefits are indexed to the cost of living. In May a holiday allowance is paid. If married, both partners have a right to half of the pension, granted to them as a couple.

Private pension plans are supervised by the government under the Pension and Savings Fund Act *(Pensioen- en Spaarfondsenwet)*. An employer is free to choose a pension plan, unless the enterprise is covered by an industry-wide pension fund in which membership has been made obligatory by the Minister of Social Affairs and Employment. At present there are about 65 industry-wide pension funds with compulsory participation.

Pension rights are usually based on salary levels and years of service (maximum 40 years). Most schemes supplement the state retirement pension *(AOW)* which is maximised, to increase retirement income to 60 - 70 per cent of the last three years' average earnings. The pension plan premiums are paid by employers and employees. Generally the employer's contribution varies.

Most people usually retire at 65 years of age. This is also the age at which the AOW starts. There is, however, a tendency to retire some years before, mostly at 61 or 62 years of age. Several branches of industry do have a separate early retirement funds for that purpose.

Other benefits

The General Widows' and Orphans' Benefits Act *(Algemene Weduwen en Wezen Wet)* provides three kinds of benefits: widow's pension, temporary widow's benefit and orphan's pension. A widow is entitled to a widow's pension if:

- she has an unmarried child born before or on the day her husband died;
- she was pregnant at the time her husband died;
- she was disabled from work for a percentage exceeding 45 per cent on the date her husband died and for at least three months thereafter;
- she was aged 40 years or over on the last day of the month in which her husband died.

If these do not apply the widow may still be entitled to a temporary benefit.

The widow's benefit is payable for varying periods, according to the recipient's age, disability and so on and is payable to widowers also. An orphan's pension is granted to a child of up to 16 years of age who has lost both parents. In certain cases the orphan's pension is paid to the age of 27. The rate is dependent on the child's age. All these benefits are indexed, indirectly based on changes in the net minimum wage. In May a holiday allowance is paid, again depending on the child's age.

Family allowances

Families with children are paid a children's allowance under the General Family Allowance Act (*Algemene Kinderbijslagwet*). The allowances vary, depending mainly on the number of children and their ages. These benefits are also indexed.

The Exceptional Medical Expenses (Compensation) Act *(Algemene Wet Bijzondere Ziektekosten)* provides all residents with insurance for treatment and nursing in recognized hospitals, nursing homes, sanatoria and so on in case of long-term illnesses and physical and/or mental disability. In certain cases the employee must make a contribution.

Under the General Disability Act *(Algemene Arbeidsongeschiktheidswet or AAW)*, all residents of the Netherlands above the age of 18 are entitled to disability benefits after being unable to work for 52 weeks if still suffering at least 25 per cent incapacity. A condition of entitlement is loss of income from employment due to this incapacity. In so far as someone is capable of work, an entitlement to a supplementary WW benefit exists.

Employed persons insurance schemes

Both employers and employees contribute to the social insurance funds. The premiums paid by employees are deducted from their wages by employers, who remit these amounts, together with their own contributions, to one of the Companies Insurance Boards (*Bedrijfsvereniging*) which are governmental bodies.

Unemployment Insurance Act

The Unemployment Insurance Act *(Werkloosheidswet or NWW)* insures the employed person (if below the age of 65) against the financial consequences of unemployment for which the person is not to blame. The benefit amounts to 70 per cent of the daily gross wage to a maximum daily gross wage of NLG 286.84 (1994) per day, for a maximum period that depends on the age, the length of employment prior to unemployment.

Other Acts

A law on supplementary benefits *(Toeslagenwet)* provides for the situation when income from NWW, AAW, WAO and ZW does not come up to the social minimum. After the expiring of NWW benefits the Law on Income Provision for elderly and partly incapable employees (IOAW) provides a grant up to the level of the social minimum income. Further, pensioners who may be able to work can apply for a benefit pursuant to the General Unemployment Act *(Rijksgroepsregeling Werkloze Werknemers)*.

Health and safety

The Working Conditions Act *(Arbeidsomstandighedenwet)* provides for rules concerning the safety, health and well-being of employees at work. The Act provides a number of guidelines the employer should observe when organizing work (that is, when laying out workshops and selecting production and working methods). Cooperation between employer and employees on matters relating to working conditions is of paramount importance. Cooperation with government authorities, such as the Factory Inspection Board is also regulated by the Act.

Anti-discrimination regulations

The 1980 Act on equal rights for men and women provides for equal treatment of men and women as to employment, transfer, or promotion.

In addition men and women who work at the same workplace must be treated equally with regard to working conditions, pay, training, dismissals and so on. If not, the employer can seek the advice of the Committee for Equal Rights or the employee can seek a remedy through the judicial system.

Regulatory bodies

District Labour Offices

The principle function of district labour offices is to mediate between persons who are looking for work and employers. The labour offices maintain data banks.

These offices provide employers with information on such subjects as conditions of employment and terms of dismissal. They also advise employers and employees when minor labour controversies arise (in major labour disputes the unions are involved).

District labour offices can be found in most cities. They are part of the Ministry of Social Affairs and their services are free of charge.

Joint Industrial Labour Council

In 1945 the central organization of employers and employees set up the Joint Industrial Labour Council (*Stichting van de Arbeid*) as a body for joint consultation and, if possible, negotiations at a national level in the area of labour agreements.

Social and Economic Council

The Social and Economic Council (*Sociaal Economische Raad, or SER*), based on the Industrial Organization Act of 27 January 1950, also has a positive influence on industrial relations. The council is composed of 45 members: 15 appointed by the employers' organizations and 15 by the union groups, together with 15 independent experts appointed by the government. The government is required by law to seek the advice of the council on all major social and economic matters.

Foreign employees

Work and residence permits

Under Dutch legislation, in the event of a job vacancy preference should be given to unemployed citizens of the Netherlands. Should a foreign national be employed, then preference is given to citizens of the European Union. To be employed, a foreign national must be able to earn his or her own living and should not constitute any danger to public order or national safety.

There are no rules concerning the maximum number of foreigners which may be employed by a Dutch company, but the employer must request a special licence if he or she proposes to employ more than 20 foreigners. Unless such a licence is granted by the Minister of Social Security and Employment, a work permit (if required) will not be issued for the foreigners concerned.

Nationals of EU Member States

Nationals of member states of the EU and the EER, who intend to work in the Netherlands can enter the Netherlands with a valid travel document. They must register at the local administration office for foreigners within eight days after arriving. They do not need any authorization to work. Any EU national who contemplates working for more than three months in the Netherlands must apply for a residence permit. He or she will obtain such a permit on production of a confirmatory statement by the employer. If the employment is for an indefinite period, the residence permit will only be issued for five years; otherwise it is issued for the period of employment. Residence permits can be renewed on the same conditions as for their original issue.

Nationals of non-EU countries

Nationals from countries outside the EU and the EER are not allowed to work in the Netherlands unless the jobs concerned are ones for which no unemployed Dutch citizens, unemployed foreigners legally in the country or EU nationals are qualified. In addition, the foreigners work must serve the economic interest of the Netherlands.

Before commencing employment, the foreigner must apply for and be granted a work permit from the Government Labour Office (even if the employee is to be a management board member). Work permits are issued for one year (or for the period of employment if shorter), but are renewable. After three years of consecutive legal employment, the permit will, on request, be replaced by a declaration that needs no renewal. Foreign unskilled workers cannot easily obtain work in the Netherlands at present.

Nationals from countries other than the EU, the EER, Liechtenstein, Monaco, Switzerland, Canada, Australia, Japan, New Zealand or the USA who intend to work in the Netherlands must additionally apply at the

Dutch embassies or consulates in their home countries for provisional residence permits before they travel to the Netherlands. A provisional residence permit is not granted unless the applicant can prove that a work permit will be issued.

Apart from nationals from the EU and the EER, nationals from one of these other countries (mentioned above) who intend to stay longer than three months in the Netherlands are not obliged to apply for visas or provisional residence permits before travelling to the Netherlands, but should ensure beforehand that they will be able to obtain work and residence permits once they arrive.

Nationals from countries outside the EU must register themselves at their local administration office for foreigners within eight days of arriving in the Netherlands, and must apply for a residence permit.

This chapter was written by Rob Faasen, Coopers & Lybrand, Netherlands.

Norway

Introduction

Employment regulations are based partly on written law and partly on the basic agreement (*Hovedavtalen*) between the employers confederation (NHO) and the federation of trade unions (LO).

The basic legislation is the Working Environment Act (WEA) of 1977, the Labour Conflict Law of 1927 and the Holiday Act of 1988. These laws are supplemented by provisions in the Social Security Act of 1966.

Individual employment regulations

Contracts

From 1 July 1994 Norwegian law requires contracts to be in writing, if the period of employment exceeds one month. Contracts are mandatory for 'hired out labour'.

Permanent employment can be terminated by notice of termination, dismissal or retirement. The law only allows employers to employ persons on a temporary basis in certain cases which are strictly defined. Employment on a temporary basis terminates at the end of the agreed period and there are in practice, no requirements to give notice.

Wages and salaries

Minimum wage provision - There is no minimum wage provision. However, the agreement between the LO and NHO contains minimum wages for members of the different labour unions.

Method of payment - In accordance with the provisions of the Working Environment Act, wages shall be paid in cash unless the parties agree that payment shall be made through a wage account, cheque or postal giro. If the employer and the majority of employees have made an agreement in writing concerning the method of payment, the employer may extend the agreement to all employees of the enterprise.

Employees paid by the hour, day or week receive their wages at least once a week. Employees paid by the month or year receive their wages at least twice a month. The pay day stipulated by the Act may be altered by agreement.

Deductions from pay - Wage deductions are not legally permitted, except in the following cases:

- where authorized by law, for example tax deductions;
- in the case of prescribed contributions to pension or medical schemes;
- where stipulated in advance by written agreement;
- when the employee has agreed to take responsibility for damages, or where this is decided by a court;
- where the collective agreement stipulates deductions for trade union subscriptions.

Itemized pay statement - At the time of payment or immediately afterwards, the employee must receive a written statement of the amount, method of calculation and any deductions from wages or salaries.

Hours of work/shift work/overtime

The main rule according to the Working Environment Act is that ordinary working hours shall not exceed nine per day and 40 hours per week. However ordinary working hours are limited to nine hours per day and 38 hours per week for:

- discontinuous round-the-clock shift work;
- work in two shifts;
- work involving individual employees working on every third Sunday;
- work mainly carried out at night.

Ordinary working hours shall not exceed nine hours per day and 36 hours per week in:

- continuous round-the-clock shift work;
- work below the ground in mines;
- tunnel blasting when the distance between the tunnel openings is at least 50 metres and blasting subterranean rooms when the room has at least 25 metres depth measured from the opening.

Any work done in addition to the employee's ordinary working hours is overtime. Overtime must not be introduced as a regular system and it may only be worded where:

- unforeseen events or the absence of employees disturb or threaten to disrupt normal operations;
- overtime is necessary to prevent damage to plant, machinery, raw materials or products;
- there is excessive pressure of work due to seasonal fluctuations or the like.

Together with ordinary working hours, the overtime must not result in any employee working for more than 14 hours on any one day. It must not exceed 10 hours in any week, 25 hours during four consecutive weeks or 200 hours per calendar year.

Holidays

Employees are, according to the Holiday Act 1988, entitled to 25 days' leave per holiday year, which coincides with the calendar year. Employees who have reached the age of 60 by 1 January of the holiday year are entitled to leave for an additional six days. An employee is entitled to holiday pay calculated as 10.2 per cent of work income received from the employer during the year before the holiday year.

Maternity provisions

An employee is entitled to leave of absence for up to 12 weeks during pregnancy, and is obliged to take leave for the first six weeks after the birth.   The labour inspection may grant exemption from this rule, where the mother proves by a medical certificate that it is better for her to work.

After the birth, the father is entitled to up to two weeks' leave of absence, provided he lives with the mother and uses the leave of absence to take care of the family and home. The parents are entitled to additional leave throughout the child's first year.

The mother is covered by national insurance up to 42 weeks, or 52 weeks at reduced rates. Four of these weeks are however, allocated to the father. If the father chooses not to make use of his leave, the period of leave shall as a rule, be reduced accordingly.

Time off

There are a number of legislative provisions which directly or indirectly entitle employees to paid time off, for holiday, sickness, pregnancy and military service. Under existing collective agreements employees with at least six months service are entitled to pay when called up for military service:

- for the full length of initial service:
  half pay for up to three months, less allowances paid by public authorities, except family allowances;
- for subsequent services:
  full pay for up to one month, less allowances paid by public authorities, including family allowances.

Disciplinary and grievance procedures

An employee may be summarily dismissed when 'guilty of gross breach of duty or other substantial breach of the contract of employment'. Refusal to work overtime or to comply with the employer's reasonable orders may be grounds for dismissal, or taking part in an illegal strike.

The employee may require the employer to consult with the employee's shop stewards prior to initiating any summary dismissal.

Lay-off and guaranteed payments

The right to lay-off employees because of lack of work is not regulated in any legislation, but is settled by the collective agreement between the NHO and the LO. According to this agreement the employee remains employed during the lay-off and has a right and an obligation to return to work when the lay-off ceases.

Under the lay-off agreement the employee is entitled to the following benefits:

- daily cash benefit during unemployment;
- grants to cover expenses in connection with travel, removal and establishment at another place of work;
- grants during training for the purpose of obtaining suitable work;
- help towards earning a livelihood;
- grants in connection with vocational rehabilitation;
- wage subsidies for unemployed persons who are given work for a municipality or a county.

Period of notice

The following periods of notice apply where there is no other written agreement or where notice is not stipulated in the collective agreement:

- one month's notice shall be given by either party;
- in the case of employees who have been employed for at least five consecutive years in the same enterprise, at least two months' notice shall be given by either party;
- in the case of employees who have been employed for at least ten consecutive years in the same enterprise, at least three months' notice.

Where the employee has at least ten consecutive years' employment in the same enterprise, the period of notice shall be increased as follows:

- at least four months' notice if the employee is aged 50 plus;
- at least five months' notice if the employee is aged 55;
- at least six months' notice if the employee is aged 60.

In the case of employment under a written agreement for a specified trial period, either party should give 14 days' notice.

If the business operation has to be suspended in whole or in part as the result of an accident, act of God or other unforeseeable event and the employees have to be given notice for that reason, the period of notice may be reduced to 14 days from the date of the event.

Dismissal

The basic rule is that any dismissal is unfair unless it is objectively justified. The law does not define the meaning of 'objectively justified', but lack of work is deemed to be a justified reason for dismissal.

Personal reasons may under certain circumstances be regarded as justified grounds for dismissal. Incompetence, failure to cooperate and negligence are examples of objectively justified grounds. Dismissals in these circumstances are normally rather complex and are affected by matters such as the size of the company, the employee's position, length of service, age and the frequency of offenses.

Reasons for summary dismissal may in less severe cases be regarded as objectively justified grounds for dismissal. The law specifies that a dismissal is not objectively justified if the employee can reasonably be assigned to other duties within the company.

The law states that an employee cannot be given notice for the following reasons:

- because of sick leave;
- as a result of the employee's pregnancy;
- after the employee has attained 61 years of age;
- during a trial period;
- during military service.

Notification of dismissal must be in writing and the employer must specify the reason for the dismissal if requested by the employee. The employee must be informed about the procedures for challenging the validity of the dismissal. [In a recent bill submitted to Parliament, it is proposed that from 1995 it will be mandatory for the employer to inform the employee about how to seek damages and whether there are grounds for reinstatement or re-engagement]

The law contains detailed provisions about the procedures for settling disputes.

Redundancy

An employer must inform the employment authorities if more than ten employees are dismissed at the same time.

Collective employment regulations

The main agreement between NHO and LO regulates provisions for the right of association, representatives, protected work, work conflicts and so on. Both these groups are umbrella organizations for others who represent different occupations.

Using the model agreement between NHO and LO as a basis, the unions negotiate with the employers association regarding salaries and wages and work conditions. These agreements are normally concluded for a limited period of two years, with the possibility of renegotiation. During the period of agreement strikes and lockouts are prohibited. The right to form and join a trade union is regulated in the main agreement between NHO and LO. The provisions include both the positive and the negative right of association. The right to negotiation is also a part of the collective employment law and relates to all matters between the employer and employees.

Employee participation

Where a company has had an average of more than 30 employees over the last three financial years, two-thirds of the employees may demand that one director and one observer (and their substitutes) be elected by and from the employees.

Where a company, not having a corporate assembly, has had an average of more than 50 employees over the last three financial years, a majority of the employees may demand up to one-third, but at least two, of the directors and their alternatives be elected by and from the employees.

A company which has had an average of 200 employees over the last three financial years should have a corporate assembly of at least 12 members, of whom two-thirds are elected by the general assembly and one-third by and from the employees.

The employer must negotiate with the employee representatives on redundancies.

Pensions, tax and insurance

Income tax and national insurance

The employer is obliged to withhold income tax as well as social security contributions. Amounts to be withheld are calculated separately for each employee on the basis of their tax cards, which are issued by the Tax Assessment Office. The employees must give their tax cards to the employer, otherwise the employer should withhold 50 per cent of the employee's salary. Deductions which are withheld should be forwarded to the tax collector every two months.

The national insurance is a public social security scheme comprising a number of various benefits, such as:

- sickness benefits: sickness allowance, medical benefits;
- pregnancy and maternity benefits: maternity allowance, medical benefits;
- unemployment benefits: daily allowance, training grants;
- disablement benefits: pension when at least 50 per cent disabled, basic benefits;
- old age pension: from 67 years.

To qualify for most of these cash benefits, the employee must have been insured for a certain period of time. Cash benefits include daily allowance during unemployment, sickness allowance and pension.

For 1994 the employee will have to pay one premium of 7.8 per cent of gross earnings. The employer is charged an employer's tax for national insurance at a rate of 14.3 per cent of gross paid salaries and wages for 1994. The employer's tax is charged at lower rates if his employees are residents of certain appointed areas.

Everybody, regardless of nationality, who works in the employ of another person (whether a foreign company or local company) is covered by national insurance and is required to pay social security contributions from the first day of work. The EU regulations concerning social security and social security conventions concluded between Norway and other countries may lead to exemption from these charges. Persons who are not employed are also covered by national insurance if they stay in Norway for at least one year.

Norway has joined the European Economic Area, and as from 1 January 1994 the EU regulations concerning social security are applicable. Norway has also concluded social security conventions with Switzerland, Turkey, the United States, Canada and Quebec

(Canadian province). In addition Norway has concluded a new social security convention with the Nordic countries which is more comprehensive than the EU regulations.

Usually foreign nationals and Norwegian citizens are covered by national insurance in the same way. Special exceptions from the obligatory insurance are provided for foreign nationals who work in Norway for a foreign state or international organization.

'Continental shelf' employees resident in non-Nordic countries are not covered by the national insurance but may be entitled to occupational injury insurance.

Sickness benefit

Employees are entitled to a daily sickness allowance equal to 100 per cent of their gross income up to a limit of six times the basic benefit from the national insurance scheme (which until spring 1995 is NOK 38 080), from and including the first day of absence. Tax and national insurance premiums are payable on the sickness allowance and the allowances count as pensionable income. The employer pays the sickness allowance for the first two weeks which is known as the 'employer's period'. After 14 days of absence because of sickness, the national insurance scheme covers the expenses.

Employees themselves can give notice of sickness covering the first three days. Employees are also entitled to a sickness allowance for up to ten days per calendar year when absent from work owing to the sickness of children under the age of ten.

Retirement pensions

The pensionable age is 70, but retirement can be taken at 67. Some professions have a lower pension age, which is either based on law or on an agreement between the employer and employee. Because the national pension scheme is limited, employers often offer an additional private pension scheme to their employees.

Health and safety

Health and safety at work is primarily governed by the Working Environment Act.   The purpose of the Act is to safeguard all employees against harmful physical and mental influences at work.

It is the duty of the employer to ensure that the enterprise is arranged and maintained so that the working environment is fully satisfactory. Employees are empowered to stop working if they find that it would be dangerous for them to continue. At all enterprises covered by the WEA a safety delegate must be elected to safeguard the interests of the employees in matters relating to the working environment. If there are less than ten employees in an enterprise, the employer and employees may agree in writing that a safety delegate need not be elected. The Act entitles the safety delegate to halt work if life or health is considered to be in immediate danger and that danger cannot be averted by any other means.

If there are more than 50 employees at an enterprise, a working environment committee must be elected.   The employer and employees have an equal number of representatives on the committee. This committee takes part in planning safety and environment work at the enterprise. It has a special duty to ensure that conditions which have caused accidents or injury to health are altered. The committee has responsibility to ensure that dangerous conditions do not arise when the enterprise reorganises production or expands.

Anti-discrimination regulations

Anti-discrimination legislation provides for equal treatment of men and women in employment, transfer or promotion. An employer cannot dismiss an employee on grounds of trade union membership.

Regulatory bodies

The *Rikstrygdeverket* is the main authority administering the national pension scheme and the sickness allowance scheme. The *Arbeidstilsynet* supervises working conditions at most enterprises covered by the WEA and is also responsible for enforcing a state guarantee for wage claims in the event of bankruptcy and so on.

Foreign employees

Work permits must be obtained before a foreign national may start work in Norway. The Directorate of Immigration is responsible for issuing residence and work permits.

Initial work permits are issued for a particular job for a specified period of time not exceeding one year. These permits may be applied for, either as an individual permit or as group permit.

For citizens of the European Economic Area (EU and EFTA) work permits are not required, but they must be registered with the police before commencing work in Norway.

Applications for individual permits should be made personally through the Norwegian consulate or embassy in the country where the applicant is a citizen. An individual application should be accompanied by an offer of employment on a prescribed form which is obtainable from employment service offices in Norway. A general application to employ a group of foreign nationals in Norway should be submitted to the Directorate of Labour.

Work permits are, with some exceptions, only granted to specialists, skilled personnel and key personnel who are absolutely vital for the success of the enterprise and where such personnel are not available in Norway.

Recruitment and training

There are no special regulations or provisions for employee recruitment or training.

This chapter was written by Per Arne Damm, Coopers & Lybrand Tax Services A.S., Norway.

Poland

Introduction

Under an employment contract, an employee is obliged to perform certain work for an employer and the employer is obliged to pay for this work.

An employer cannot generally employ persons younger than 18 years of age, except in certain circumstances. The employer may employ persons older than 15 years of age, if the person has graduated from primary school and has obtained a health certificate appropriate to the kind of work to be performed.

Individual employment regulations

Contracts

Contracts of employment should be specified in writing and should contain the following information:

- the description of the work to be performed;
- a date specifying the commencement of employment;
- the salary to be paid;
- an agreement by the employee to follow the regulations in the workplace.

Contracts may be concluded for a fixed term period or may be concluded for an unlimited period of time. Where a contract of employment is for an unlimited period of time, the employer may include a trial period. The duration of the trial period is strictly regulated by law. For most employees, the trial period is limited to two weeks. In the case of managers, employees who perform independent work and employees who are financially liable for their work, the trial period is extended to three months.

As a way of increasing the duration of the trial period, employers may employ persons on a fixed term contract, with a right of renewal.

Wages and salaries

Minimum wage provision - The minimum wage or salary is stipulated by the Minister of Finance. Currently it is approximately 2 400 000 Plz.

Method of payment - Salary or wages are usually paid on a monthly basis, but can be paid more frequently, at such intervals to be agreed between the parties. Generally payment should be paid on or before the last day of the month. If the last day of the month is a holiday, payment should be made the day before.

Deductions from pay - The employer is obliged to deduct personal income tax from the employee's salary and pay it to the tax office. The employer may explicitly deduct the following payments:

- alimony payments and any other obligations pursuant to an executory document with a writ of execution;
- advance payments;
- penalties imposed by labour law.

The employer may deduct alimony payments up to an amount equivalent to three-fifths of the employee's total remuneration. Any other deductions can only be deducted up to 50 per cent of the employee's total remuneration.

The employer is fully entitled to deduct any money previously paid to the employee, for any absences for which the employee is not entitled to receive payment.

Itemized pay statement - There is no statutory requirement for the employer to provide employees with an itemized pay statement. The employer must however, give the employee's all documents relating to their salary calculation.

Hours of work/shift work/overtime

The maximum number of hours of work are eight hours a day and 42 hours per week. Any time worked in excess of these hours, or during the night or holidays is classified as overtime. An employee cannot work more than 120 hours of overtime in a calendar year.

Managers, supervisors and employees who perform independent work are not entitled to payment for overtime hours.

Holidays

An employee becomes entitled to paid holidays after the completion of one year's employment. The employee's holiday entitlement is based upon the employee's total years of employment, rather than service with the current employer, as illustrated in Table 1.

Table 1

Total years of employment	Number of days paid holidays
After 1 year's employment	14 working days' holiday
After 3 years' employment	17 working days' holiday
After 6 years' employment	20 working days' holiday
After 10 years' employment	26 working days' holiday

When calculating the employee's holiday entitlement, the number of years spent in educational institutions count towards the employee's total period of employment as follows:

- years at high school are equivalent to four years of employment;
- two years of college education are equivalent to six years of employment;
- years at college and university are equivalent to eight years of employment.

Maternity provisions

The employment contract cannot be terminated during the employee's pregnancy or during maternity leave.

If a fixed term contract expires after three months of the employee becoming pregnant, the contract is automatically extended to the day of child birth.

A pregnant woman cannot work overtime and/or work night shifts, and cannot be sent on a business trip unless she agrees. The same applies to a mother of a child up to one year of age.

The period of maternity leave is specified in Table 2.

Table 2

Period of maternity leave	Number of children
16 weeks	For the birth of the first child
18 weeks	For the birth of each following child
26 weeks	For a multiple birth

The employer is obliged to provide the pregnant employee with necessary time off during working hours for medical check-ups, if the employee is unable to receive such check-ups in her own time. The employer cannot deduct this time from the employee's salary.

A breast-feeding mother is entitled to two breaks of 30 minutes each, every day. An employee with a child younger than 14 years of age is entitled to two days paid leave per year. This leave does not affect the employee's entitlement to a child allowance in the event of the child's sickness.

Time off

An employee is entitled to paid time off in the following circumstances:

- young employees still attending school   18 hours per week
- mothers with children aged less than 14   two days per year
- wedding   two days
- paternity leave   two days
- child's wedding   one day
- funeral of spouse, child or parent   two days
- funeral of sibling, in-laws, grandparents one day
- calling at the administrative offices or courts at their request
- voluntary participation in rescue operations
- voluntary blood donations

The employee is entitled to time off to resolve any private or family affairs, provided that the employee makes up this time in his or her own time.

Lay-off and guaranteed payments

Where the employer does not provide the employee with work during the employee's normal working hours, for reasons wholly attributable to the employer, the employee is entitled to his or her normal remuneration. Where the work stoppage is caused by the employee, there is no right to remuneration.

During the period of work stoppage, the employer can provide the employee with alternative 'appropriate' work, provided that the employee receives his or her normal rate of pay.

Period of notice

The length of the period of notice is dependant upon the employee's total period of employment. Once again, this period of employment is not restricted to service with the employee's current employer, but includes all previous employments and some educational activities.

Table 2 illustrates how the period of notice is calculated.

Table 2

Notice period	Length of service
2 weeks' notice, with notice expiring on a Saturday	Less than 1 year's service
1 month's notice, with notice expiring on the last day of the month	More than 1 year's service
3 months' notice, with notice expiring on the last day of the month	More than 10 years' service

An employer is able to reduce the period of notice from three months to one month under the following circumstances:

- in a redundancy situation;
- where the scope of the business activities of the company is limited;
- where a division or branch of the company is closed down.

In the case of bankruptcy or where the company closes down completely, the employer may terminate the employees' contract of employment by giving the employee two weeks' notice. In these circumstances, the employee remains entitled to payment for his or her entire notice period.

Dismissal

A contract of employment may be terminated:

- by mutual agreement;
- by notice of termination;
- without notice of termination;
- upon the expiry of a fixed term contract.

Either party can terminate the employment relationship by giving notice, with the exception of employees who are within two years of their retirement. In these circumstances, the employer is prohibited from giving notice to the employee to terminate the employment contract, but the employee is free to terminate the employment relationship, with notice, at any time.

Any unilateral change in the employee's terms and conditions of employment, including changes in his or her remuneration, will be regarded as notice of termination of employment.

The employer can terminate the employee's contract of employment without notice in certain circumstances. Examples of where termination without notice has occurred are as follows:

- where the employee did not comply with the by-laws of the company (for instance disturbance of the peace at the workplace, unjustified leave of absence, use of alcohol during work hours and so on);
- where the employee was convicted of an offence;
- where the employee has his or her licenses or permits evoked, which are necessary for work, as a result of his or her own behaviour;
- where the employee was continually sick for more than three months;
- where the employee was unjustifiably absent for more than one month.

Where the employee is represented by a trade union, the trade union must be informed of the contemplated termination of employment, prior to the termination taking place. The employer is not required to inform the trade union of any terminations in the event of bankruptcy or liquidation of the company.

In the case of a fixed term contract, the employment shall terminate automatically upon the expiry of the fixed term. However, where a fixed term contract is concluded for a period of more than six months, the contract can only be terminated by mutual agreement or by giving two weeks' notice.

Redundancy

There is a special law dealing with redundancies which result from economic causes or changes within a company. A redundancy occurs when within a period of three months:

- 10 per cent of the workforce are dismissed, where the workforce numbers at least 1 000 people;
- at least 100 persons are dismissed in a workforce exceeding 1 000 persons.

The employer must inform the relevant trade union and the local job centre, in writing, of the proposed redundancies and the reasons for the redundancies no later than 45 days before giving notice to the employees.

Within 30 days of notifying the trade union, the employer should try to reach an agreement with the union concerning the redundancy procedure, the list of employees and such other matters as necessary. If agreement cannot be reached, the director of the company must determine all the issues related to the redundancy, including those issues previously agreed with the trade union. If there is no trade union operating in the company, the director must consult directly with the employees.

Employees who have been made redundant are generally entitled to redundancy compensation as set out in Table 3.

Table 3

Total period of employment	Compensation
Does not exceed ten years	One month's salary
More than ten years but less than 20 years	Two months' salary
At least 20 years	Three months' salary

This compensation is subject to a maximum ceiling, as payment cannot exceed 15 times the minimum salary.

In certain circumstances, the employee will not be entitled to receive redundancy compensation. These circumstances are as follows:

- where the employee accepts employment with the new company;
- where the employee starts his or her own business;
- where the employee is working part-time and receives a pension;
- where the employee runs his or her own farm.

Where the employee is entitled to both retirement and redundancy compensation, the most profitable option should be chosen.

The Minister of Labour may ask the employer to suspend the redundancy procedure for a period not exceeding three months, if the Minister is requested to do so by the employment authorities or by the national trade union organization.

Collective employment regulations

Trade unions

The Trade Union Law of 23 May 1991 governs the establishment and operation of trade unions. A trade union may be established pursuant to a resolution, passed by a minimum of ten employees. Once established, an establishing committee should be formed and articles of association drafted. The committee should then submit a registration application to the court within a period of 30 days. The court should also be notified of any changes to the articles of association.

A trade union will be dissolved if any of the following events occurs:

- the statutory body passes a resolution to dissolve the trade union;
- the enterprise where the trade union operates is struck off the register as a result of liquidation, bankruptcy or restructuring;
- the total number of members is lower than ten for a period of more than three months.

The trade union may participate in any of the following activities within the enterprise:

- dealing with individual cases pursuant to labour law regulations;
- dealing with an employer in relation to collective matters and employees' rights;
- regulating and controlling labour law and safety regulations;
- supervising the activity of social labour inspection and cooperation with public labour inspectors;
- taking care of the living conditions of pensioners.

Furthermore the trade union may participate in establishing a remuneration system and granting bonus rules.

Trade disputes

In any dispute between the employees and employer, the employees may be represented by a trade union. Disputes may arise in relation to work conditions, wages, social benefits, union rights and so on.

A dispute commences when a trade union makes demands which are unacceptable to the employer. A trade union may warn the employer that if these demands are not met, a strike will be called. A strike cannot begin until the expiry of 14 days, after the day the dispute started.

The employer must begin negotiations immediately and inform the local labour inspectorate about the dispute. If the negotiations are successful, the parties must sign an agreement. If the parties cannot reach a consensus, they must sign a protocol identifing their different positions.

If the demands continue, the parties may require the assistance of an independent mediator. At the conclusion of the mediation process, the parties must either enter into a mutual agreement, or sign a protocol identifying their different positions. The union is entitled to call a strike if mediation fails.

The other option available to the parties is to submit the case to the Social Arbitrary Board. The Social Arbitrary Board is situated at the Voivodship Labour Court, where the labour court is established. If the dispute involves a number of enterprises then the case must be submitted to the Social Arbitrary Board at the Supreme Court. The jury consists of the judge appointed by the Chairman of the Court and six members appointed by the parties (each party appoints three members). The Board's decision is a majority vote and is binding upon the parties.

Where there is a dispute, the ultimate option available to the employees is to strike. Participation in the strike is not obligatory on the employees. A strike can only be called by the trade union if at least 50 per cent of the employees have voted in favour of the strike. The union should then give at least five days notice prior to the date of the strike. The strike leaders must cooperate with the management of the enterprise in matters concerning the safety of the workplace and the necessary operation of some instalments or units.

Participation in a strike does not violate the employees' obligations or affect their rights deriving from employment law.

Employee participation

The employees of state-owned enterprises may participate in the decision making process through the employees' council or through general meetings of employees (or delegates).

Employees may address the following issues in the general meeting of employees:

- introduction of the statute of the enterprise;
- passing resolutions regarding the division of profit allocated to employees;
- annual reviewing of management and employees' council's activities;
- setting forth long-term plans for the enterprise;
- giving opinions in any cases related to the enterprise.

The members of the employees' council are elected by all employees for a period of two years. The employees' council is entitled to the following:

- setting forth the annual plan for the enterprise and implementing any changes;
- approving the annual balance sheet;
- passing resolutions regarding any investment;
- granting permission to access the commercial company;
- passing resolutions regarding merger or division of the enterprise;
- passing resolutions regarding changes within the enterprise's activities;
- giving permission to transfer fixed assets;
- making decisions regarding membership in an organization;
- setting forth the internal by-laws of the enterprise;
- passing resolutions concerning referendums in the enterprise.

Pensions, tax and insurance

Social security contributions

Social security contributions ('ZUS') are levied at the rate of 48.5 per cent of gross remuneration. This includes a 3 per cent contribution to the unemployment fund and 0.5 per cent contribution to the employees' guaranteed benefit fund. Generally, all Polish employees are liable to pay social security contributions.

Where there is an agency agreement, both the principal and agent are liable to pay 20 per cent social security contributions. In addition, the agent is liable to pay a 3 per cent contribution towards the unemployment fund.

Employees of a foreign employer seconded to Poland for a specific task, are not subject to ZUS.

Under current legislation, persons engaged under a contract for service for a period of less than 30 days are not be liable for ZUS. There are however, proposals to amend this legislation. Social security contributions will be payable on a contract of services entered into for periods longer than 14 days. ZUS will also be payable on consecutive contracts, even if these contracts are only for short periods of time.

Where an employee has separate employments, in which he or she works more than half the standard working week (generally 40 hours), the employee will not have to pay social security contributions on his or her part-time work.

Nationals of countries who have entered into a social security treaty with Poland, namely, Belgium, the Czech Republic, France, Germany, Greece, Hungary and Libya will be exempt from social security contributions. It is possible for these persons to obtain a statement from the foreign social security office stating that social security contributions are being paid, and that they are exempt from Polish ZUS. Generally, no ZUS needs to be paid for the first 12 months which may be extended for a second period of 12 months.

ZUS payments are tax deductible for the employer and for self-employed persons. These payments must be paid on a monthly basis by the company, on the fifteenth of the following month.

A Polish national gains the following benefits from the social security system:

- sick leave allowance;
- re-qualification allowance;
- rehabilitation allowance;
- funeral gratuity;
- childbirth allowance;
- maternity allowance (for bringing up a child). A mother is entitled to an allowance ranging between 112 and 182 days, depending upon the number of children;
- allowance for unemployment caused by sickness of a child (14 years of age or younger). It may be granted for up to 60 days per year for both parents (jointly);
- a monthly children allowance (for having to support children up to the age of 25);

- a monthly children allowance (for children requiring special care);
- a monthly allowance for the spouse (in case of men over 65, women over 50 and for disability).

Generally a foreign national will not benefit from the Polish social security system, even if he or she has made ZUS contributions.

If a Polish national has a period during which he or she does not make social security contributions, that person will not be entitled to enjoy the benefits of the social security system for the duration of that period. In addition, that person will not benefit from a full old age pension.

Retirement pensions

Private pensions are not recognised in Poland and do not confer any taxation advantages, for example neither corporate or personal pension contributions are tax deductible. All receipts from a private pension scheme are taxable.

Health and safety

The employer is obligated to ensure that employees have a safe and hygienic work environment. Where the employer employs more than ten employees, the employer must set up a work safety and hygiene service ('BHP service'). The BHP service acts as a consultative, executive and supervisory body for the chief manager of the establishment, in all matters of work safety and hygiene.

Where the employer employs less than 100 employees, the employer may assign the tasks of the BHP service to an employee carrying on other work. Where the employer employs less than 50 employees, the employer may assign the tasks of the BHP service to a specialized third party.

The Minister of Labour and Social Policy may issue general regulations concerning work safety and hygiene for particular industries or for certain types of work, with the agreement of the Minister of Health and Social care, and after consultation with a national trade union association.

The Labour Inspectorate supervises work safety and hygiene, and ensures that labour law regulations are observed.

Anti-discrimination regulations

The Polish constitution, which is supreme law, guarantees all people equal rights. The constitution provides legal grounds for making a claim if a person's rights are violated as a result of discrimination.

Foreign employees

Foreign nationals employed, either directly or pursuant to a secondment agreement, within the territory of the Polish Republic must have a work permit.

Employment under a secondment agreement

Foreign nationals employed by foreign employers, who are seconded to a Polish company in the Polish Republic to perform specific work, must have a written and signed secondment agreement between the foreign employer and the Polish company.

Foreign nationals employed under a secondment agreement to perform any of the following tasks do not require a work permit:

- contract for the supply of artistic services;
- contract with a foreign broadcasting station;
- activity at an exhibition and/or market fair;
- an export contract to make machines.

An application for a work permit under a secondment agreement by a foreign entity should include the following:

- a statement of application;
- a copy of the secondment agreement (with a sworn translation);

- a summary of the agreement;
- personal details of the employee;
- copy of the employee's passport;
- an excerpt from the company's register (with sworn translation);
- the employment contract (with sworn translation).

Each of these documents should be submitted with six copies to the Voivodship Labour Office (*Wojewódzki Urzad Pracy*).

Once the foreign employee has a certificate of issuing agreement, the employee may apply to the Polish embassy or consulate abroad for a long-term visa. The following documents should be presented:

- a certificate of issuing permission for the secondment agreement;
- an application for a visa with the employee's signature;
- a declaration from the employee concerning the performance of a registration obligation;
- the secondment agreement;
- temporary residence;
- stamp duty;
- a declaration that all taxes shall be paid;
- an excerpt from the company's register.

Promise of work permit

A foreign national entering Poland should submit an application to obtain a promise of work permit. The application should be submitted to the Voivodship Labour Office not later than six weeks before the period of employment commences.

The application for the promise of work permit should contain the person's:

- forenames and surnames;
- father's name;
- date and place of birth;
- nationality;
- passport number;

- a permanent address in the host country of the foreign national;
- professional qualifications (degree, professional training and so on);
- remuneration;
- the period of service:

In addition, the company will have to justify the necessity of employing a foreign national instead of a Polish national, and will have to disclose details of the company's employment structure (including information on the number of Polish and foreign employees).

The following documents should be presented with the application:

- a statement of application;
- copy of the person's passport;
- copies of any diplomas and/or other certificates confirming the person's qualifications;
- a copy of the REGON certificate number of the employer;
- an opinion from the District Labour Office about the proposed position;
- an excerpt from the company's register;
- a copy of the employment contract.

Visa

Once the foreign employee has a promise of work permit, he or she may apply to the Polish embassy or consulate abroad for a long-term visa.

The following documents need to be presented when applying for a long-term visa:

- the promise of work permit;
- an application for a visa, signed by the employee;
- a declaration of circumstances by the employee (registration obligation);
- stamp duty;
- the employee's address in Poland;
- excerpt from the company's register;

- a declaration that all taxes shall be paid.

Work permit

To get a work permit, the employer must notify the relevant Voivodship Labour Office within seven days from the commencement of the employment contract (as stated in the promise of work permit).

This chapter was written by Margaret Karpowicz and Hanna Wijkowska, Coopers & Lybrand Sp. z o. o., Poland.

Portugal

Introduction

Labour relations in Portugal are founded principally on individual employment contracts which are signed by both the employer and employee. The terms of the individual employment contract are regulated by a voluntary agreement between the parties concerned. However statutory minimum rights do exist and such rights must be respected, with any variation being more generous to the employee than the basic statutory minimum.

The two principal statutes restricting the negotiation of terms and conditions of employment are the General Employment Law (based on Decree Law No. 49 408 of 24 November 1969) and when applicable the Collective Statutory Instruments of Labour Relations (IRCT).

The General Employment Law (LGT) applies to most employment contracts, with the exception of domestic service, dock labour or rural work, for which there are special rules. The IRCT applies where the employers or their representatives and employee representatives specifically agree to apply these statutes, whether to a specific industrial sector, specific profession or a specific company.

Individual employment regulations

Contracts

The most widely used employment contract is an agreement for an indefinite period, or permanent contract, which can only be terminated by the employer under stringent conditions. Although it is not necessary to sign a formal employment contract, the employer should inform the employee in writing about the major conditions governing the employment relationship.

The general law also provides for the use of fixed term contracts in very specific and tightly defined circumstances, such as:

- temporary replacement of other employees;
- temporary or exceptional increases in the activity of the company;
- launch of a new activity;
- seasonal activities or occasional work;
- precisely defined construction or repair works and development of projects.

Fixed term contracts must always be specified in writing for a definite term, normally lasting up to six months. They must also provide the following information:

- the names and addresses of the parties to be bound by the contract;
- the employee's job title and salary;
- the employee's place and hours of work;
- the date on which the employment agreement commences and the expiry date or, alternatively, in the case of indefinite contracts the reason justifing its signature;
- the reason for the fixed term contract;
- the date of signature.

Fixed term contracts may be renewed twice but must not exceed a total of three years (two years in certain cases). In contrast, agreements for an unspecified duration can last as long as the work or task which justified their signature.

Employee register - Employers have a statutory obligation to keep the following registers in relation to employees:

- register of employees;
- disciplinary action register;
- time register;
- shift register;
- overtime register.

Wages and salaries

Minimum wage provision - The current minimum national wage is PTE 49 300 per month (1994), paid 14 times a year.   Nevertheless, collective agreements (IRCT) quite often provide minimum wages which are higher than those laid down in the general law.

Method of payment - There are no legal requirements restricting the method of payment of salaries. The money must be at the disposal of the employee on the normal payment date.

Where the employees' salary is partly paid by a non-cash benefit, the amount of the non-cash benefit must not exceed the part paid in cash, unless otherwise agreed by the employee.

Deductions from pay - Employers have a statutory obligation to deduct income tax, social security and stamp tax from the salaries of their employees. Employees are expressly prohibited from making these contributions themselves.

Apart from these legal deductions, the law provides for other deductions to be made from salaries pursuant to a judicial decision or with the prior agreement of the employee.

Itemized pay statement - Every employee has a right to an itemized pay statement, at the time payment is made, showing the following details:

- the employee's full name;
- the employee's social security number;
- the period to which the salary corresponds;
- the amounts paid in respect of overtime, extraordinary services rendered on bank holidays and days off;
- the amounts and purposes of deductions made;
- net amount to be received.

Hours of work/shift work/overtime

The normal hours of work for employees is generally limited to a maximum of eight hours a day, up to 44 hours a week and, for office employees, seven hours a day and 42 hours a week. In most cases, however, these periods are shortened by the IRCT.

Employees are entitled by law to one day off per week, normally Sunday, although the IRCT has the right to increase the time off to two days a week.

Employers are also obliged by law to define the employees' working day. Each working day must include a break of at least one hour and not more than two hours, and established in such a way that no working period exceeds five consecutive hours.

Employees in managerial positions are exempt from these requirements.

If the company so requires, employees except for disabled workers, pregnant women or persons under 18 years of age, may be obliged to work overtime or shift hours. As a general rule, women and persons under 18 years of age may not work night shift, especially without a doctor's medical certificate and annual medical check-up.

The number of hours to be worked in shift work are subject to approval from the Labour Ministry, and the employee may only be moved to a different shift after a day off. Except for services normally rendered at night (night guards and so on), night shift work wages are calculated at a rate of 125 per cent of daytime rates of pay. Overtime rates are calculated as follows:

- overtime worked on a weekday:
  150 per cent of the normal basic rate of pay for the first hour, 175 per cent of the normal basic rate for any time exceeding the first hour;
- overtime worked on the employee's weekly day off or on a bank holiday;
  200 per cent of the normal basic rate.

Additionally, employees who work overtime have the right to time off in lieu, calculated at 125 per cent of the overtime worked. Shift work generally compensates the employee for the irregularity of his or her working period, which is normally regulated by the IRCT.

Although not stipulated by law, incremental pay in relation to the number of years of service in the same professional category is generally applicable by a rule of the IRCT, and is paid monthly with salary.

Holidays

Paid holidays are considered to be an employee's constitutional right. Employees are not allowed by law to waive this right to holidays.

The normal annual holiday entitlement is 22 working days. This entitlement is calculated on the basis of work provided in the previous year, however employees joining a company in the first half of the year are entitled to eight working days holiday during that year. Employees employed under a fixed term contract for less than one year are entitled to two days' leave for each month of service rendered.

In addition to paid holidays, employees are entitled to the following bonuses:

- holiday bonus (or thirteenth month payment) which is equivalent to the amount of the employee's holiday pay. Both holiday pay and the holiday bonus must be paid to the employee before the holiday commences. Employees are entitled to a full year's holiday if they are employed on 31 December of the previous year.
- christmas bonus (or fourteenth month payment) was established by the IRCT, and is equivalent to the amount of the employee's monthly salary. This bonus is paid proportionally in the first and last years of service.

Maternity provisions

A period of 90 days' paid leave is provided for maternity leave. The employee is entitled to maternity pay during this period, paid by the social security, at 100 per cent of the average salary for the last three months.

Time off

Absences from work may be either justified, as in the case of disease, marriage or the death of a relative or unjustified, which by default are all those reasons not considered by the law to be justified.

Unjustified absences from work are considered to be a breach of the employees' obligations towards the employer and may be punished by various penalties, going as far as dismissal if the employee exceeds five successive or ten non-successive absences in a year.

Justified absences may or may not give the employer the right to deduct pay from the employee's wages, according to the underlying reasons.

Disciplinary and grievance procedures

The law provides various general sanctions and permits the IRCT to establish other sanctions. However, the application of these sanctions, which may go from a simple admonishment to dismissal, requires a formal procedure, so that the employee has a right to defend his or her case.

Lay-off and guaranteed payments

Lay-off may only take place when the viability of the company and maintenance of jobs are at stake, and is taken as a preventive measure. In the case of lay-off, the employee's contractual rights, for example social security contributions, holidays and, where applicable the Christmas bonus will continue.

The period of lay-off, which must be previously defined and strictly fixed, may not exceed six months if it is due to market, economic or technological reasons or one year if due to a catastrophe. In both cases, the period of lay-off may be renewed for a further six months. At the end of this lay-off period the employees' contracts automatically regain full force.

Any employee affected by a lay-off is entitled to a guarantee payment, which usually equals two-thirds of the employee's normal salary; provided however that it may not be less than, or more than triple, the national minimum wage. The employer and the unemployment fund are equally liable for payment of this compensation.

Trial periods

A trial period always exists under general law, regardless of whether it is specified in the contract of employment. Under general law the trial period is as follows:

- the first 240 days for directors and top company officers;
- the first 180 days for employees holding positions of technical complexity, or involving a high degree of responsibility or trust;
- the first 60 days for other employees (90 days if the company employs less than 20 employees under the normal permanent employment regime);
- the first 15 days for temporary employees employed for a period of less than six months, or the first 30 days for employees employed for a longer period.

Collective or individual agreements may reduce the trial period, but may not increase them. It is a general rule that either party may terminate the employment relationship during the trial period without notice and without payment of compensation, provided the parties have not agreed otherwise in the contract of employment.

Period of notice

In the case of a lay-off, employees are entitled to a period of notice which must be fixed when the lay-off conditions are established. No time limit is fixed by law for this period of notice.

The minimum period of notice to be given when terminating the employment relationship depends upon the employee's length of service, as specified in Table 1.

Table 1

Length of service	Period of notice
Less than 2 years' service	30 days' notice
More than 2 years' service	60 days' notice

Where there is 'just cause' for the dismissal, no period of notice is necessary.

Termination of employment

Contracts of employment may be terminated by:

- expiry in the case of fixed term or temporary contracts or retirement of the employee;
- frustration;
- mutual agreement between the parties on specified date;
- dismissal where the grounds set out for fairly dismissing an employee must be strictly adhered to - reasonable grounds include poor conduct, absenteeism and so on;
- notice by the employee or without notice if the employee has 'just cause';
- during the trial period.

Redundancy

Employers must strictly adhere to the rules relating to dismissal when collectively terminating the employees' contracts of employment. Collective termination or redundancy, may only take place in the case of a definite cessation of activity of the company, or of one or more departmental sections, for structural, technological, or macroeconomic reasons.

Employees are entitled to a period of notice of 60 days, which must be preceded by notification to the employees' organizations.   This notification must be made in writing, specifying the economic reasons for the terminations and the procedures to be followed when terminating the employees' employment.   The Minister for Labour may participate in negotiations between the employer and employees in an attempt to minimise the redundancies.

In the absence of any objection by the Minister in relation to the redundancies, any employee declared redundant is entitled to a statutory redundancy payment calculated as one month's salary for each year or partial year of service, the minimum payment being at least three months' salary.

Collective employment regulations

Collective labour regulations may be determined by a Collective Labour Convention (CCT) which has been voluntarily negotiated by the employer or employers and the trade unions.   These Conventions may be adopted by an entire industry.

The CCT may not contradict the fundamental legal rules or be to the employees detriment.   These agreements bind the subscribing employers and all those employers registered in recognized employers' associations and their employees who are members of the recognized trade unions.   In order to be legally binding these agreements must be registered with the Minister of Labour.

Portuguese law provides various mechanisms for overcoming collective labour conflicts relating to the negotiation or revision of an agreement or in its interpretation.   One of these mechanisms is by administrative order.

Administrative order is a substitute for the collective agreement and is applied when the application of an agreement is not possible.   The administrative order is exercised through governmental decree with the following objectives:

- Extension Decree (PE): extends the applicability of a CCT to employers or employees not covered by the CCT, but who belong to the same economic sector, industry, profession or field that has a CCT; provided they do not have their own employers' associations or trade unions and their type of employment corresponds to a CCT category;
- Labour Regulation Decree (PRT): applied by the Ministry of Labour when no extension decree is appropriate and there is a lack of consensus between the parties.

Trade unions and employee organizations

Employees have the statutory right to form workers' associations with the object of defending their interests and for the purpose of democratic representation within the company. They are free to be or not to be a member of a trade union and to take part in lawful trade union activities.

Employees' associations are created and function in accordance with Law 46/79. This law states that these associations must be elected by permanent employees and that they have the following rights:

- to any information necessary for their activities;
- that they may participate in management, intervene in productivity organization and participate in the preparation of industrial legislation and socio-economic plans of the respective sector.

Management control is achieved by the management of the company meeting periodically with the employees' associations who are asked to give written opinions on certain matters.

Trade union liberty and the legal system of trade unions are regulated by Decree Law 215-B/75. It is illegal to make membership of a particular trade union a condition of employment. For the same reason it is also illegal to dismiss or discriminate against any employee on the grounds of union membership.

The Decree Law 215-B/75 also gives various rights to union delegates, one of which is the right to paid time off work for trade union duties.

Trade disputes

The right to strike is considered a constitutional right. The decision to strike may be made by a trade union or by a workers' assembly, providing secret ballots have been obtained from the majority of the workers, and a simple majority of those voting are in favour of the strike. The employer must be given a minimum of 48 hours' notice.

Employees on strike automatically lose all their contractual rights and duties, including the right to remuneration. The employer is not allowed to substitute any employees for the employees on strike and it is illegal for the employer to discriminate against any employees because they have participated in a strike.

Lockouts are absolutely prohibited.

Employee participation

The representatives of workers' commissions and registered trade unions have the right to participate in the formation of labour legislation. No legislative development can be discussed or voted on by the government, or by local government, without the participation and agreement of the abovementioned employee entities.

Law 46/79 obliges company management to actively consider written opinions of employee commissions in the company's administrative decision making. Employers are required to inform the representatives of employee commissions and trade unions of proposed lay-offs or redundancies, including the names of those employees to be affected. The intention is to obtain general agreement through negotiation.

Pensions, tax and insurance

Income tax and national insurance

All obligatory contributions are deducted from the employees' wages and are duly accounted for and paid to the respective entities by the employer. The obligatory contributions are income tax (calculated according to the employee's rate of pay) and social security (11 per cent).

Employers are also obliged to make social security contributions, calculated at 24.5 per cent of the company's total wage expenditure.

Sickness benefit

Employees who have subscribed to national insurance for at least six months are entitled to statutory sick pay on account of illness, providing they can produce a doctor's medical certificate. The statutory sick pay is calculated as 65 per cent of the employee's wage, and is paid directly by the Social Security Institution. In the case of less than three days' sick leave, the employee is entitled to his or her full pay from the employer.

Retirement pensions

The Social Security Institution has various types of pensions for employees and their families, including a disability and retirement pension. Pensions may be paid to non-contributors if the person's total income justifies it.

Retirement pensions become payable at the age 65 for both men and women. Under a transitory regimen, the retirement age of women will increase progressively from the previous age of 62 to the ordinary retirement age of 65 (for example the retirement age will be 62.5 in 1994, 63 in 1995, 63.5 in 1996, and so on). The total value of the employee's pension is calculated in accordance with the number of years' service and the rate of salary paid during those years. The value of the pension is also influenced by any contributions made after the official retirement age.

Health and safety

Apart from health and safety legislation established by the constitution, the General Employment Law obliges employers to observe rigorously the guidelines set down by health and safety bodies; the most important of these guidelines is the employers' liability insurance. Employers must take out insurance against liability for personal injury and disease suffered by employees in the course of, or arising out of, their employment.

Anti-discrimination regulations

Discrimination on the grounds of gender, race, colour, political inclination or religious affiliation is prohibited. The law does however, permit certain legal restrictions in respect of certain employees for reasons either in the collective interest or related to an employee's capacity (for instance, young persons under the age of 14 and certain work for women).

The law guarantees equal rights for men and women in respect of employment, and the Labour Ministry and Equal Rights Commission are responsible for putting this policy into effect. In addition, there are various clauses in the law that refer to anti-discrimination policy, such as the stipulated prohibition of discrimination on the grounds of membership or not of a recognized trade union.

Regulatory bodies

Labour Ministry

The Labour Ministry is a division of central government and its principal functions are to study, define and promote labour and employment policies. It also plays an important part at the IRCT level in negotiations or revision of CCT either as conciliator or through its decrees.

Permanent Council for Social Conciliation

Made up of representatives of employees, employers and the Labour Ministry, the main objective of the Council is to achieve a climate of industrial peace.

Foreign employees

Nationals of EU Member States

EU nationals wishing to work and reside in Portugal may freely enter the Portuguese territory by presenting their passport or identity card. These nationals should be registered with the relevant authorities which will issue Residence Cards accordingly. Individuals working for periods up to three months and seasonal workers (up to eight months) do not require specific documents.

Nationals of non-EU countries

Nationals of non-EU countries wishing to work in Portugal for periods up to 90 days (an extension is obtainable once in Portugal for a period not exceeding 60 days) must obtain a working visa at a Portuguese consulate, unless otherwise defined by bilateral or multilateral agreements. If these nationals wish to work in Portugal for longer periods, residence and work permits are necessary.

Employers may not hire nationals from non-EU countries over and above 10 per cent of their total workforce, unless special authorization is obtained upon request.

Employment contracts must be written and registered with the Labour Inspectorate.

Recruitment and training

EU funds are available for the training and specialization of employees. There are also some incentives for the creation of first jobs for employees. For instance, employers may be exempt from social security contributions on salaries for a period of two years, when they hire employees aged less than 30 years in their first job.

This chapter was written by Paulo Barreto, Coopers & Lybrand, Limitada, Portugal.

Slovakia

Introduction

The basic statutory instruments regulating industrial relations are:

- the Labour Code;
- Order on the Labour Code;
- the Act on Severance (Redundancy) Pay When Employment is Terminated;
- Order on Industrial Relations with Private Entrepreneur Activities of Individuals;
- the Act on Collective Bargaining;
- the Act on Wages;
- the Act on Travel Costs;
- the Act on Salary;
- the Act on Employment Fund;
- Order on Minimum Wage Rates;
- Order on Minimum Wage.

The first five statutory instruments stipulate the basic employment law provisions, the remaining instruments supplement these provisions by providing a much wider range of issues than just those concerned with industrial relations. The Constitution of the Slovak Republic also contains information on employment rights, which has been reflected and developed in the Labour Code and other statutory instruments.

The fundamental principles contained in the Labour Code include:

- all citizens have the right to work, the right to a free choice of employment, to decent working conditions, and to protection against unemployment;
- employees are entitled to remuneration for their work; the level of remuneration to be determined by the quantity, quality and social importance of the work;

- employees are entitled to occupational health and safety, and to rest and recreation after work;
- employees have the right, through their trade unions, to be informed about the activities of the organization and the key issues concerning the organization's economic situation and development;
- employees shall be obliged to properly fulfil their employment duties and the position (function) entrusted to them by the employer;
- women shall have the same status as men;
- adolescents shall have the right to vocational training, including good working conditions which will enable them to develop their physical and intellectual abilities;
- employers are obliged to take measures to protect the health of their employees at work, and are liable for any injury caused to employees as a result of an accident at work or for any occupational disease affecting the employee;
- trade unions are entitled to engage in industrial relations, including collective bargaining.

Collective bargaining between trade unions, employers and/or employers organizations is regulated by the Act on Collective Bargaining. Collective agreements are legally binding agreements which regulate:

- individual relations between employers and employees;
- collective terms and conditions of employment, for example wages;
- rights and duties of the contractual parties.

Many employment law issues are still determined through the process of tripartite negotiations between representatives of the trade unions, employers and the Government of Slovak Republic. Tripartite bargaining takes place at the Council of the Economic and Social Agreement.

The General Agreement stipulates the agreed procedures and obligations to be observed in the individual industrial and social sphere and is signed on an annual basis by the representatives of Government and the social partners.

Although the General Agreement is not legally binding, it does constitute a gentleman's agreement between the parties. The Government does however, have the power to transform the government's obligations under the General Agreement into legal regulations.

As many employment law issues are determined in this manner, it is expected that there will be some changes in employment law in the foreseeable future.

Individual employment regulations

Contracts

An employment relationship commences upon the signing of a contract of employment between the employer and employee. The contract of employment must describe:

- the type of work the employee is employed to do;
- the place of work (town, organizational unit or other description);
- the day on which the employment commences;
- any other relevant information.

The employer must provide the employee with a copy of the contract of employment.

It is possible for the parties to agree upon a trial period up to a maximum of three months duration. This period cannot subsequently be extended.

The contents of the contract of employment may be amended if both parties agree to the changes. If the contract has been concluded in writing, any subsequent amendments must also be in writing.

The employment relationship is normally established for an indefinite period of time.   Where the parties have agreed to a fixed term contract, this contract may be extended, but only for a period of three years at any one time.

The employment of children is prohibited.   Persons under the age of 18 may only be employed with the consent of their lawful guardians and cannot be employed for night work.

Wages and salaries

Minimum wage provision - Wages in Czechoslovakia, under the former tariff wage system, were severly restricted as they reflected
social norms rather than embodied human capital or the relative scarcity of special skills.   In 1990, wages were liberalized and an excess wage tax was imposed to control costs.   The excess wage tax was then suspended in December 1992.

Wages are now mainly set by tripartite 'rational' collective bargaining agreements in enterprises, or alternatively determined in accordance with a schedule of occupation-and-industry-specific minima set by the Ministry of Labour, Social Affairs and Family.   The general minimum wage is currently Sk 2 450 per month (the maximum level of minimum wage is Sk 9 800 according to the Slovak Statistic Office).   The minimum hourly wage is currently 13.30 Sk per hour (the maximum level of minimum hourly wage is Sk 41.50 per hour according to the Slovak Statistic Office).   Premium payments are made for arduous or hazardous work, as well as for night work.   These premiums are paid at a minimum of 2.50 Sk per hour.

Method of payment - Wages are paid monthly in arrears and unless there is an agreement to the contrary, should be paid by the last day of the following calendar month.   Wages should be paid in cash during the employee's working hours, but can in extraordinary circumstances, be paid by a valid wage measure.   The employee may request the employer to transfer an amount specified by employee to any Slovak financial institution.

Deductions from pay - The employer is entitled to make such deductions from the employee's wages as required by law, the courts or some other authority. The employer may also deduct any wage advances and similar amounts which the employee has subsequently failed to repay, without obtaining the employee's agreement. All other deductions however, must be made on the basis of an agreement between the employer and employee.

Itemized pay statement - Every employee has a right to an itemized pay statement, at or before the time payment is made. The itemized pay statement must show, in writing, the gross wage, amount and purpose of any deductions, and the net amount of pay.

Hours of work/shift work/overtime

The maximum working week is 43 hours. Certain high risk industries have a 35 or 36 hour week. Employees aged less than 16 may not work for more than 33 hours in any one week.

Contracts of employment should provide a 30 minute meal break and a rest period after five hours of uninterrupted work.

The shift schedules used are as set out in Table 1.

Table 1

Shift	Time
First shift	6am to 2pm
Second shift	2am to 10pm
Third shift	10am to 6pm

Any work performed in excess of the hours stipulated in the weekly schedule or outside the work shift schedule is considered to be overtime. The employer can only require the employee to work overtime in exceptional cases.

Overtime must be limited to eight hours per week and 150 hours per calendar year. Compensation for overtime is salary plus at least 25 per cent for normal days, and at least 50 per cent for holidays. The parties may however, agree to the employee taking time off in lieu of overtime, in which case overtime will not be paid. Any employees employed in risky conditions are not permitted to work overtime.

Holidays

The minimum annual leave entitlement is three weeks per annum for employees who have worked for at least 60 days' with the same employer. Where the employee has 15 or more years' service with the same employer, he or she will be entitled to four weeks annual leave per annum. For those employees who have worked for more than one employer during the requisite 60 day qualifying period, they will be entitled to one-twelfth of the annual leave entitlement for every 22 days worked.

Employees can only be required to work on days declared as state holidays or official commemoration days under special conditions. Payments for working on state holidays is regulated by a special system, set out in the industrial relations regulations.

The following days are public holidays in the Slovak Republic:

1 January	Slovak Republic Founding Day
6 January	Appearance of God Day
March - April	Good Friday
March - April	Easter Monday
1 May	Labour Day
5 July	St. Cyril and St. Methodius Day
29 August	Slovak National Uprising Day
1 September	Slovak Republic Constitution
15 September	Feast of the Seven Sorrows
1 November	All Saints Day
24 December	Christmas Eve
25 December	Christmas Day
26 December	Boxing Day

Maternity provisions

There are special working conditions for women generally and for pregnant women specifically:

- women may not be employed to work underground;
- women may not be engaged in work which is physically inappropriate for them or which may cause physical harm, especially work threatening their ability to conceive;
- a pregnant woman or a woman caring for a child under the age of one year may not be sent on business trips;
- a woman caring for a child aged between one and three years may only be sent on business trips with her consent.

The Ministry of Health maintains a list of jobs which prohibits the employment of women, pregnant women, or women working less than nine months after the birth of their child.

Women are generally entitled to 28 weeks maternity leave. If however, the women gives birth to two or more babies at the same time, or if she is a single parent with no other income besides her employment, she will be entitled to 37 weeks maternity leave.

The employer is required to grant additional maternity leave to women who request it for such periods up until the child reaches three years of age.

Time off

The employer is obliged to provide necessary time off to trade union representatives to enable them to perform their trade union responsibilities. The amount of compensation to be paid to the trade union representatives during these periods is a matter of agreement between the employer and the trade union. Such agreement may be specified in the collective agreement, or the parties may apply the measure stipulated by the Ministry of Work and Social Affairs.

Disciplinary and grievance procedures

The Labour Code stipulates the basic disciplinary or working responsibilities of the employer and employee. The employer is entitled to develop a working rules document which specifies the employees' duties. Prior to issuing this document, the employer is obliged to discuss the contents of the document with the appropriate trade unions.

Lay-off and guaranteed payments

The employer is obliged to compensate employees, in accordance with the wage regulations and provisions of any applicable collective agreements, in the case of work interruption caused by the employer. In certain circumstances, for instance operational problems, the employer and trade union can conclude a written agreement whereby the employer can reduce the employees average wage by 60 per cent for the duration of the problem. This agreement cannot be replaced by an employers' decree.

Supplemental employment

'Supplemental employment' is defined as any employment relationship other than the one in which the employee works the stipulated working hours. In other words, the supplemental contract of employment can only be for less hours than the normal weekly working hours. Therefore a second job taken during the employees' annual leave is not considered to be 'supplemental employment'.

If the employee wishes to be engaged in secondary employment, identical to that of his or her primary employment, the employee must first obtain the written permission of the employer.

Supplemental employment may be terminated by either party giving at least 15 days' notice of termination.

Period of notice

Either party may terminate the employment relationship by giving written notice. This notice must be delivered to the other party in order to be valid. The employment relationship will then end upon the expiry of the notice period.

The standard period of notice is two months for both employer and employee. The period of notice commences on the first day of the calendar month following the date on which the notice is delivered, and expires on the last day of the next calendar month.

Dismissal

The contract of employment may be terminated in any of the following ways:

- by the written agreement of both parties;
- by either party giving the requisite period of notice;
- by instant dismissal in the case of disciplinary breaches or criminal acts;
- at any time during the trial period;
- upon expiration of employment relationship;
- unless terminated in another manner an expatriate's employment expires on the day on which the person's presence on the territory of Slovakia is to end as a result of a valid ruling cancelling his residence permit.

An employer may give notice to an employee for the following reasons:

- the company is in whole or in part abolished, or it moves to a new location;
- the company ceases to exist or a part of it is transferred to another company and the latter organization has no possibility of providing work for the employee in accordance with the employment contract;

- the employee is not willing to be transferred to a different, although still suitable job that the employer offers him or her at a location agreed upon as the employee's workplace;
- the employee becomes redundant as a result of decision on the part of the organization or relevant body regarding a change in the company's production, or other organizational changes;
- the employee has lost the capacity to perform his or her tasks due to long-standing health problems verified by a medical doctor's certificate or the decision of a public health board or social security board;
- the employee does not meet the conditions set forth in the legal provisions for the performance of the agreed work and in the last 12 months the employee was asked in writing to eliminate the deficiencies in his or her work, but failed to do so within an appropriate period;
- the employee has seriously breached work discipline, or has consistently committed infringements against work discipline, provided he or she was warned in writing within the previous six months of the possibility of being given notice.

Restrictions on giving notice

Employers may not give notice during a 'protection period', that is, when the employee is:

- temporarily incapable of working due to an illness or accident that has been certified by a medical doctor, provided that the employee did not cause the incapacity through his or her own wilful acts, or in a drunken state;
- called up for duty in the armed forces, from the day when he receives the call up order, or from the day when an ordinance containing a general call up order is published, until two weeks following the employee's release from such service;
- a pregnant woman or a single female or male employee who has no other income but his or her wage, and who must care for at least one child under three years of age.

In the case of a trial period, both the employer and the employee may terminate the employment relationship at any time, on any grounds, and without having to state those grounds.

Immediate termination

An employer may dismiss an employee immediately only by submitting the reasons for the dismissal in writing, and only in the following exceptional cases:

- the employee is sentenced to a prison term exceeding six months for committing a wilful criminal act related to his or her work activity;
- the employee is sentenced to a prison term exceeding one year for committing a wilful criminal act not related to his or her work activity;
- the employee breaches work discipline in a particularly gross manner.

Employers may not immediately dismiss a pregnant woman or a single female or male employee who cares for at least one child under three years of age.

The employee may terminate the employment relationship with the organization immediately if, according to a medical doctor's certificate, he or she cannot continue working without seriously impairing his or her health and the employer has failed to transfer the employee to an alternative and suitable job within 15 days of the submission of the doctor's certificate.

Redundancy

If redundancy is due to organizational changes the company is required to find suitable employment for the following two special categories of employees:

- single female or male employees having no other income source and permanently caring for a child or children younger than the age of 15;
- disabled employees not in receipt of a pension.

Collective employment regulations

Collective creation of law

The Act on Collective Bargaining has been in force since 1990. The provisions of this Act comply with the ILO convention No. 154 on collective bargaining and stipulates that collective bargaining occurs between the relevant trade union bodies and employers.

Collective agreements regulate individual and collective relations between employers and employees as well as rights and duties of both contractual parties.

The types of collective agreements are as follows:

- a company collective agreement, concluded between a relevant trade union and an employer;
- higher level collective agreements, concluded between relevant trade union branches and the organization or organizations of employers (for example within an industrial sector);

The collective agreement becomes valid if concluded in a written form and signed by the authorized representatives of relevant trade union bodies and employers.

The collective agreement can become invalid if the provisions are in contradiction with the legal regulations, or if it stipulates rights of employees of a lower standard or level than the higher level collective agreement or if wages are higher than those stipulated by higher level collective agreement.

Trade disputes

Collective disputes and grievance procedures may arise during the process of concluding the collective agreement or from obligations under that collective agreement.

Collective disputes or grievances can be settled by:

- a mediator, elected by the contractual parties or appointed by the Ministry of Work and Social Affairs of the Slovak Republic, who is obliged within 15 days from investigating the grievance to submit a proposed solution. If the grievance cannot be settled within 30 days from the date of submission of the grievance to the mediator, the grievance settlement is considered unsuccessful;
- an arbitrator, the parties can refer the grievance to an abitrator where mediatiation has been unsuccessful. An arbitrator is obliged to submit a solution within 15 days from investigating the grievance. The arbitrator's opinion should be considered final and the grievance procedure should be considered finished. In some cases however, a court ruling may be gained by any of the contractual parties to cancel the arbitrator's decision.

Employee participation

As stipulated by legal regulations of the Slovak Republic, trade unions and trade union bodies are considered to be the employees' representatives. Employers have a duty under the provisions of the Labour Code and other employment regulations to:

- provide information to the trade unions or trade union bodies;
- to consult and discuss problems with them;
- to invite them to participate in the decision making process;
- to accept any control procedures submitted by the trade unions and/or trade union bodies.

The present legal environment generally complies with the relevant measures of the International Labour Organization.

Pensions, tax and insurance

Income tax

Remuneration received by the employee includes gross salary from his or her employment together with the income from any dependent personal services plus:

- benefits-in-kind (for example use of a company car for private purposes, living and houses allowances, reimbursement of travel expenses above regulated limits);
- other taxable income (such as dividends, interest received from abroad, income from running private business, and so on).

The net taxable income is calculated by taking the gross taxable income minus the social security contributions paid by the employee:

- Sk 3 600 per annum for employment expenses and so on;
- Sk 21 000 for every taxpayer;
- Sk 9 000 per annum for each dependent child living with the taxpayer in a common household (this is paid in respect of the first four children only);
- Sk 12 000 per annum as allowances for a spouse living with the payer in a common household;
- other allowances (for example for disabled taxpayers)

The tax payable on a person's taxable income, less any relevant tax allowances is set out in Table 2.

Table 2

Net taxable income sk	Annual tax payable sk
0 - 60 000	0 + 15 % on excess over 0
60 000 - 120 000	9 000 + 20% on excess over 60 000
120 000 - 180 000	21 000 + 25% on excess over 120 000

Net taxable income sk	Annual tax payable sk
180 000 - 540 000	36 000 + 32% on excess over 180 000
540 000 - 1 080 000	151 200 + 40% on excess over 540 000
over 1 080 000	367 200 + 42% on excess over 1 080 000

Social insurances

As from January 1993 employers and employees are required to contribute to a new insurance fund for pensions, health care, sickness benefits, and employment benefits according to specified contribution rates (expressed as a percentage of base wages) as shown in Table 3. Combined together these contributions total 50 per cent of the base wage. The National Health Insurance is responsible for operating the health and social insurance.

Social security contributions are divided into four funds:

- health fund;
- sickness fund;
- pensions fund;
- employment fund.

The employee must contribute in aggregate 11 per cent of their income to the health, sickness and pension funds, while the employer must contribute 35 per cent. In respect of the employment fund, the employee must contribute one per cent and the employer must contribute three per cent. The base for calculating these contributions is gross salary minus deductible items.

Table 3

Type of insurance	Employer	Employee	Total
Health fund	10%	3.7%	13.7%
Pensions fund	20.6%	5.9%	26.5%
Sickness fund	4.4%	1.4%	5.8%
Employment fund	3%	1%	4%
Total	38%	12%	50%

The base for calculating the social security contributions cannot be lower than the minimum wage which is currently Sk 2 450.

Sickness benefit

The sickness benefit covers the employee against loss of income where the employee is absence from work on account of personal illness, or illness of a family member or is absent due to the birth of a child. The employee receives the sickness benefit from the employer, who is reimbursed by the state. The sickness benefit equals 70 per cent of the employee's salary for the first three days of illness and 90 per cent of the employee's salary for the remaining period of sickness. There is however, a maximum benefit of Sk 180 per day, if the employee's net salary is more than Sk 4 500 per month.

Retirement pensions

Men are entitled to a retirement pension at the age of 60, while women can retire earlier, between the ages of 53 and 57 years. A woman who has not had any children may retire at the age of 57, a woman with one child may retire at the age of 56, while a woman who has brought up two children may retire at 55 years and so forth.

Employees who have been given notice of termination as a result of structural or organizational changes in the company and who cannot find alternative employment may retire two years early.

It is expected however, that in the future the retirement age for both men and women will be increased to 65 years.

Health and safety

The employer is primarily responsible for ensuring that all the basic standards and regulations concerning and safeguarding health and safety at work are complied with. However, employer's bodies and trade union bodies can provide control procedures. Trade union bodies provide these procedures on two levels, by the trade union body of individual companies and by higher level trade union bodies.

Trade union bodies are entitled to issue a decree on the removal of investigated shortages and if necessary to interrupt operations, to remedy any shortfalls.

Anti-discrimination regulations

Race and sex discrimination

The Labour Code states that 'all citizens shall have the right to work, and to a free choice of employment, along with decent working conditions, and protection against unemployment. These rights belong to all citizens regardless of race, colour, language, sex, social origin, age, religion, political or other opinion, political party membership, trade union activity, national or ethnic group or other status.'

Women have the right to the same status at work as men. Working conditions for women must not only conform to their physiological constitution, but must also take into account the women's social role as mothers and their obligation to care for children.

Regulatory bodies

The Confederation of Trade Unions of the Slovak Republic participates on a national level in negotiating settlements on behalf of employees with the Government and employers' groups.

Employers may belong to various employers' organizations. The Association of Employers' Unions of Slovakia negotiates with the Government on behalf of employers.

Mediation authority and reconciliation board

Mediation and arbitration authorities assist in settling collective disputes and grievance procedures between employers and employees.

Legal institutions

The Slovak Republic does not have independent Labour Courts as labour disputes and grievances are settled by courts who also deal with other grievances under the Labour Code, Commercial Code and Penal Law.

Foreign employees

Foreigners can work in the Slovak Republic provided they have been granted:

- a permit for stay;
- a work permit, which is granted by the relevant Work Authority.

A work permit may only be granted for a maximum period of one year and the Work Authorities must have regard to special regulations governing the protection of the national work market, when issuing a work permit.

Employers are obliged to transfer appropriate deductions to individual funds for employed foreigners.

Recruitment and training

Recruitment

The Act on Employment stipulates provisions for the recruitment of employees. The state authorities, namely the labour offices and natural or juristic persons, licensed for such activities by the Ministry of Work and Social Affairs, provide recruitment services.

Labour offices provide recruitment services free of charge and deal primarily with unemployed job seekers. Natural and juristic persons have the right to charge for their services, but such fees are regulated by internal regulations. There is no limitation on recruitment activities developed through the mass media.

Apprenticeship

Apprenticeship is part of occupational education.   Secondary Apprenticeship Schools are managed and regulated by the Ministry of Education and by individual economic ministries (for instance the Ministry of Agriculture, the Ministry of Economy, the Ministry of Transport, the Ministry of Communication, the Ministry of Public Works and so on).   Some apprentices conclude an apprenticeship agreement with employers in order to cover their study costs and to have guaranteed employment after finishing school. The study costs of apprentices who have not entered into an apprenticeship agreement are reimbursed by the State. After finishing school these apprentices must compete for work on the job market.

This chapter was written by Monika Peschlová (MCS), Michal Cibira and Caroline Woodward (Tax Advisory) and Magdaléna Forrová (Consultant to Coopers & Lybrand), Coopers & Lybrand, Slovakia.

Spain

Introduction

In Spain, there are many different types of labour regulations which are being changed periodically. This diversity is reflected in differences in the legislative level of the regulations. Labour regulations also emanate from collective agreements.

The Constitution of 27 December 1978 forms the basis of labour law. It provides a structure for and implements a set of rights and liberties for the individual - in the case of labour law, employee's rights. Employment regulations and labour law are based primarily on the Labour Statute ('the Statute'), in force from 10 March 1980.

The Statute specifies basic rights and conditions which may not be relinquished. Such conditions are usually improved upon by collective agreements. Collective agreements are concluded between employers and trade unions in the various manufacturing and service industries, and have full legal effect. They are usually agreed on an annual basis.

Where two regulations conflict, the most favourable regulation is applied in accordance with the *in dubio pro operario* principle. This principle holds that the interpretation most favourable to the employee must be adopted.

The original Labour Statute has been revised by Law 11/1994 of 19 May 1994 which modifies a great number of the articles. These reforms have been based on two basic pillars which notably affect labour relations. These pillars are:

- priority is given to collective negotiation and agreements between the parties concerned, eliminating, in part, the protectionist style of the State;

- flexibility of labour relations to better adapt to the present needs of business, which facilitates the management of human resources within a company.

The Statute applies to all salaried work carried out for the account of, and dependent upon a third party, with the following exceptions:

- public servants;
- company directors;
- work performed out of friendship, benevolence or neighbourliness;
- work within the family;
- independent commercial representatives;
- transport services provided by a person who owns the vehicle used.

The application of the Statute is extended to certain employment relationships of a special nature, which includes:

- senior company managers or executives;
- domestic servants;
- artists in public shows;
- dependent commercial representatives.

Individual employment regulations

Contracts

In Spain, employment contracts may be concluded orally, except in the following situations where they must be concluded in writing:

- training and apprenticeship contracts;
- contracts for part-time employment;
- contracts for homeworkers;
- contracts for the performance of a specific job or type of service;
- contracts with employees hired in Spain by Spanish companies operating abroad;
- contracts for a period exceeding four weeks;

- contracts that are required by law to be in writing (temporary, job creation, launching of a new activity, and so on).

Failure to observe these requirements will result in the presumption that the contract has been entered into indefinitely and for full-time employment.

Employers who enter into written contracts of employment with persons, regardless of whether such persons are registered with the employment office, must register the contracts with the employment office within ten days.

The employment office must be notified of any contract concluded orally within the same period.

In addition to public employment offices, the Law 10/1994 of 19 May now permits, under certain circumstances, private, non-profit making employment agencies to conclude employment contracts between employees and employers.

To facilitate the flexibility of labour relations, the Law 14/1994 of 1 June 1994 now regulates the workings of new businesses called Temporary Employment Companies. Temporary Employment Companies subcontract employees to other companies ('user companies') on a temporary basis.

These subcontracts can only be used to cover certain temporary needs of the 'user company', as specified by law. For example:

- to carry out a specific job or service;
- to attend to circumstantial market requirements;
- to substitute 'user company' employees who have retain their previous positions;
- to cover a position during a selection or training process.

The employment contract may be concluded for an indefinite period or for a specified period, although temporary contracts concluded fraudulently will be presumed to be indefinite contracts.

There are several different types of employment contracts, the most common being:

- indefinite contracts (no time limit);
- training and apprenticeship contracts;
- part-time contracts for any employment less than a normal working day;
- temporary contracts for the launching of a new activity.

Where certain requirements are fulfilled, the employer may be entitled to an incentive, such as reductions in social security contributions or capital grants.

Wages and salaries

Wages and salaries consist of the total remuneration received by the employee in return for working for the employer. The employer may, with the agreement of the employee, pay up to 30 per cent of the remuneration by benefits in kind.

Minimum wage provision - The minimum wage or salary is determined by the government on an annual basis. The minimum wages (in pesetas) applicable during 1994 to all sectors of the economy are set out in Table 1.

Table 1

Employees	Per day	Per month
Under 18 years of age	1 334	40 020
18 years of age and over	2 019	60 570

Minimum salaries for different categories of employees are often laid down in collective agreements, which improve upon the minimum wage fixed by the government. Minimum salaries may also be increased according to length of service, nature of work, bonuses, allowances, productivity incentives, and so on.

Method of payment - There are no legal requirements restricting the method by which salaries must be paid (cash, cheque, bank transfer, and so on). The frequency cannot exceed one month, and the payment itself must be evidenced by a receipt, issued in duplicate by the employer in an official form.

The original statement must be signed by the employee upon receipt of his or her salary and returned to the employer; the copy is for the employee's files.

The employee is entitled to two special bonus payments per year, one in December and the other as laid down in the collective agreement (usually in July). Notwithstanding the foregoing, collective agreements may provide that such bonuses be paid in 12 monthly instalments.

The employee or employee's representative may legally ask the employer for advance payments on work already performed.

Late salary payments may give rise to interest accruing at 10 per cent per annum, payable by the employer.

Deductions from pay - The only deductions which the employer can make without the express agreement of the employee, are those in respect of income tax and social security. It is the employer's obligation to deduct the employee's social security contributions and to withhold income tax. Any provision or practice to the contrary will be null and void.

Itemized pay statement - Salary payments must be evidenced by issuing an official form, itemizing the different types of payment. Salary consists of base salary and where applicable, complementary salary. The payment of complementary salary is dependant upon the employee's personal circumstances, the requirements of the employee's position and the company's financial situation.

Wage Guarantee Fund - This fund, administered by the Ministry of Labour and Social Security, guarantees the payment of outstanding salaries, wages and redundancy pay within certain limits and under certain conditions.

The Wage Guarantee Fund is financed by employer contributions. The rate of the contribution is fixed by the government on the basis of wages currently paid to employees.

Salaries and wages will be paid to the employee in the event of insolvency, suspension of payments or bankruptcy of the employer. The maximum amount paid is calculated by multiplying twice the minimum daily wage by the number of days for which salary is unpaid, up to a maximum of 120 days. These payments must be recognised in a settlement or court order.

Employees will also be compensated where they voluntarily rescind the employment contract in the following circumstances:

- where the employer has not complied with his or her obligations;
- for technological or economic reasons;
- force majeure;
- where the employer is insolvent or bankrupt, or where payments have been suspended.

The maximum amount of compensation is one year's salary and is limited to twice the minimum wage.

Hours of work/shift work/overtime

Hours of work are either fixed by collective agreement or by individual employment contracts. The Labour Statute states that the maximum number of hours of work shall not exceed 40 hours per week. The normal number of hours per day shall not exceed nine.

This maximum can, however, be increased or decreased for certain activities in specific economic sectors. Separate regulations specify which activities in which sectors these exceptions apply to. They also make provision for minimum rest periods.

Night shift work is considered to be from 10pm to 6am. Such work must be paid at the compensation rate specifically laid down in the collective agreement, unless consideration was given to the employee working such shifts when the employee's salary was set, and such compensation is adequate.

Any employer who regularly requires employees to work at night must inform the labour authorities.

The Labour Statute sets out certain limits on overtime. Overtime may not exceed 80 hours per year. Where the employee receives time off in lieu of overtime (within four months of the overtime entitlement becoming due) such overtime is not included in the accumulated total.

The collective agreement or, where there is no such agreement, the individual contract of employment will stipulate the amount to be paid for overtime. The employee will be compensated for overtime by receiving payments, which may not be lower than the employee's normal pay, or by receiving time off in lieu. In the absence of any agreement, the employee will be compensated for overtime by receiving time off in lieu, to be taken within four months of the entitlement occurring.

Persons under 18 years of age are not allowed to work overtime. In addition, overtime cannot be worked at night subject to certain exceptions.

Holidays

Employers are under a statutory obligation to provide annual paid holidays to their employees. The holiday entitlement fixed by the collective agreement or individual contract may not be less than 30 days per working year, which must be allotted pro rata in accordance with the effective working period during the first year of employment.

Holiday periods must be agreed between the employer and the employee. Where there is a collective agreement in force, holidays must be determined in accordance with that agreement. In the event of a disagreement between the parties, the labour authorities will set the date for holidays, their decision being final.

In addition, employees are entitled to not more than 14 paid public holidays per working year.

Maternity provisions

A pregnant employee is entitled to maternity leave of up to 16 weeks. The employee is allowed to allocate her maternity leave at her own convenience, provided that at least six of the 16 weeks are taken after the actual date of birth. These six weeks may be taken by the father in the event of the mother's death.

If the employee contributed to the social security system for at least 180 days during the year preceding the date of birth, and has been affiliated during at least nine months preceding that date, she is also entitled to 16 weeks' maternity pay, calculated at 75 per cent of her average pay. Maternity pay is fully recoverable by the employer from the Spanish Social Security.

The employee is entitled to return to work after completion of maternity leave. Failure on the part of the employer to allow her to return to her original job constitutes unfair dismissal.

Employees are entitled to time off at work to breast-feed babies under the age of nine months.

Military service or social service leave

Military service leave (either voluntary or compulsory) or social service leave constitutes an interruption of employment, during which the employee is not statutorily entitled to any remuneration from the employer.

The employee is entitled however, to return to work within 30 days of completing such leave. Failure on the part of the employer to permit the employee to return to his or her original job constitutes unfair dismissal.

Any service period counts towards the employee's seniority for purposes of salary increases, compensation allowance or otherwise.

Time off

The employer has an obligation to provide employees with paid leave in specified circumstances. For example:

- 15 days' leave for the employee's marriage;
- two days' leave for the birth of a child;
- two days' leave for serious illness or death of a close relative (this increases to four days leave where travel is involved);
- one day's leave when moving to a new permanent residence;
- where the employee is a member of a recognized trade union and holds union appointments, paid leave to take part in union activities;
- leave for sitting professional examinations.

In addition, the employer has the statutory obligation to provide time off (without pay) to employees who are elected to hold public office or to carry out union activities on a provincial or national basis.

Where other conditions are satisfied, the employee may request time off without pay. However, in these circumstances, the employee's job is not protected and any return to work will depend upon suitable vacancies being available.

Disciplinary and grievance procedures

General disciplinary rules are included in the Labour Statute, although collective agreements may mention specific rules and procedures to which the employee is subject. Furthermore, employers may adopt appropriate disciplinary rules and procedures in order to provide safe working conditions.

The employer may impose sanctions on any employee who breaches the statutory or internal rules, but they must always be reviewed by the labour authorities.

Where the breach of discipline leads to dismissal, the employer must notify the employee in writing, detailing the events which led to the dismissal.

Trial periods

The employment contract may contain a trial period, subject to such limits as specified in the collective agreement, if applicable. Where there is no collective agreement governing the relationship, the trial period may not exceed six months for technical graduates or two months for all other employees. In companies with less than 25 employees the trial period may not exceed three months for employees who are not technical graduates.

In order to be legally effective, the trial period must be specified in writing. During this period the employee has the same rights and obligations as if he were a member of the permanent staff. Either party may terminate the employment relationship at any time during the trial period, without paying compensation.

Once the trial period has elapsed without termination having occurred, the employment becomes permanent. The trial period is then taken into account when calculating the employee's length of service.

Termination of employment

Under the Labour Statute, a contract of employment may be terminated in the following circumstances:

- by agreement between the parties;
- on the grounds validly stipulated in the contract, unless such reasons are a manifest abuse of law by the employer;
- on expiry of the agreed term or completion of the work or service which is the subject of the contract;
- on the employee's resignation;

- on the employer's death, disability or retirement;
- in cases of force majeure, making it permanently impossible to do the work;
- for collective dismissals, based on economic, technological, organizational or production reasons which must be authorized in accordance with the stipulations laid down by the Statute;
- at the employee's dismissal;
- for legally valid reasons of an objective nature.

Termination at the employee's request

The employee can validly terminate the employment contract in the following circumstances:

- where there has been a substantial alteration in the conditions of employment to the detriment of the employee's professional training and/or dignity;
- where there has been a failure to pay the employee or a repeated delay in paying the employee;
- where there has been any other serious failure on the part of the employer to discharge his contractual duties, except in cases of force majeure.

The Statute does not prescribe any special notice requirements in these circumstances, but states that the employee shall be entitled to compensation set out for unlawful dismissal. Compensation for unlawful dismissal equals 45 days' pay for every year of service, up to a maximum of 42 months' pay. Any periods less than one year entitle the employee to a proportional fraction of such compensation for each month.

Termination for objective reasons

Termination for objective reasons may result from the employee's incapacity to adapt himself or herself to technological changes in the job, or may result from the employee's lack of necessary skills or the employee's repeated absences. In the latter case, absences from work, including justified absences, will count against the employee if it represents 20 per cent of working days in any two consecutive month period or 25 per cent of the working days in any four non-consecutive months, over a 12 month period.

Alternatively, an employee's employment contract may be terminated for accredited objective reasons, when the employer needs to reduce the number of employees for economic, technical, organizational or production reasons within the following limits:

- ten employees in a company engaging less than 100 employees;
- 10 per cent of the total number of employees in companies engaging between 100 and 300 employees;
- 30 employees in a company engaging more than 300 employees.

Procedure

The employer must comply with the following procedures when terminating the employee's employment contract for objective reasons.

- the employee must be notified of the termination in writing, with an indication of the reason for the termination;
- the employer should provide the employee with compensation at the rate of 20 days' pay for each year of service, up to a maximum of 12 months' pay, at the same time as notice is given.   Periods of service less than one year entitle the employee to a proportional fraction for each month;
- the employer must allow 30 days between delivery of the notice of termination and actual termination.   During the notice period, the employee shall be entitled to six hours off each week, without loss of pay, to look for other employment.

Effect

The employee has 20 working days from the end of the period of termination to lodge an appeal against the termination.

Where the termination is declared to be valid, the employee shall be entitled to retain the compensation he or she has received (20 days' salary for every year of service up to a maximum of 12 months' pay) and shall be deemed to be unemployed for reasons beyond the employee's control.

Where the Labour Tribunal finds that the employer has failed to comply with the procedural requirements, or that the decision to terminate is motivated by a reason prohibited by the Constitution or by law, or that the employee's basic rights or liberties have been violated, the termination will be null and void.

The employer's subsequent compliance with the procedures will not validate the termination, but will constitute a new decision to terminate the employment contract, with effect from the date the latter decision is taken.

Where the termination is found to be null and void, the employee will be entitled to immediate reinstatement and payment for any loss of income between the period of termination and the date of judgment.

Where the termination is declared to be invalid (for instance notice of termination has not been provided or an indemnity not paid) and the employer reinstates the employee, the employee shall reimburse the employer any compensation he or she has already received.

Alternatively, where the employer pays the employee compensation in lieu of reinstatement, the amount of compensation previously paid to the employee will be deducted from the final amount due.

Termination on disciplinary grounds

The employer may terminate the employee's employment contract on disciplinary grounds where the employee is guilty of a serious and blameworthy breach of contract. Such conduct is defined as:

- repeated and unjustified unpunctuality or absence from work;
- indiscipline or disobedience at work;
- verbal or physical offensive behaviour towards the employer, any persons working in the undertaking or relatives living with such persons;

- lack of good faith in the performance of the contract and breach of trust in the performance of the work;
- consistent and wilful reduction of the normal or agreed output;
- habitual drunkenness or addiction to drugs, if it adversely affects the work.

Procedure

The employer must notify the employee in writing that the employment contract is terminated, expressing the reasons for the termination. The employer must indicate the date on which the termination takes effect, as there is no statutory period of notice to observe in these circumstances.

Collective agreements may establish other formalities for the termination of employment contracts.

Effect

The employee has 20 working days from the date that the termination takes effect to lodge an appeal with the Labour Tribunal. The Labour Tribunal will declare the termination to be lawful, unlawful or null and void.

A termination will be considered lawful where the reason alleged by the employer in the written notice is accredited. In these circumstances the employee is not entitled to any indemnity or salary.

An unlawful termination occurs where the employer cannot substantiate the reasons for the termination or where the employer has not complied with the formal requirements.

Where the termination is declared to be unlawful, the employer has five days, after notice of the decision, to opt to reinstate the employee or pay the employee compensation in lieu of reinstatement. Where the dismissed employee is a representative, the employee has the right to determine whether he or she will be reinstated or will receive compensation in lieu thereof, not the employer.

The amount of compensation equals 45 days' salary for every year of service, up to a maximum of 42 months' pay. Any periods less than one year entitles the employee to a proportional fraction for each month of service.

The employee will also be entitled to an amount equal to the salary that the employee has forfeited between the date of termination and the date of judgment, or if earlier, the date that the employee commenced alternative employment. The salary is limited to the amount of salary accrued from the date of termination to the date of reconciliation. Reconciliation occurs if the employer recognizes that the dismissal was unfair and offers the employee an indemnity equal to 45 days' salary for each year of service. The employer should deposit the payment with the Tribunal within a period of 48 hours following reconciliation.

Termination will be null and void if it results from any type of discrimination prohibited by the Constitution or by law, or if it occurs in violation of the employees basic rights and liberties. Termination in these circumstances requires the immediate reinstatement of the employee and payment of any outstanding wages, accruing from the day termination came into effect.

Force majeure

Where force majeure is the cause for termination of employment, it must be verified by the labour authorities regardless of the number of employees affected.

The process is initiated by the petition of the company, provided the employees' legal representatives are informed simultaneously.

Once all required actions have been taken and the reports filed, the labour authorities' will announce their decision within five days of the issuing of the petition. The decision will be effective from the date of the event determined to be a result of force majeure.

Changes in work conditions

The management of a company may, for accredited economic, technological, organizational or production reasons make changes to work conditions in respect of working days, working hours, shifts, salary systems, work system, output and work posts. Such changes may be done on an individual or collective basis.

Changes to an individual employee's work conditions must be notified to the employee and the employee's legal representatives at least 30 calendar days before the changes take effect. Collective changes to the employees' work conditions must be preceded by a consultation period with the employees' legal representatives.

Where the employee is affected negatively by substantial changes to his or her work conditions, the employee may terminate the employment contract and receive an indemnity amounting to 20 days' salary for each year of service, up to a maximum of nine months pay.

Employee transfers

The employer may, for the same reasons as outlined above, transfer employees between different work centres to improve the company's competitiveness.

The decision to transfer an employee must be notified to the employee as well as the employee's legal representatives at least 30 calendar days before the transfer takes effect.

In this situation, the employee is entitled to choose between the transfer and compensation for his or her expenses, or termination of employment and an indemnity amounting to 20 days' salary for each year of service, up to a maximum of 12 monthly payments.

Non-competition clause

An employee cannot perform services for two or more employers during the same period, if such employments will create unfair competition, or if the employee has entered into agreement with the employer that he or she will devote all of his or her efforts to the employer's service, in exchange for compensation.

A non-competition clause may be entered into restraining the employee's activities after the termination of employment, if the following conditions are satisfied:

- the clause cannot be valid for more than two years in the case of technicians, or six months in the case of any other employee;
- the employer must be protecting a genuine industrial or commercial interest;
- the employer must pay the employee suitable compensation in return for restraining the employee's employment.

The employee can terminate the non-competition clause by giving the employer 30 days' written notice, in which case the employee forfeits the right to compensation and any other rights deriving from the agreement.

Collective employment regulations

Collective termination

Collective termination occurs when, within a period of 90 days, employment contracts are terminated for accredited economic, technical, organizational or production reasons and affect at least:

- ten employees in companies employing less than 100 employees;
- 10 per cent of the total number of employees in companies employing between 100 and 300 employees;
- 30 employees in companies employing more than 300 employees.

The termination of all employees' contracts in a company will also be a collective termination, provided there are more than five employees and it is the result of the company ceasing its activity for the above-mentioned reasons.

Procedure

The employer must file a petition with the competent labour authority and begin consultations with the employees' legal representatives. The petition must be accompanied by all the necessary documentation, which accredits the reasons for the petition and justifies the measures to be adopted.

The discussion and consultation with the employees' representatives lasts for at least 30 calendar days (15 in the case of companies with less than 50 employees). During this time, the parties must discuss all the reasons for the petition and any possibilities of avoiding or reducing the effects of the terminations. They must also consider any measures necessary to minimize the effects on the employees and the possibility of continuing the business and making it viable.

In any event, companies with more than 50 employees must provide a plan covering the abovementioned measures with their initial petition.

When the consultation period ends the employer must inform the labour authorities of the outcome.

Where the parties reach an agreement, the labour authorities must decide, within 15 calendar days, whether to authorize the termination of the employment contracts. If this period elapses without the labour authorities making a decision, the measure will be considered to be authorized under the terms of the agreement.

Where the parties are unable to reach an agreement the labour authorities will decide whether to permit or bar (partially or fully) the employer's petition. The decision will be announced within 15 days following the date on which the labour authorities are informed that the consultation period has ended. If this period elapses without the labour authorities making a decision, the measure will be considered to be authorized under the terms of the petition.

Authorization will be given where the documentation included with the petition, reasonably indicates that the measures proposed by the company are necessary to reach the goals laid down therein.

Indemnity

Employees who have their employment contracts terminated as a result of a collective termination are entitled to an indemnity amounting to 20 days' salary for each year of service, up to a maximum of 12 months' pay. Any periods less than one year entitle the employee to a proportional fraction for each month.

For those companies engaging less than 25 employees, the Wage Guarantee Fund will pay 40 per cent of the legal indemnities for these employees.

If the labour authorities verify the existence of a force majeure they may authorize partial or total indemnity payments to be paid from the Wage Guarantee Fund. This does not waive the right of the Wage Guarantee Funds to seek repayment from the employer.

Transfer of a company

Any change in the ownership of the company, work centre or independent production unit will not terminate an employment contract. The new employer is subject to the same rights and obligations as his predecessor.

Where the change is a result of inter vivo transactions, the transferor, or in his absence the transferee, is required to inform the legal representatives of the transferred company's employees of the change. Both parties must respect the labour obligations entered into prior to the transfer, which have not been fulfilled, for a period of three years.

Bankruptcy

Where the court appointed official receivers agree that the company cannot continue in business (or in other cases where business activities have ceased as the result of a court order), employees affected by the bankruptcy will be given access to the unemployment system.

Lay-off and guaranteed payments

Salaries and wages are privileged guaranteed payments as they are preferential over any other loan, except loans with real rights. The amount of the guarantee results from multiplying the minimum wage by three and by the number of days pending until payment.

Salaries for the last 30 days of work, provided they do not exceed twice the minimum wage, are preferential over any other loan, even if such loans are secured by a pledge or mortgage.

Salary liabilities are preferential over any other loan in respect of the objects manufactured by the employees while they are the property of or in the possession of the employer.

Employee participation

Employees have a right to participate in their company's organization through employee representatives and works' committee, though this does not preclude other forms of participation.

All companies with 11 to 30 and 31 to 50 employees can statutorily nominate one or three delegates, respectively, to represent the employees before the company. Companies employing more than 50 employees can constitute a works' committee, which will be composed of a minimum of five and a maximum of 75 members, depending upon the total number of employees.

Representatives and committee members must be elected by the employees for a period of two renewable years through personal, direct, free and secret ballot.

Any employee, including representatives and council members, is free to join or not to join a trade union and to take part in the activities of such union. Recognition of trade unions by the employer is not statutorily required, although it is in practice made through recognition of the employees' representatives or committee members.

The representatives and the works' committee are entitled to undertake the following functions, among others:

- to receive information on a quarterly basis regarding the general development of the company's economic sector; the company's production and sales figures and the company's production programme and development of employment;
- to be informed of the contents of the balance sheet, the profit and loss account, the notes to these accounts and, in the event that the company is formed by the use of share or holdings, the same documents that are provided to the shareholders;
- to issue information, prior to action being taken by the employer, in relation to the following areas:

    - staff restructuring; and total or partial, definitive or temporary lay-offs;
    - reductions made to the working day as well as the total or partial transfer of the installations;
    - the company's professional training plans;
    - implementation of or changes to organizational systems and work controls;
    - time studies: the establishment of bonus or incentive programmes and work post evaluations.

The representatives and members of the works' committee, including the committee as a whole, must observe professional secrecy with regard to information released pursuant to these functions. This obligation continues even after such people cease to be representatives or members of the works' committee, especially where management has specifically indicated that such information is privileged.

In addition, the representatives and the works' committee are entitled to:

- be informed of any fines imposed for serious infractions;
- be informed on at least a quarterly basis of the statistics regarding absenteeism and the reasons for the absences; work related accidents and professional illnesses (and their consequences); the accident rate; regular or special studies on the labour environment and preventative measures used in the workplace;
- verify the employer's compliance with labour, social security and employment regulations;
- verify and control safety and hygiene conditions within the company;
- work with management in establishing measures necessary to maintain and increase productivity in accordance with the collective agreements;
- verify that the terms and conditions of the employment contracts comply with the legal requirements (employees must provide the representatives and works' committee with copies of all employee contracts).

Any documents provided to the representatives and works' committee by the company may not be used outside the company's environment, or for reasons apart from those for which the document was provided.

The employee representatives and members of the works' committees are protected by law, from any arbitrary decision of the employer that could infringe their rights or functions.

Trade disputes

Trade disputes may statutorily consist of collective disputes, strikes and lockouts expressly recognised by labour legislation in Spain. Collective disputes can arise among the parties during collective negotiations, with respect to the modification or the termination of a provision. Such collective disputes may be resolved through a special expedited procedure, involving either the labour courts or arbitrators. Other disputes arise from the application or interpretation of some provision or regulation.

The right to strike is recognized by the Spanish Constitution of 1978 and by the labour regulations. In order to be legal, the employer and labour authorities must be informed of the strike at least five days in advance (ten days for public services). Where the strikes affect essential services, a reasonable proportion of those services must be maintained between the minimum services imposed on the striking workers and the inconveniences imposed on the users of the service.

The employer may not impose any sanction on any employee for being legally on strike, and is bound to negotiate the alternatives proposed by the strike committee. In certain special circumstances the Ministry of Labour may have a hand in the final decision.

The employer may have recourse to lockout when a strike or any other collective dispute may lead to violence or to a dangerous situation, or when the employer's premises have been or may be illegally occupied, or when labour absenteeism, including abusive strikes, may seriously affect the normal course of production.

Details must be communicated to the labour authorities within 12 hours following the lockout, which is limited to the period required to ensure the resumption of the company's activity or the removal of the reasons for the lockout.

Pensions, tax and insurance

The social security system

The social security system is designed to protect workers, and their dependents in the event of incapacity, old age, unemployment, and so on.

The employer is required to register the employee with the social security system within five days of beginning to work. Autonomous workers are also required to register with the Social Security office.

Social security contributions are divided between the employee and the employer based on certain percentages and the employee's salary.

Income tax

The employer is obliged to withhold individual income tax from the pay of the employees (as well as their contribution to the Spanish social security system). Income tax withholdings must be paid over to the tax authorities on a quarterly basis, within 25 days of the end of each quarter, whereas social security contributions must be paid over on a monthly basis, within 30 days of the end of each month.

The employer is liable for any deductions that should have been made from the employee's pay and which has been omitted.

Sickness benefit

Any employee who has satisfied certain conditions regarding contributions to the social security system, will be entitled to sick pay. Sick pay is calculated at 60 to 75 per cent of the employee's average pay, depending upon the length of sickness, seniority and whether it is related to work. The entitlement is limited to 12 consecutive months, which can be extended for an additional six months under certain circumstances.

Sick pay is fully recoverable by the employer from the Spanish social security system, except for the wages relating to the first three days of sickness.

Retirement pensions

Both employees and employers are required to make contributions to the state pension scheme, under the general social security system. In addition, many companies operate occupational pension benefit schemes, which are of a complementary nature to the state pension scheme.

State retirement pensions become payable at age 65, as a general rule. Early retirement may be available at age 60, but will result in a pro rata reduction in the amount of the pension.

The amount received under the retirement pension may vary in accordance with the years of employment and the period of contribution to the social security system. This amount is calculated on the actual pay declared for contribution purposes during the eight year period preceding the date of retirement. The minimum contribution period for a retirement pension is 15 years.

Health and safety

Employees are statutorily entitled to an appropriate health and security policy at work. Legislation has not been developed to a great extent in the Labour Statute, but is covered by several resolutions, the most important being the Ministerial Order on the General Aspects of Health and Safety Policy ('*Ordenanza General de Seguridad e Higiene en el Trabajo*'). Similarly there are several specific orders which cover specific sectors of the economy, circumstances, operations, premises, types of machinery, materials, substances, and so on.

In addition, companies may develop their own specific and detailed health and safety policies.

Organization of health and safety at work

Companies and premises with more than 100 employees must have a committee in charge of all matters relating to health and safety at work. Companies in certain sectors of the economy must form a committee when engaging more than 50 employees.

The committee must submit an annual report to the labour authorities and to the labour inspectors regarding the activities performed during the whole year. Committee members are nominated by the employer and employees.

Companies may nominate a committee but, if it engages more than five employees, must nominate a safety watchman (*vigilante de seguridad*) to be in charge of setting out the necessary arrangements for health and safety and ensuring the implementation and monitoring of such policies.

In addition, companies employing between 100 and 1 000 employees must provide medical facilities in conjunction with similar companies. Companies with more than 1 000 employees must have their own medical services.

General duties of the employer

The employer's principal obligations under the general regulations regarding health and safety at work are as follows:

- to provide safe systems of working;
- to provide information about personal safety at work;
- to observe the legal limitations with regard to work performed by young persons and women;
- to follow the recommendations of the health and safety committee or watchman;
- to provide adequate premises and persons for the running of statutory medical services;
- to encourage the cooperation of all the members of the company in connection with health and safety matters.

General duties of the employee

The employee is subject to statutory obligations under the general regulations regarding health and safety at work, as follows:

- to follow the instructions received from the employer regarding health and safety policy;
- to attend any course or discussion regarding health and safety at work provided by the employer;
- to make adequate use of personal safety systems;
- to inform the employer of any damage or breakdown which may cause dangerous situations;
- to cooperate in rescue operations following accidents at work.

The employees' representatives may complain about any breach of health and safety regulations to the employer or to the labour authorities.

Anti-discrimination regulations

The Labour Statute precludes any discrimination in employment based on sex, marital status, age, race, social status, religious beliefs, political opinions or membership of a trade union. Discrimination based on physical or psychological disability is statutorily precluded, as long as the work performed is not affected by such disability.

The government may approve general employment policies which provide special incentives to employers to encourage the favourable treatment of certain individuals (for example disabled or unemployed persons).

Regulatory bodies

Arbitration procedure

Any individual labour dispute is subject to a prior reconciliation attempt, before the Labour Courts, at the Arbitration Service ('*Servicio de Medición, Arbitraje y Conciliación*'). This service is provided by regional labour authorities.

The employer and the employee may act without any legal representation for reconciliation purposes, although common practice is to appear before the arbitrator with a lawyer.

National Tribunal

The National Tribunal has jurisdiction to hear certain trials, basically relating to conflicts concerning collective agreements and unions. Decisions of the National Tribunal may be appealed to the Supreme Court.

Labour Courts

The Labour Court is the competent authority to be the court of first hearing. Decisions of the Labour Court may be appealed to the High Court of the Autonomous Region concerned, which also has the jurisdiction to be the court of first hearing. Decisions of the High

Court of the Autonomous Region may be appealed to the Supreme Court.

The procedure before the labour courts may have different levels, based on the subsequent appeals which can be made against a court's decision. The parties may act without any legal representative before the Labour Court; however, an attorney must act before the National Tribunal, the High Courts of the Autonomous Regions and the Supreme Court.

Foreign employees

As a general rule, foreigners must have a residence permit and a work permit to work in Spain. There are different types of work permits, depending upon the duration of employment.

Any employer who contracts foreign workers without the necessary permits will be subject to sanctions.

Application for work permits

Because of the high unemployment rate in Spain, the government is particularly reluctant to grant work permits to foreigners in respect of jobs which can be equally performed by Spaniards. In this connection, the applicant must obtain a certificate from the local employment office, testifying that no Spaniard is available to do the work. At the same time, the foreigner must apply for a residence permit. As a general rule, residence permits will not be granted without the corresponding work permits, except under certain circumstances (involving, for example, retired individuals or students).

The permits may be granted for different periods, depending on the specific circumstances involved.

Nationals of EU Member States

Nationals from Members States of the European Union have the same rights as Spanish nationals in respect of employment. The concept of 'priority' for the national market, which precluded employment of other nationals when a Spanish national could perform the work, has been eliminated. The immediate result has been the elimination of work permits for European Union nationals, although the labour authorities must still be informed.

This chapter was written by Antonio L. Bañón and Eduardo Tejero, Coopers & Lybrand, S.A., Spain.

Sweden

Introduction

The trade unions and the employers' associations in Sweden have for many years tried to regulate their relationship by means of agreements to avoid government intervention. However this relationship has recently been increasingly regulated by law.

Many of the new laws are optional as collective agreements are allowed to supersede a number of provisions, provided the employees' position is improved. Some laws assume that certain matters will be resolved through collective agreements. Many of the laws and the supporting agreements are complex and there may be deviations between different sectors of industry.

The main parties of the labour market are the Swedish Employers' Confederation (SAF), the Swedish Trade Union Confederation (LO) and the Federation of Salaried Employees' in Industry and Services (PTK). PTK is, however, only empowered to sign recommendation agreements on behalf of its affiliated organizations. LO has well over two million members and PTK represents, through its affiliated organizations, about 580 000 union members.

Individual employment regulations

There are a number of laws regulating the relationships between employers and the individual employee. The more important among these are:

- the Employment Security Act 1982;
- the General Hours of Work Act 1982;
- the Holiday Act 1977;
- the Act on Employer's Right to make deductions on account from employees' pay 1970;

- the Act on the Position of Trade Union Representatives 1974;
- the Act on Employees' Right to Educational Leave 1974;
- the Act on the Right to Leave for Care of Children 1978.

The laws are supplemented by provisions in the Social Security Act and in the collective agreements.

Contracts

The Employment Security Act stipulates that employment shall be permanent unless otherwise agreed. The employer is obliged to inform the employee, within a month, of the terms of employment.

Permanent employment can be terminated through notice, dismissal or retirement. Temporary employment is allowed by law only in certain cases which are strictly defined. It terminates at the end of the agreed period and there are in principle no requirements for period of notice.

The law allows the following types of temporary employment:

- work of a 'stand-in' nature: the period must be fixed to end at a certain date or to end on the return of the regular employee;
- excess work load: in temporary circumstances, such an individual large orders or during rush periods, an individual employee may be employed for an aggregate period of 12 months during two consecutive years;
- trial periods with a maximum length of 12 months: the employer must give notice before the end of the trial period, otherwise the employment will be regarded as permanent;
- special circumstances such as a specific project (for example in the building industry) or seasonal variations (as in farming, forestry or the tourist trade);
- traineeship and work during school holidays;
- periods in excess of three months for employees waiting to fulfil their compulsory military training;
- after retirement.

Wages and salaries

Minimum wage provision - The various employment laws do not contain any minimum wage or salary provisions. The collective agreements may include such provisions, however.

Method of payment - There are no statutory requirements regarding the method of payment. The agreements on general employment conditions which are incorporated in the collective agreements normally regulate these matters. Agreements may also be reached at company level, between the individual employer and the local trade unions.

Salaried employees are in most cases paid by a transfer of the net amount after deductions to individual bank accounts.

Deductions from pay - According to the tax laws, employers are obliged to make deductions for taxes withheld whenever remunerations are paid. The tax laws contain detailed provisions about the deductions and the employer's liability to account for deductions made. Deductions from pay following proper decisions about attachment of wages or distraints are also compulsory.

The Act on Employers' Right to make deductions on account from pay, lists three cases where deductions can be made without the consent of the employee:

- where the employer has a claim against the employee which was originally agreed to;
- following damages due to intentional negligence by the employee;
- deductions arising from provisions in a collective agreement.

The definition of deductions on account from pay does not include deductions due to sickness or other absence from work, advances, adjustments of preliminary payments or deductions on behalf of a third party as per collective agreement.

Itemized pay statement - The requirements for wage and salary slips are to a certain extent prescribed by law. The employer is obliged to inform the employee about deductions related to taxes withheld by means of a receipt or similar arrangements. Otherwise the details of the wage and salary slips may be specified in the collective agreements or follow from local custom. The slip normally contains information about accrued holiday and overtime. It is a general rule that all deductions from the gross pay are specified on the slip.

Hours of work/shift work/overtime

The General Hours of Work Act is in principle applicable to all employees carrying out work on behalf of an employer. The law is valid within Sweden only. A Swedish company located outside Sweden with Swedish employees is exempted. A non-Swedish entity employing Swedish or non-Swedish residents within the country must adhere to the law.

The law does not apply to what is defined as uncontrolled work: that is, work carried out in an employer's home and in cases where the employer cannot be assumed to be responsible for the way the work is organized (travelling sales staff).

The working week is in principle 40 hours. It is, however, possible in certain cases to compute the statutory working week as an average of four calendar weeks. Shift work falls under this exception from the general rule. There are three different categories of working hours:

- normal working hours, which are defined as hours during which actual work is performed;
- duty hours, which means hours during which the employee must stay within the premises to be able to work if the need arises;
- on-call hours, when the employee is at the employer's disposal without any liability to stay within the premises.

Normal working hours (including overtime) and duty hours are regulated by law.   On-call hours are regulated by collective agreements. Duty hours may amount to 48 hours during four consecutive weeks or to 50 hours during a calendar month. Duty hours are not included in the provisions for overtime.

There are two categories of overtime - general overtime and special overtime. General overtime can be utilized for up to 48 hours in a four week period or 50 hours in a calendar month. Total maximum general overtime allowed per calendar year is 200 hours. Special overtime is hours worked in excess of normal working hours and general overtime. Special overtime requires either provisions in a collective agreement or a permit from the Board of Occupational Health and Safety.

The law also contains regulations about work during the night, working hours for young persons under the age of 18, rests and intervals and verification of overtime and duty hours.

The law permits extensive deviations through collective agreements. (Overtime in the meaning of the law may not always correspond to the definition in a collective agreement.) The agreement on a flexible working day means that employees may start and end their work within certain limits at their own discretion. Agreements on flexible working days will normally apply to salaried employers.

Holidays

The statutory holiday entitlement is five weeks during each holiday year. The holiday year runs from 1 April to 31 March the following year. The employee is entitled to holiday from the first year of employment. If, however, the employment starts after 31 August the statutory holiday entitlement for the actual holiday year is reduced to five days. It is possible to accumulate part of the holiday entitlement. During a period of five years an employee may accumulate five days for each holiday year. After five years an employee will be in the position to have ten consecutive weeks' holiday.

Holidays should normally be arranged to enable the employee to have four consecutive weeks of holiday during the period June to August. An employer is obliged to negotiate or consult with the employees as regards the arrangement of the holiday period.

Without the employer's consent holidays cannot be arranged to take place during a period of notice. Holiday pay is only paid if it has been accrued during the 12 month period preceding the holiday year and is computed as 12 per cent of the income during the relevant 12 month period.

The Holiday Act contains provisions about periods of absence or leave which qualify as employment periods when computing holiday. Absence due to illness for up to 180 days each holiday year qualifies, as does maternity leave, up to 120 days.

When a contract of employment is terminated the employee is entitled to the holiday pay accruing at the termination date. The right to holiday pay exists irrespective of the reasons for the termination of the employment. The law contains provisions which regulate the right to holiday in cases of transfer of employment and of ownership.

The main rule is that the provisions in the Holiday Act are compulsory in favour of the employee. However the law allows extensive deviations based on collective agreements. Certain deviations based on agreements at company level are also possible.

Maternity provisions

Pregnant employees are entitled to be reassigned to less demanding work without any reduction of their benefits. This right can be exercised from 60 days prior to the estimated date of the birth of the child. If the employee cannot be reassigned she is entitled to pregnancy leave, which will be compensated by the social security system.

A parent is entitled to leave without pay in connection with the birth of a child until the child is three years old. Part of the leave will be compensated through the social security system. The parents themselves decide who is going to utilize the leave to care for the child. The father is always entitled to ten days' leave compensated through the social security system in connection with the birth of the child.

Both parents are entitled to part-time work until the child has reached the age of eight years. The part-time working day corresponds to three-quarters of a normal working day.

Time off

Union representatives appointed by a local trade union bound by collective agreements are entitled to time off for union activities. Where these activities relate to union activities within the company there will be no reduction in pay.

According to an arrangement between SAF and LO/PTK, members of a trade union are entitled to five paid hours per year to take part in union meetings dealing with matters related to the company.

Employees who hold public office are entitled to leave to carry out their duties. The employer is not obliged to pay any remuneration during the leave period. Members of parliament have their employment protected by the Constitution Act. The right to time off can be based on law as well as custom.

Employees who have been given notice are entitled to leave with pay to arrange for alternative employment. According to law, employment cannot be terminated in connection with compulsory or voluntary military or civil defence service. The Act on Educational Leave entitles every employee employed for more than six months or in aggregate at least 12 months during the two preceding years to time off for education. There is no limitation on the length of leave for education. The social security system entitles parents to leave for care of minor children.

Immigrants are entitled to be trained in the Swedish language without pay. Hours used for training are included in the normal working hours, even if the training takes place outside the normal working day. This means that training hours qualify as employment time when computing holiday.

Collective agreements can provide for time off during part of the working day without reduction in pay, normally for personal reasons.

Disciplinary and grievance procedures

According to the Employment Security Act an employer may terminate an employment summarily on disciplinary grounds. The employee must be informed and notification to the trade union given at least one week in advance.

Summary dismissal must be based on serious and intentional offences such as prolonged absence without permission, refusal to carry out duties in contradiction of agreements, participation in certain illegal actions, violence and certain crimes. The employee must be informed in writing and the notification delivered to the employee in person.

Employees have the corresponding right to terminate the employment immediately if the employer has seriously neglected liabilities by, for example, permitting prolonged delays in paying out wages.

Lay-off and guaranteed payments

Employees may be laid off during periods of shortage of work. This is not regulated in any statute. The question is settled in accordance with case law and provisions in the collective agreements. The employment is not considered to have been terminated by the lay-off when lay-off occurs. The employees are deemed to be liable to resume work when the reason for the lay-off has come to an end. During lay-off an employee is entitled to normal benefits of employment.

The employer is not obliged to pay wages or salaries if the lay-off is due to seasonal variations or to the intermittent nature of the work.

Period of notice

The general rule is that both employers and employees are liable to observe a statutory period of notice of one month.

If an employee has been employed for six consecutive months or an aggregate of 12 months during the two preceding years the length of the period of notice will be as shown in Table 1.

Table 1

Age	Period of notice
25 - 29 years	2 months
30 - 34 years	3 months
35 - 39 years	4 months
40 - 44 years	5 months
45 years and over	6 months

The collective agreements may contain other rules which are not less favourable than those in the table. The length of the period of notice may be related to a combination of the employee's age and length of employment, an arrangement which may also apply to an employee giving notice.

Length of employment

Length of service is an important concept as it is the basis for the length of the period of notice, priority rating in connection with redundancy, priority for re-employment and the right to special damages.

Each day of service is considered, including days of granted leave and days during which no work has been done. Different positions with the same employer are regarded as part of a continuous period of employment.

The Employment Security Act provides that employments with different companies belonging to the same group are for these purposes regarded as continuous employment. This is valid even if the parent company is a foreign entity (although only employment in Swedish companies is considered).

Transfers of undertakings, formation of an enterprise into a limited company and mergers do not constitute a new employment in this respect.

In certain areas the provisions are more favourable for employees above the age of 45.

Dismissal

The basic rule is that any dismissal is unfair unless it is justified objectively. The law does not define this, but lack of work is deemed to be a justifiable reason for dismissals.

Personal reasons may under certain circumstances be regarded as justified grounds for dismissal. Incompetence, failure to cooperate and negligence are examples of objectively justified grounds. Dismissals due to such personal reasons are normally rather complex and are affected by matters such as the size of the company, the employee's position, length of service, age and the frequency of offences. A guideline may be whether the employee can be expected to behave properly if the employment is allowed to continue.

Reasons for summary dismissal may in less severe cases be regarded as objectively justified grounds for dismissal. The law specifies that a dismissal is not on objective grounds if it can be reasonable to reassign the employee to other duties within the company.

Notification of dismissal must be in writing. The reason for the dismissal must be stated if required by the employee. The employee must be informed about the procedures for challenging the validity of the dismissal, how to seek damages and if there are grounds for reinstatement or re-engagement.

The law contains detailed provisions about the procedures for settling disputes.

Collective employment regulations

Co-determination at work

The most important piece of collective labour law is the Act on Co-Determination at Work (MBL) effective as of 1 January 1977, which regulates the operation of collective agreements and the relationship between the parties in the labour market. MBL can be described as framework legislation which assumes that the parties in the labour market will draw up more detailed regulations for the participation of employees by means of collective agreements.

Sphere of application - The provisions of MBL are supposed to be applied to all matters regarding the relationship between employers and employees, such as:

- terms of employment;
- entering into and terminating the contract of employment;
- supervision and assignment of work;
- management.

The provisions apply to all work places irrespective of size, within certain limitations. Compulsory provisions in the Swedish Companies Act in favour of creditors and shareholding minorities cannot be superseded by agreements based on negotiations. Decisions which are the prerogative of the shareholders' meeting cannot be transferred to any other party by means of a collective agreement. On the other hand, it is possible to reach agreements on co-determination of matters which normally are the responsibility of the Board of Directors and of the managing director. The effect of co-determination is not allowed to have legal implications on the company's responsibilities to society and third parties.

Right of association - An employer or employee has the right to belong to an organization of employees or trade unions; to utilize the membership of such an organization and to be active in the organization or for the establishment of an organization. The negative right of association - the right not to belong to an organization - is not protected. Violations of the right of association are not valid, and the violating party will be liable to pay damages.

General right of negotiation - Every organization of employees and every employer or organization of employers is entitled to ask for negotiations on any matter related to the relationship between employer and employees, where there is or has been a contract of employment between a member of the trade union and the related employer.

The general right of negotiation applies to matters of interest (questions which are unresolved by the parties and which are to be regulated through an agreement) and to legal disputes, including individual cases. If no agreement can be reached the parties involved are entitled to take offensive actions such as strike or lockout or to appeal to a court in cases of legal disputes. Refusal to negotiate can lead to the paying of damages.

Collective agreements - The collective agreement must be evidenced in writing and cover conditions of employment and other matters related to the relationship between employers and employees. A collective agreement is binding on the organizations which have entered into the agreement and on the members of these organizations. It is also binding on members who joined the relevant organizations before and after the signing of the agreement and on members who have left the organizations.

It is generally assumed that an employer bound by a collective agreement shall not offer inferior benefits to employees who do not belong to the contracting trade union. Normally, however, deviations which give improved terms are permitted.

A number of laws become applicable when a collective agreement has been signed. Parts of the MBL, such as the extended right of negotiation and the extended obligation to inform, are not enforceable until an agreement has been signed. Another example is the employee's right to be represented on the board of directors.

Co-determination through collective agreements - A number of collective agreements on co-determination have been reached. In the private business sector the collective agreement has been replaced by an agreement between SAF, LO and PTK about further development of the provisions of MBL. The agreement contains provisions for the following:

- agreements at company level;
- design of co-determination;
- trade union meetings during working hours;
- trade union representation in small companies;

- cooperation, within group companies;
- employee consultations in companies with at least 50 employees;
- council for the consideration of development.

Trade disputes

Parties in the labour market who are not bound by collective agreements are normally entitled to take industrial action: this may be a strike or lockout, refusal to work overtime, blockade or boycott to prevent the hiring of new employees or delivery of goods. The basic right to take industrial action is established through the Constitution Act.

The provisions of MBL imply that employers and employees bound by collective agreements are generally not allowed to take part in industrial action during the period of agreement, with one exception. If a party has requested regulation of a question dealt with in the co-determination provisions in a collective agreement and the negotiations have failed, industrial action is allowed.

Agreements on remuneration and terms of employment are normally signed for shorter periods than the principal collective agreement and lately industrial action in connection with these negotiations has increased.

MBL does not include any provisions about industrial action for political purposes. Secondary industrial action to support a trade union in another country is permitted provided the actions of the foreign trade union are legal.

If employees bound by a collective agreement have taken industrial action both the employer and the local trade union are mutually obliged to negotiate immediately in order to settle the issue.

Arbitration - If offensive action is contemplated, the party in question is obliged to give notice in writing, at least seven days in advance, to a central organization of arbitration. The parties concerned are obliged to appear before the arbitrator to negotiate. The arbitrator cannot force any party to delay offensive action.

In cases of extensive industrial disputes the government can appoint a special arbitration commission.

Damages - Any employer, employee or organization who breaches the MBL or a collective agreement is liable to compensate the other party for damages suffered. The compensation can relate to financial and general damages. For employees, the normal level is SEK 2 000 per individual involved.

Employee participation

Negotiations

Trade unions which are bound by collective agreements with the employer have the right to seek to initiate negotiation. This applies to all places of work where the trade union has a member. The employer has an obligation to delay a decision until the necessary negotiations have been concluded.

The primary obligation to negotiate refers to major changes in the company's activities and to major changes in working or employment conditions for one or more members of the trade union.

Decisions to appoint management at all levels, adoption of a budget and smaller acquisitions affecting the employees have been regarded as subject to the primary obligation to negotiate.

Major changes in the conditions of an individual employee may be:

- a change of duties;
- relocation;
- prolonged transfer within the company;
- lay-offs or dismissal due to lack of work.

The employer may in emergency situations disregard the obligation to negotiate before the decision is taken. The trade union - if bound by a collective agreement - has the right to ask for negotiations about all matters not included in the employer's primary obligation to negotiate, though this must be related to a specific case.

Information

Where there is a collective agreement, an employer has a primary obligation to inform about the development of production and financial matters within the company and about guidelines for the company's personnel policies. The employer must continuously and without prior request provide information about these matters.

In addition an employer must, if requested, allow the trade union to review any material required for the purpose of protecting the employees' collective interests in relation to the employer. The law allows certain exceptions, such as information about research of a confidential nature, data supporting tenders in a competitive situation and the employer's intended arrangements in connection with a dispute.

Employee representation

The Act on Representation on the Board of Directors for Employees of Limited Companies and Economic Associations 1988 states that, in companies or associations with at least 25 employees, the employees are entitled to appoint two members to the Board of Directors and two deputies. In companies with more than 1 000 employees and operating different lines of business, the employees are entitled to appoint three members to the Board of Directors and three deputies.

The employee representatives are normally a minority on the Board of Directors. The objective is to provide the employees with general information about the company's affairs and about the company's plans for the future.

Pensions, tax and insurance

An employer has a statutory obligation to pay social security contributions. The 1994 social security charges amount to 31.36 per cent of the total remuneration paid to employees and consist of the following:

- national basic pension (AFP);
- national supplementary pension (ATP);
- partial pension insurance;
- statutory sick pay insurance;
- unemployment and training allowance;
- occupational insurance;
- safety at work;
- continuing education;
- child care;
- charge for remuneration guarantee;
- general charge on remunerations.

The employees do not contribute to the above social charges. The additional charges for employees belonging to a trade union within the LO area amounted in 1994 to 6.6 per cent of the total remuneration paid to employees. The major part of these charges covers special complementary pensions and sick pay insurance.

For salaried employees belonging to the PTK group the 1991 charges based on agreement are estimated to amount on national average to 7.9 per cent of total salaries. Approximately 90 per cent of the charges apply to private complementary pension plans.

Depending on the provisions in the relevant collective agreement, there may be additional benefits such as complementary sick pay or additional charges for company health services.

The rules relating to and the benefits from the statutory social security system and the system based on collective agreements are complex. Only the sick pay insurance and pension benefits will be described below.

Sickness benefit

Every person above 16 years of age - irrespective of nationality - must be registered with the local social insurance office. The sick pay insurance consists of three parts: daily compensation; compensation to parents with minor children; and reimbursement of expenses for medical care. The daily compensation is based on the estimated annual remuneration from work with a maximum of 7·5 times the base amount which is calculated once every year by the Central Bureau of Statistics and is linked to the consumer price index.

No compensation is paid for the first day of absence - the qualifying day. After that the compensation for the first 14 days is paid by the employer. As from the fifteenth day, the compensation is paid by the social insurance office. In cases of permanent illness the local social insurance office normally converts the daily compensation into disability pension after approximately 12 months.

The compensation to parents with minor children is payable during maternity and periods when parents have to stay home to take care of sick children below the age of 12. Both types of compensation are treated as taxable income and also qualify for national supplementary pension.

Reimbursement of expenses for medical care includes hospital and dental fees and medicine at reduced prices.

Retirement pensions

There are in principle three different types of pension. The national basic pension (AFP) applies to every person irrespective of earlier employment and amounts for a single person to 96 per cent of the base amount. For a married couple where both spouses are entitled to the basic pension the actual amount corresponds to 157 per cent of the base amount.

The national supplementary pension covers all salaried employees and wage earners including self-employed persons. The service period for full pension is 30 years, and is calculated on the 15 years in which income has been highest.

The special complementary pension for wage earners requires a service period of 30 years. The pension amounts to 10 per cent of the average income during the three best years between the age of 55 and 59. The complementary pension for salaried employees (PTK) requires a service period of 30 years and contribution payments up to pensionable age.

Normal retirement age for all three types of pension is 65. If the required service period has not been met there will be a corresponding reduction of the pension benefits. Early retirement and widow's pension are included in all pension schemes with the exception of the special complementary pension.

Partial pension between the age of 61 and 64 years is available for employees as well as for self-employed persons.

Health and safety

Health and Safety at work is regulated in the Working Environment Law of 1978 with amendments and in the Working Environment Ordinance.

The Working Environment Law is a framework law with general provisions which are supplemented by directives from the Board of Occupational Health and Safety.

Scope and objectives

The Working Environment Law covers almost every type of working environment. Safety regulations regarding technical facilities and dangerous materials are applicable also to individual enterprises. The Board of Occupational Health and Safety has issued a number of directives which are compulsory. The directives are supplemented by instructions and notifications.

If an employer disregards the directives, sanctions may include fines or, in severe cases, imprisonment. Employees in every place of work are supposed to have access to the contents of the law and the ordinance and to the directives issued by the Board.

Responsibility for the supervision of implementation has been delegated to the Labour Inspectorate.

General responsibilities

Work must be arranged so that the environment is acceptable and the individual employee's conditions are considered. Due regard must be paid to handicapped persons.

The working environment requirements must be considered when premises, equipment and systems are planned. The employer is obliged to ensure that the employees have the proper training and education to avoid injury and bad health.

Employees are obliged to utilize safety arrangements and to take proper care. Furthermore, safety responsibility rests with the manufacturers of machinery and equipment or dangerous materials and with parties who grant the use of premises and land.

The Board of Occupational Health and Safety has far-reaching powers to prescribe testing of processes, systems and facilities and can prohibit their use if deemed to be dangerous.

The law contains special provisions regarding working conditions relating to minors.

Cooperation between employers and employees

Safety committees and safety representatives are supposed to participate in the planning phases. The individual employee is entitled to interrupt work in case of a dangerous situation to be able to consult with supervisors or with the safety representative. The safety representative is entitled to intervene in situations where an employee is alone carrying out dangerous work.

Rehabilitation

As from 1992 there are rules on rehabilitation in connection with illness for the purpose of restoring employees to working life, with the employer taking an active part.

Anti-discrimination regulations

Act on Equality between Women and Men at Work 1980

The law is divided into two main parts. One part contains prohibition against sex discrimination and the other prescribes active arrangements to achieve equality. The law applies to every category of employer irrespective of size and to employees and applicants for employment.

Sex discrimination is prohibited in connection with employment, promotion and selection for training and promotion. It applies to pay, conditions of employment, supervision and assignment of work, notice, relocation, lay-off, termination and similar arrangements. The law allows the intentional recruitment of persons of one sex to achieve a better balance within an area dominated by the opposite sex and defines this arrangement as positive discrimination.

The rules about sex discrimination are compulsory and cannot be superseded by collective agreement. An employer who disregards them may be liable to pay damages. The employer must arrange working conditions equally suitable for women and men. Training and education must be arranged in such a way that equality is promoted. Fines may be paid in cases breaching the provisions.

Supervision of the observance of the law is the responsibility of the Parliamentary Commissioner for Equality. A special board on equality matters has the responsibility to act upon the Commissioner's requests for actions against employers who disregard the rules about active arrangements to achieve equality.

Race discrimination

The criminal code states that, if anyone, who is carrying on any kind of business, discriminates on grounds of race or nationality or religion by not applying the same conditions as apply to others, fines or imprisonment may result.   A new Act was passed in 1994, which prohibits ethnic discrimination or undue treatment of applicants for employment or existing employees on ethnic grounds.

Regulatory bodies

The Act on Litigation in Labour Disputes 1974 contains provisions regarding disputes over collective agreements and other disputes related to the relationship between employers and employees.   The Labour Court has nationwide jurisdiction.   It is made up of judges and representatives of employers and employees.   An organization may appeal on its own behalf or on behalf of members.   The Labour Court's rulings are final.

Other types of disputes are dealt with by the district courts.   Appeals against the district courts' rulings are made to the Labour Court.

Foreign employees

Nordic nationals

The Nordic countries constitute a joint labour market.   Nordic nationals may work and live in any of the Nordic countries (Denmark, Finland, Iceland, Norway and Sweden).   This privilege is based on the 1982 agreement.

Non-Nordic nationals

Citizens of EU or EFTA member states do not require a work permit to work or seek employment within the EEA.   For stays longer than three months, a residence permit is required.

Other nationals

Other nationals must have residence and work permits arranged before they arrive in Sweden. Work permits are issued by the Swedish Immigration and Nationalization Board after consultation with the Labour Market Board.

This chapter was written by Stefan Carlsson, Coopers & Lybrand, Öhrlings Reveko AB, Sweden.

Switzerland

Introduction

Swiss labour law can be classified into three main subdivisions, namely private labour law, public labour law and collective labour law.

Private labour law regulates legal relations between employers and employees under private law. The most important law being the Swiss Code of Obligations (CO), in particular Articles 319-362 CO, which regulate individual employment contracts and the standard employment contract.

In addition, the Federal Law is important as it regulates the information and participation of employees in enterprises. This law came into force on the 1 May 1994 (*Bundesgesetz über die Information und Mitsprache der Arbeitnehmer in den Betrieben*).

Public labour law is binding on all employers and employees as it contains provisions concerning the protection of employees. This law is contained in a variety of statutes, the most important being the Federal Labour Statute of 13 March 1964 (*BG über die Arbeit in Industrie, Gewerbe und Handel*) and its executive orders. The Federal Labour Statute details the necessary requirements for the employees' sanitary protection, regulates work hours (with special provisions for women and young employees) and regulates for the prevention of accidents, illnesses and overstrain.

Another important statute is the Accident Insurance Statute of 20 March 1981 (*BG über die Unfallversicherung*) as it contains provisions concerning safety at work.

Basically the supervision and enforcement of public labour law is under state control (administrative procedure). Nevertheless, according to Art. 342 para. 2 CO, any provisions of public law which can become incorporated into an individual employment contract, can be subject to a civil action.

Collective labour law regulates the law of trade associations and their relationship to their respective social partners.

The CO includes dispositions about the collective employment contract (Art. 356 - 358 CO). Other federal laws include:

- The Federal Statute of 28 September 1956 declares the collective employment contract to be generally binding (*BG über die Allgemeinverbindlicherklärung von Gesamtarbeitsverträgen*).
- The Federal Statute on the Federal Conciliation Office for collective labour disputes of 2 February 1949 (*BG über die eidgen. Einigungsstelle zur Beilegung von kollektiven Arbeitsstreitigkeiten*).

In each case, the parties must examine which provisions of a standard or collective employment contract supplement or even modify the statutory provisions.

Individual employment regulations

Contracts

Provisions of the CO which govern the employment contract are subdivided as follows:

- the individual employment contract (Art. 319-349; 361-362 CO);
- the special employment contracts;
  - apprenticeship contracts (Art. 344-346a; 361-362 CO);
  - the travelling salesman's contract (Art. 347-350a; 361-362 CO);
  - the home work contract (Art. 351-354; 361-362 CO);
- the collective employment contract (Art. 356-358 CO);
- the standard employment contract (Art. 359-360 CO)

According to Art. 355 CO, general provisions of the individual employment contract shall supplement special employment contracts.

With the exception of apprenticeship contracts and contracts for travelling salesmen, the form of the individual employment contract is left to the discretion of the parties, although a written form is highly advisable.

A contract normally specifies the beginning and duration of the employment relationship, the parties to the contract, title or function, trial and notice periods, normal hours of work and overtime, details of salary and bonus, holiday, accident, sickness and pension payments, and occasionally restraint of trade clauses.

Under Art. 361 and 362 CO, certain provisions of an individual employment contract cannot be modified either by a collective employment contract or by a standard employment contract to the detriment of the employee or to the detriment of the employee and the employer.

Swiss law specifically authorizes the use of fixed term contracts and regulates their termination.

Standard employment contracts are enacted at a federal or cantonal state level to protect employees whose trade or profession is not sufficiently organized to negotiate a collective agreement.

Wages and salaries

Minimum wage provision - There is no statutory minimum wage. Public law may however, stipulate a minimum wage as a precondition to granting foreign employees (without a permanent residence in Switzerland) a work permit.

Furthermore collective employment contracts often contain a minimum wage clause.

Method of payment - There are no legal requirements as to the form of salary or wage payments, although salary is generally paid by cash, bank transfer, cheque and so on. In certain specified professions payment can also include non-cash compensation such as lodging, food and supplies; this must be expressly agreed between the employer and employees. Salary payments can be calculated on a time basis (annual, monthly, weekly, hourly) or according to a price-per-piece basis (mainly used in factories).

Bonus - It is becoming customary, especially in service companies (for instance offices and banks) to pay employees an annual bonus in the form of a month's salary (thirteenth month salary). This bonus payment could become a contractual payment if specified in the employment contract or if granted for many years, without a reserve clause.

Deductions from pay - Compulsory deductions on all salary payments including bonuses are:

- AHV/AVS - minimum federal old age and survivors plan;
- IV/AI - disability insurance;
- EO/APG - aims at the insurance of, or at least partial compensation for the loss of wages due to military or civil service;
- BVG/LPP - additional compulsory private old age pension scheme;
- ALV/AC - federal unemployment insurance;
- UVG/AA - compulsory insurance against accidents.

For optional benefits such as the additional pension scheme, sickness insurance policy, non-professional accident insurance and so on, any deductions from salaries must be agreed between the parties.

Hours of work/shift work/overtime

In accordance with the Federal Labour Statute, the hours of work are restricted to a maximum of 45 or 50 per week for all employees, depending on their category of employment. These hours can only be extended with the prior authorization from the state. Working hours may not be more than 14 hours during the day for men and 12 hours for young people and women.

Night work is permitted only temporarily, with the employee's consent, and must be remunerated at a minimum rate of 125 per cent of the usual salary payment. Night work is also subject to prior authorization from the authorities.

Overtime is usually not authorized at night, on Sundays or statutory public holidays except where specifically mentioned in the law. Employees may be remunerated for overtime by receiving 125 per cent of their salary (unless some other rate is specified in the employment contract, collective agreement or by written notice) or may agree to equivalent time off in lieu of payment.

Holidays

The CO provides that all employees are entitled to four weeks' leave per year of service, with young persons and apprentices under the age of 20 being entitled to five weeks leave. There are eight official public holidays during which employees do not work. Salaried employees are paid for such holidays. For those paid hourly, payment is left to the employer's discretion.   There may be other additional holidays according to cantonal, religious or other events.

Maternity provisions

The Federal Labour Statute contains special provisions concerning the employment of pregnant women. A woman is not allowed to work during the eight weeks following the birth of her child. If the woman wishes, this period can be reduced to six weeks, provided that her doctor confirms that she is able to work. The employer must give a nursing mother necessary free time to nurse her child while at work.

In accordance with the CO, employers cannot give a woman notice to terminate her employment during her pregnancy or for 16 weeks after childbirth. If notice is given prior to the woman's pregnancy, the notice period for dismissal is delayed for an equivalent time period.

For absences before and after childbirth, the employer must pay the woman a minimum salary, provided that she has been or was contracted to be employed for more than three months. The woman is paid three weeks' salary during the first year of service with further periods being paid in accordance with the cantonal calculation scales. Maternity leave is not always covered by the employers' loss of salary insurance schemes.

Time off

Time off must be granted to male employees taking part in military service and female employees involved in military service on a voluntary basis. In these circumstances, the employee will be entitled to compensation for a limited period of time, provided he or she has been or was contracted to be employed for more than three months. The employee is entitled to at least three weeks wages during the first year of employment, and for such further periods as specified in the cantonal scales.

Special paid leave is often granted to employees for a wedding, birth or death in the family, for moving house or for such other activities as specified in the employment contract or company rules. This is not regulated by law but is often subject to collective agreements. Time off without any reduction in salary is also granted to employees looking for a new job while working out their notice period.

Disciplinary and grievance procedures

Disciplinary measures can only be taken if the employer's rules provide for such measures. Where the employer is subject to a collective agreement, such disciplinary measures must comply with terms of that agreement.

Trial periods

It is general practice to consider the first month of employment as a trial period. This period may be extended by written agreement, up to a maximum of three months.

Unless agreed otherwise, either party may terminate the contract of employment during the trial period (without showing cause) by giving the other party seven days' notice. Where a trial period is interrupted due to sickness, accident, or the performance of a legal duty which is not voluntarily assumed, the trial period shall be prolonged correspondingly.

Termination of employment

Either party can terminate an indefinite employment contract by giving the requisite period of notice, or where there is a valid reason without notice. Generally the employer is not required to give the employee reasons, unless requested to do so by the employee.

Period of notice

The CO specifies a statutory minimum period of notice where no alternative period of notice has been agreed. This notice may be given in writing or may be given verbally, unless specified to the contrary in the collective agreement or employment contract.

Either party may terminate the contract of employment, at the end of the month, by giving the statutory periods of notice as illustrated in Table 1.

Table 1

Notice period	Service period
1 month	Less than 1 year
2 months	1 year or more, but less than 10 years
3 months	10 or more years

The employer may not give notice of termination in any of the following situations:

• during the employee's performance of compulsory Swiss military service, civil defence service, women's military service or Red Cross service and, in cases where such service lasts for more than 12 days, during the four weeks prior to and after the service;

- during the period that the employee is prevented from performing his or her work (fully or partially) as a result of sickness or accident which has been caused through no fault of the employee. The employee is entitled to 30 days in the first year of service, 90 days for the second year of service up to and including the fifth year of service, and for 180 days after the sixth year of service;
- during the employee's pregnancy and for the first 16 weeks following the birth of the child;
- during the employee's participation in a foreign aid service assignment (in another country), which has been ordered by a competent federal agency and agreed by the employer.

Notice given to the employee during any of these periods is void. Where the notice was given prior to the commencement of any of these periods, the notice remains effective, but does not run for the duration of the period.

Swiss law does not specifically provide for the payment of salary in lieu of notice, but does provide that the employer must pay the employee's salary for the duration of the notice period. Where the employer pays the employee's salary in lieu of notice, the employer cannot demand repayment of the salary (or part of it) if the employee subsequently commences new employment during that period, unless it was a condition of payment at the time payment was made.

Termination with notice

Notice must be given in all situations where a valid reason for terminating the employment without notice does not exist, or where there is no power to end the employment relationship for a valid reason.

Termination without notice

An employer or employee can terminate the contract of employment at any time without notice for a valid reason. Such a valid reason is considered to exist where it is no longer reasonable to expect the parties to continue in the employment relationship with loyalty and trust. To terminate a contract for a valid reason, the following requirement must be satisfied:

- the offending act must be of a type which destroys the trust between the parties;
- the act must have actually destroyed that trust.

Examples of where a valid reason has been established include:

- gross dishonesty, for example, deception, embezzlement or theft;
- consistent refusal to perform lawfully requested work;
- competing with the employer;
- after repeated warnings, failure to attend work.

Whether or not a valid reason exists is a question of fact for the judge to determine on a case by case basis.

The law prohibits termination without notice in circumstances where the employee is unable to perform his or her work for reasons outside the employee's control. In these cases, the employer must give the employee his or her requisite period of notice.

Abusive notice of termination

Termination is considered to be abusive if one party gives notice because:

- of a quality inherent in the personality of the other party (for example sex, race, age) - unless such quality relates to the employment relationship or significantly impairs cooperation within the enterprise;
- the other party exercises a constitutional right (for instance religion or membership of a political party) - unless the exercise of such a right violates a duty of the employment relationship or significantly impairs cooperation within the enterprise;
- to prevent the other party from filing claims arising out of the labour relationship;

- the other party asserts, in good faith, claims arising out of the labour relationship;
- the other party performs compulsory Swiss military service, civil defense service, military women's service, or Red Cross service, or a legal duty not voluntarily assumed;
- of the employee's affiliation, or non-affiliation with a union, or lack thereof, or because the employee performs work for a union;
- the employee is an elected representative of an employee or a labour organization, unless the employer proves grounds for notice;
- a large-scale dismissal is in defiance of the provisions concerning consultation of the labour union in respect of the employees.

The party who has given abusive notice of termination has to pay an indemnity to the other party, which will be determined by a judge after taking into account all the circumstances. This indemnity may not however, exceed six month's wages, except in the last two situations where the indemnity cannot exceed two month's wages.

The party who files a claim must give written notice to the other party before the end of the notice period. If the parties do not agree to maintain their employment relationship, the plaintiff must file a claim within 180 days after the employment relationship has ended.

Redundancy

Employers can terminate the employment relationship for a justified reason, which includes reorganization or economic reasons. In these circumstances, trade unions may request arbitration to determine the amount of compensation.

Severance payments

The employer is required by law to pay a severance payment to any employee aged at least 50 years, with at least 20 years' service, who has had his or her employment terminated. The amount of this payment may be fixed by written agreement, standard employment contract or collective employment contract, but may not be less than two months' salary. Where the parties have not specified an amount, a judge will determine the amount of the severance payment after considering the employee's personal circumstances and the employer's financial resources. Such payments cannot exceed eight months' salary.

The amount of the severance payment may be reduced or eliminated in the following circumstances:

- where the employee terminated the employment relationship without a valid reason;
- where the employer has a valid reason to terminate the contract of employment without notice;
- where payment of the severance payment would cause hardship to the employer.

The Code of Obligations entitles the employer to reduce the amount of the severance payment if the employee receives a benefit from a personnel welfare institution which has been either fully or partially financed by the employer.

These provisions have, to some extent, become redundant as a result of the Occupational Pension Plan Law. The Occupational Pension Plan Law affects all employees over 17 years of age, who receive an annual salary of SFr 22 560 or more. Both the employer and employee contribute equally to the employee's private occupational pension fund, on a monthly basis. On termination of employment, the employer's contributions are transferred to the employee's new pension fund, in whole or in part. As the employer's contributions normally exceed the amount of the severance payment, the employee does not receive an additional severance payment.

At present, the employee will only receive the total amount of the employer's contribution if he or she has had 30 years' service or more with the employer. A partial amendment to this law, which should come into effect on 1 January 1995, will enable the employee to obtain all the employer's contributions, regardless of length of service.

Employees not covered by the Occupational Pension Plan Law will receive a severance payment under the Code of Obligations.

Contracting out

The general principle is that statutory provisions may be modified by agreement between the employer and employee; however there are numerous exceptions to this principle. For example, the standard notice of termination may be modified by written agreement, standard employment contract or collective employment contract, but the notice period during the first year of employment can only be modified by the collective employment contract.

Collective employment regulations

A collective employment contract is a contract whereby employers or employers' associations and employees' associations jointly establish provisions concerning the conclusion, content and termination of the individual employment relationships of the participating parties. The parties cannot exclude any of these provisions, unless expressly authorized by the collective employment contract.

These contracts or agreements may be concluded for a definite or indefinite period of time, and may be cancelled with six months' written notice.

Collective agreements will only bind those individuals who are parties to it. Where the provisions of a collective agreement are applicable to an individual employment contract, a specific reference to the existence of the collective agreement should be made.

In addition, these agreements are usually made in order to preserve a peaceful working environment. If mention is made of that concept in the agreement, any action that would endanger it, such as strikes, would become illegal.

Federal or cantonal authorities may declare collective agreements as generally applicable to all parties in a specific industry or professional group.

Collective termination for economic reasons

The new provisions of the Swiss Code of Obligations governing business transfers and collective terminations for economic reasons came into force on 1 May 1994.

The law defines a collective termination as a number of dismissals which an employer announces within 30 days for reasons which are not connected with the characteristics of the employee, and which affect:

- at least ten employees of enterprises which employ as a rule more than 20 and less than 100 employees;
- at least 10 per cent of employees of enterprises which employ as a rule more than 99 and less than 300 employees;
- at least 30 employees of enterprises which employ as a rule at least 300 employees.

Where the employer intends to make a collective termination, the employer must contact the employees' representatives, or if there are no employee representatives the employer must contact the employees themselves, and give them an opportunity to propose measures on how to avoid or reduce the collective terminations, or how to mitigate its consequences. Moreover, the employer must give the employees or their representatives detailed information on the collective termination.

If the employer is in breach of these regulations the collective termination is considered to be abusive. In this case the indemnity, which will be determined by the judge, must not exceed the employee's wages for two months.

The collective termination has to be notified to the cantonal employment service. The employment relationship terminates 30 days after notification to the cantonal employment service, unless there are statutory or contractual provisions which stipulate that notice takes effect at a later period.

Payments

Where it is proposed to make a large number of employees redundant, it is common practice for employers, unions and/or employee organizations, and the pension funds to enter into a voluntary plan to mitigate hardship for ex-employees ('Sozialplan'). The Sozialplan may include such options as early retirement, assistance in the search of new employment, severance pay, agreement that all the employer's contributions to the pension plan be paid out in full. Such agreements are in addition to any severance payments required by the law.

Closure of companies

In a closure situation, the employer may terminate the employee's employment by ordinary termination or in the case of a collective termination, by following the collective termination procedures. Where the company is declared bankrupt, severance pay, like unpaid wages, belong to the first privileged class of debt and therefore receive priority.

Employee participation

On 1 May 1994 the Statute on information and consultation of the employees of enterprises (*BG über die Information und Mitsprache der Arbeitnehmer in den Betrieben*) of 17 December 1994 came into force.

In accordance with the law, the staff of an enterprise which employs more than 50 employees, are entitled to elect from their midst one or more representatives. If they fail to designate a representative, the information and consultation rights belong directly to the employees.

At least once a year the employer has to inform the employees' representatives about the effects of the course of business on the employment situation.

The employees' representatives have a right of co-determination in the following matters:

- health protection and security at work;

- collective termination of employment;
- business transfer.

Pensions, tax and insurance

Individuals must pay income tax on salaries at two levels: direct federal tax and cantonal/communal tax. There is no deduction of income tax from salaries, at source, by the employer unless:

- the employee is a foreign citizen, living but not permanently authorized to live and work in Switzerland (that is, subject to work and residence authorization) and not having a minimum amount of real assets in Switzerland;
- living across the border of Switzerland (France, Italy, Germany): a so-called 'cross-border-worker'.

Employers must deduct from salaries the employee's contribution to Swiss social security (AHV/AVS), to the disability insurance (IV/AI), to the military compensation plans (EO/APG), to the unemployment insurance (ALV/AC) and to the compulsory occupational pension plans (BVG/LPP). The employer must account periodically to the authorities for these contributions.

Sickness benefit

In cases of sickness, the employer is bound by the Code of Obligations to pay the employee's salary in full for up to three weeks during the first year of employment, unless provided otherwise by contract, collective or written agreement; and provided that the employment relationship has existed for more than three months, or was concluded for more than three months. The employer has to pay for longer periods of sickness, depending upon the duration of the employment relationship and the particular circumstances. Different cantons have elaborated scales which are generally considered as guiding rules by the judges.

If the employee is compulsorily required by law to be insured against any economic consequences arising from being prevented from performing his or her work, for reasons inherent to the person, the employer is not required to pay wages; provided that the insurance covers at least four-fifths of the employee's wages. If the benefits under the insurance policy are lower, the employer has to pay the difference between the benefits and 80 per cent of the employee's wages. If the benefits are only granted after a waiting period, the employer must pay at least 80 per cent of the employee's wages for that period.

More and more employers are taking up insurance coverage for loss of salary caused by sickness, pregnancy and/or accident and for time off not compensated by compulsory salary. This coverage starts after an initial period and is computed as a percentage of the employee's salary, which tends to vary as there is no established practice.

There is no legal requirement, either for the employer or for the employee, to take out insurance coverage for doctors' bills or prescriptions and hospital costs in the case of sickness. Some cantons have recently introduced legislation concerning mandatory sickness coverage for specific categories of employees.

Retirement pensions

All employees aged 17 or over must contribute to the basic federal Swiss social security and disability scheme (AHV/AVS).

Starting at the age of 17, all employees who earn a specified minimum annual wage (currently SFr 22 560) are compulsorily insured under an occupational pension plan (BVG/LPP) against disability and risk of death. When the employee reaches 25 years, the new plan combines insurance against disability and risk of death and coverage for pension on retirement.

The retirement age in Switzerland is at present 65 for men and 62 for women.

Health and safety

Employers must take all necessary measures, including safe and adequate premises, machinery and tools equipped with safety devices and so on, to protect employees' health and well-being. Cantons exercise the right to check that all measures for safeguarding the health and life of employees are enforced.

All employers must cover their employees under a professional and non-professional accident and professional sickness insurance policy. The premiums for professional risks are paid in full by the employer; the premiums for non-professional risks can be charged to the employee, at the employer's discretion or according to the employment contract. These insurance policies are routinely contracted with private insurance companies duly agreed as per the Statute of 23 June 1978, on supervision of insurance companies. Policies are also issued by the state-run Swiss Accident Insurance (*Schweizerische Unfallversicherungsanstalt/Caisse nationale suisse d'assurance en cas d'accident*). This federal agency sets the standards of health and safety at the workplace.

Depending upon the category of applicant, the insurance may be contracted with a private insurance company or with the Swiss Accident Insurance.

Employers' liability insurance

According to the Swiss Code of Obligations the employer is responsible for damages caused to employees in the execution of their work if it can be proved that the employer did not take all due care to prevent such damages. The employer can appeal against the decision by attempting to establish the employees' responsibility.

Anti-discrimination regulations

The Swiss Federal Constitution guarantees equality for all citizens. On 14 June 1981 the Swiss Federal Constitution was amended to include a new paragraph on equal opportunity between men and women, particularly in respect of family, education and labour matters. Men and women have the right to be equally paid for equivalent work. The federal law of application is in the course of being implemented and will probably come into force in 1995.

Regulatory bodies

Federal Office of Industry, Trade and Labour

The Federal Office of Industry, Trade and Labour (*Bundesamt für Industrie, Gewerbe und Arbeit*) promotes industry, trade and commerce. Besides a variety of other tasks, this Federal Office takes part in the preparation of legislation and conducts surveys in the following areas:

- labour market;
- economic development;
- professional training;
- labour legislation;
- safety at work;
- unemployment insurance;
- statistics and so on.

Courts

Disputes can be submitted to different offices or courts depending upon the type of conflict.

For the settlement of private law disputes, approximately half of the cantons have special prud'hommes courts (labour courts) which deal with conciliation and issue judgments. Most labour courts are restricted to hearing disputes up to a certain maximum value in litigation. The other cantons have charged the ordinary civil courts to deal with these disputes. The appeal proceedings depend upon the cantonal procedural law.

It is common practice for arbitrators to settle labour law disputes. Certain cantons consider arbitration clauses, which are signed in advance of a dispute, as invalid. The canton may require the arbitration clause to be incorporated in collective employment agreements, not in the individual contracts.

Collective labour law disputes are primarily dealt with by special conciliation offices, arbitrators or civil courts. Decisions of the cantonal courts may, under certain circumstances, be appealed against in the higher Federal Court.

Most of the disputes concerning public law subjects are treated by administrative or insurance courts.

Procedural provisions of the Swiss Code of Obligations

As a principle of Swiss law the promulgation of the procedural legislation is determined by the cantons. Nevertheless the Swiss Code of Obligations contains some procedural provisions about labour disputes where the amount claimed (disregarding any counterclaims) does not exceed SFr 20 000. In these cases the cantons are required to provide a simple and expedient procedure, without charge except where a party has brought a frivolous action. The judge has to establish the facts and appraise the evidence at his discretion.

Disputes may be commenced at the place where the defendant is domiciled, or at the place of business where the employee performs his or her work.

Foreign employees

The legislation and practice concerning work and residence permits for foreign nationals is complicated and differs from one canton to another. In this respect, the following information is an outline of the legal requirements and should not be considered to be exhaustive.

The residence and employment of foreign nationals is subject to federal and cantonal regulations. The basic regulations regarding foreign nationals who reside in Switzerland are:

- the Federal Statute on the Temporary and Permanent Residence of Foreigners (*BG über Aufenthalt und Niederlassung der Ausländer vom 26.03.1991*);
- the Federal Ordinance on the Limitation of Gainfully Employed Foreigners (*Verordnung über die Begrenzung der Zahl der Ausländer vom 06.10.1986*).

The Federal Ordinance on the Limitation of Gainfully Employed Foreigners contains requirements for foreign nationals working in Switzerland.

Temporary residence permits

- *120-day permit*

  Foreign nationals residing or working in Switzerland for a period not exceeding four months in a calendar year may apply for a so-called '120-day permit'. This permit does not fall under the quota system and does not lead to residence in Switzerland. It enables the person to engage in short-term employment for a specific and limited purpose.

- *Short-term residence permit ('L permit')*

  Foreign nationals who intend to stay in Switzerland for short-term occupational activities may receive a permit of a limited duration (at maximum six, respectively 18 months) which cannot be renewed. It may be granted to au-pairs for example, or to qualified specialists being employed by a foreign academy or doing some research work or even to specialists who are necessary to fulfil some extraordinary tasks in a firm. A simplified administrative approval procedure is granted for transfers of qualified employees within a concern.

- *'Limited one year work permit'*

  Where occupational activities are limited in time, foreign nationals may receive a 'limited one year work permit', which is renewable up to a maximum of four years. It may be granted to managers for example, or to specialists engaged by a foreign academy or who will do some research work or who are necessary for the fulfilment of some extraordinary tasks in a firm. A simplified administrative approval procedure is granted for transfers of qualified employees within a concern.

- *One year work permit (B permit)*

The one year work permit is issued for a year within a given canton. It is subject to federal and cantonal quotas. An annual renewal is generally granted every year provided that all the conditions are fulfilled. As a rule it is not possible to change the employer in the first year. A short-term residence permit (L permit) or a 'limited one-year permit' may be converted into a normal one-year permit (B permit) under certain circumstances.

Permanent resident permit (C permit)

Permanent residents hold permits which bear no limit in time; they can engage in any kind of activity in the issuing canton. Foreign nationals changing residence to another canton obtain preferential treatment for a permit in the new canton. 'C permits' are generally granted to foreigners who have resided in a given canton for a specified number of years, as set by the Federal Alien Policy. The number of years can differ depending upon the citizenship of the foreigner and/or whether the foreigner comes from a country having entered into an agreement with Switzerland.

Seasonal permit (A permit)

Permits are granted to seasonal workers for not more than nine months a year, mainly for seasonal activities such as construction, hotels and so on. A change of employment is rarely permitted during the season. If the seasonal worker has worked in Switzerland for a total of 36 months within four consecutive years, he or she can apply for conversion of the seasonal permit into a temporary residence permit, although the person has no vested right thereto.

Border permits (G permit)

Foreign nationals residing in Switzerland for more than six months in the border zone of a neighbouring country can obtain a work permit while residing abroad. Before the authorities will issue a work permit to the foreign national, they will ensure that there are no similar domestic employees available. The renewal of the permits is easy to obtain.

This chapter was written by Gabriela Taugwalder, Schweizerische Treuhandgesellschaft - Coopers & Lybrand AG, Switzerland.

Turkey

Introduction

Labour law in Turkey is mainly governed by the Labour Act 1971, which sets out the rights and obligations of each party to the employment contract. This law governs all employers, representatives of the employers and employees, irrespective of their field of activity.

Individual employment regulations

Contracts

There are three main types of employment contracts. They are:

- short-term temporary contracts, up to a maximum of 30 working days;
- fixed term contracts with a specified duration (the employer cannot use successive fixed term contracts to avoid paying the employee severance pay or to avoid notice periods);
- indefinite contracts.

There is a legal requirement that contracts for a duration of one year or more should be evidenced in writing. These contracts should contain the following information:

- the names and addresses of the employer and employee;
- the duties to be performed by the employee;
- whether the contract is for an indefinite period or for a fixed term period (in the case of a fixed term contract the expiry date should be specified);
- the amount, method and timing of salary payments;
- any special conditions pertaining to the employment relationship;
- the signature of the parties and the date.

Contracts for a period of one year or more are exempt from stamp duty, other duties and fees.

Where there is no written contract, the employee may request a signed document outlining the employee's general and specific conditions of employment. These documents are also exempt from stamp duty, other duties and fees.

Another form of written contract is the group contract, which is signed by the employer and leader of the group, who is chosen as the representative. Group contracts are deemed to be concluded directly between the employee and employer, when all groups of employees who are listed in the contract, commence service.

Wages and salaries

Minimum wage provision - The minimum wage of workers, shipman and journalists is determined by the Minimum Wage Commission under the authority of the Ministry of Labour. The Commission's decisions are binding and come into force once they have been published in the Official Gazette.

Method of payment - Workers' salaries must be paid in Turkish lira, at least once a month. The frequency of payment may be increased to weekly periods, by means of an individual employment contract or collective labour agreement, but any amendment or variation must be to the benefit of the employee.

Deductions from pay - The only deductions that the employer can make from the employee's salary are those deductions in respect of income tax, social security contributions, stamp duty and other legal withholdings. The employer cannot implement penalty deductions to the employee's salary unless it is provided for in the employment contract.

Itemized pay statement - The employer is required to give the employee a written pay statement for each payment, showing the date and the related period of payment. The pay statement must also specify all types of additions to the base salary such as overtime, paid holidays and public holiday payments, and all types of deductions or withholdings such as income tax, social security contributions, advances and other legal deductions.

Hours of work/shift work/overtime

The Labour Act fixes the maximum number of working hours per week at 45 hours. These hours can be arranged over six working days, with a maximum of seven and a half hours per day. This provides flexibility to enable employees to work half days or to take a full day off on Saturdays.

The law regulates the minimum rest periods that employees are entitled to during the working day. These rest periods are illustrated in Table 1. It is possible, and quite usual for the parties to negotiate a longer rest period in the collective labour agreement.

Table 1

Hours worked	Rest break
Less than 4 hours	15 minutes
4 - 7½ hours	½ hour
More than 7½ hours	1 hour

Shift work is permitted by law, provided that the night shifts do not exceed seven and a half hours. Night shift workers can only be transferred to the day shift in the subsequent week. This interchanging of night shift and day shift workers may be done only once in 15 days, provided the employer has obtained the approval of the Ministry of Labour.

Generally overtime work may not exceed three hours a day on a maximum of 90 days a year. Overtime is paid at an increased rate of 50 per cent for the normal working hour, while payment for overtime worked on weekends or public holidays is paid at an increased rate of 100 per cent for the normal working hour.

Holidays

Turkey observes the following statutory holidays:

23 April	National Sovereignty and Children's Day
19 May	Youth and Sports Day
30 August	Victory Day
29 October	Anniversary of Republic
1 January	New Year's Day
	Religious holidays

Employees receive a full wage for these holidays, and work is generally forbidden.

Where the employee has at least one year's service with the employer, he or she will be entitled to paid annual leave as specified in Table 2. The period of annual leave increases with years of service.

Table 2

Years of service	Period of annual leave
1 - 5	12 days
5 - 15	18 days
More than 15	24 days

The period of annual leave can be extended by collective labour agreements or individual employment contracts.

Maternity provisions

Maternity leave is granted for a period of 12 weeks, beginning six weeks before the date of confinement and extending to six weeks after the confinement. This period may be extended as a result of the employee's health or because of the nature of the work itself. The employee may request, at the end of the six week period subsequent to the confinement, up to six months' leave without pay.

Time off

An employee is entitled to three days' paid leave in the case of marriage, two days' paid leave for bereavement on the death of a family member. Paid leave is also available for a number of other reasons including accidents or sickness.

Period of notice

Under the Labour Act, the termination of an employment contract must be notified to the other party, before the termination actually takes effect. Employees with three or more years' service must receive eight weeks' notice of termination. Employees with less than three years' service receive a shorter period of notice as illustrated in Table 3.

Table 3

Length of service	Period of notice
Less than 6 months	2 weeks
6 months - 1½ years	4 weeks
1½ years - 3 years	6 weeks
More than 3 years	8 weeks

As these notice periods are legal minimums, the parties can increase the periods of notice in the employment contract or collective labour agreement. Where the contract is terminated without giving the requisite period of notice to the other party, the terminating party must pay the other party compensation.

During the notice period the employee is entitled to a minimum of two hours' leave per day to search for a new job.

Dismissal

The employment contract may be terminated in the following situations:

- by mutual agreement;
- at the expiry of a fixed term contract;
- upon the death of the employee;
- by either party giving notice;
- the employer may terminate the employment contract by giving notice in the event of redundancy for economic reasons or for just cause.

The law identifies three major grounds where the employer may terminate the employment relationship for 'just cause', which do not give rise to any liability to pay compensation. These grounds are:

- *health reasons* - where the employee contracts a serious or contagious disease which is incompatible with the employee carrying out his or her work. It also applies to situations where the employee is absent for three or more consecutive days or for more than five days in a month for such reasons as drunkenness;
- *immoral or unethical behaviour* - such as false or misleading information about qualifications or experience, theft or breach of trust, breaching professional confidentiality, poor performance, unauthorized absences for two or more days, intentionally endangering and jeopardising work safety, committing any criminal act in the workplace which results in at least seven days in prison and so on;
- *force majeure* - unforeseen acts such as earthquakes, fire, floods and other acts of God. In these circumstances, the employer must wait for at least a week before terminating the employee's employment.

The employee may terminate the employment relationship for 'just cause' where actions by the employer force the employee to resign. In these circumstances, the employee will be entitled to severance compensation.

The employer is not obliged by law to give the employee any reason for terminating the employee's contract of employment. As a result, employees have significant problems in establishing that they have been unfairly dismissed.

Unfair dismissal arises where the employee is dismissed without 'just cause'. The Labour Act gives two examples of a dismissal without just cause:

- where the employee is dismissed for having filed a grievance against his or her employer;
- where the employee is dismissed for being a member of a trade union.

If a woman wants to terminate her employment after one year of being married, the employer is required to pay a severance payment, which is equal to one month's salary for each complete year of service.

Where an employee wishes to challenge his or her dismissal in court, the employee has the burden of proving that his or her dismissal was unfair. If the court finds in favour of the employee, the employee will be entitled to compensation equal to three times his or her notice period, plus compensation in lieu of notice, where notice was not given.

Redundancy

Employees made redundant within the terms of the statutory definition are entitled to a severance payment, calculated on the employee's continuous years of employment. This severance payment is financed exclusively by the employer.

Where the employer has made an employee redundant, the employer is prohibited from employing another employee for a period of six months. If the employer wishes to re-employ someone, the employer should firstly offer the position to the redundant employee.

Non-competition clause

The law does not require employment contracts to contain a non-competition clause. However, the parties may agree to include such a clause in the contract of employment.

Collective employment regulations

Workers' trade unions and employers' trade unions regulate the negotiation of collective labour agreements. The purpose of these bodies is to protect the interests of their members.

Collective labour agreements

Collective labour agreements are agreements negotiated between workers' trade unions and employers' trade unions (or the employer) to regulate the content, conditions and termination of the employment contract. They also regulate and set out procedures for settling any disputes or conflicts between the parties.

Collective labour agreements can be contracted for a minimum period of one year, up to a maximum period of three years.

Where an employees' trade union wants to be a party to the collective labour agreement, it must first apply to Ministry of Labour. The trade union must have at least ten per cent of the total workforce in that particular industry as members, in order for it to be appointed as a party to the collective labour agreement. The Ministry of Labour will make all necessary investigations before granting the trade union a licence.

An employers' trade union, or employer who is not a member of any trade union, must apply to the Ministry of Labour in order to determine whether an employees' trade union can be a party to collective labour agreement. The Ministry will appoint the employees' trade union within six days and will inform the employer.

Within the period of 15 days following the appointment of the employees' trade union, one party must invite the other party to meetings for the negotiation of a collective labour agreement. The agreed collective labour agreement must be submitted to the Ministry of Labour.

Employee participation

Trade unions

Every employee is entitled to be a member of a trade union appropriate to that sector of industry. It is unlawful however, for the employment contract to state that membership or non-membership be a condition of employment.

It is also unlawful for the employer to discriminate against a trade union member in the member's conditions of employment, including such areas as recruitment, distribution of work, salaries and so on. Where an employer is found guilty of discrimination, the employer will be liable to pay the employee compensation equal to the employee's annual salary.

Pensions, tax and insurance

The Turkish social security system

Under Turkish Social Security Law, all employees (except agricultural workers, self-employed persons and civil servants - who are subject to an alternative scheme) must be covered by the social security system. The social security system includes benefits for industrial accidents and sickness, health insurance, maternity, disability, old age and death. The system also covers nearly all the costs of medical care.

The employer is obliged to notify the Social Security Institution within 30 days of the employee commencing employment, that the employee has started work. The employer is liable to withhold the employer and employee contributions and pay the contributions to the Social Security Institution.

Social security contributions

The monthly social security ceiling has been increased to TL 7 315.020 for the second quarter of 1994. These contributions are payable by both the employee and the employer as a percentage of the ceiling, as specified in Table 4.

Table 4

	Employer %	Employee %	Total
Old age, disability and death benefits	11	9	20
Health insurance	6	5	11
Maternity benefits	1	-	1
Industrial accident	1½ - 7*	-	-
Working after retirement	18	6	24
	19½ - 25	14	33½ - 39

* Varies depending upon the risk inherent in the job

Retirement pensions

Articles 60 and 61 of the Social Security Law state that the retirement age for men is 55 years and for women it is 50 years, provided that the employee has completed 25 and 20 years of service respectively, and have paid their social security contributions.

In principle, the pension equals 60 per cent of the employee's average salary over the last five years of employment. However, in future, the pension will be calculated as the average of a variable number of years, as shown in Table 5.

Table 5

Date of retirement	Number of years of employment used to calculate the average salary
1994	6 years
1995	7 years
1996	8 years
1997	9 years
1998	10 years

Pensions are increased or decreased by one per cent for each year of employment above or below 20 years (women) or 25 years (men), with the maximum pension payable at 85 per cent of average earnings. If the employee is ineligible for a pension, all contributions paid by the employer and employee will be refunded.

Disability pension (permanent disability)

In order to receive a permanent disability pension, the employee must satisfy certain criteria:

- the employee must have lost two-thirds of his or her working capacity;
- the employee must have been insured for at least five years or made 1 800 days of contributions, or contributed for an annual average of 180 days.

The permanent disability pension equals 70 per cent of the employee's average earnings over the last five years. These pensions are adjusted every six months in accordance with changes to the cost of living and wages, and depending upon the employee's financial conditions. In addition, earnings for the prior years are adjusted according to tables published by the government.

Survivor's pension (death benefits)

Survivors of a deceased employee are eligible to receive a survivor's pension if the deceased employee was receiving a retirement or permanent disability pension at the time of death.

Under this scheme, a widow receives 50 per cent of the deceased employee's pension, and each child receives 25 per cent if they fall within the following age groups:

- under the age of 18;
- college students under the age of 25;
- high school students under the age of 20;
- unmarried daughters and invalids (no age limits apply to these groups).

Children who are orphaned by the death of the employee receive 50 per cent of the deceased employee's pension, and parents of the deceased employee may receive any remaining portion, if other pension entitlements are below the maximum.

If the survivors are ineligible for a pension, they will receive a full refund of all contributions paid by the employer and employee, according to the percentages mentioned above (for instance 50 per cent to the widow, 25 per cent for each child).

Sickness benefit

The employee will be eligible for a sickness benefit if he or she has contributed for 120 days over the last 12 month period.

Under the social security scheme, the Social Security Institution is obliged to provide health services free of charge to employees and their dependents. Employees and their dependants pay 20 per cent of their medication expenses, whereas retired individuals only pay 10 per cent except in the case of hospitalization. If the employee is on sickness leave, the Social Security Institution has to pay an amount equal to two-thirds of the social insurance contribution ceiling per month.

Sickness benefits are provided for a maximum of six months (which may be extended up to 18 months, if the medical services will 'materially' reduce the disability).

Employees must pay 20 per cent of the cost of outpatient medicine, except in the case of long-term treatment.

Health care

Health care includes hospitalization, medical treatment and surgery, medicine, appliances, and transportation. There is no limit on the period of time health care benefits are provided.

Maternity benefits

Employees will be eligible for maternity benefits after 90 days of contributions, over the last 12 month period.

The maternity benefit equals 66 per cent of the employee's earnings, paid for a period of up to six weeks before and six weeks after confinement.

Industrial injuries and sickness (workmen's compensation)

There is no minimum qualifying period for benefits in relation to injuries arising out of work.

Temporary disability benefit - This benefit equals 50 per cent of the employee's earnings, or 66 per cent of the employee's earnings if the employee has one or more dependents. The hospitalization benefit is 33 per cent of the employee's earnings, or 50 per cent of the employee's earnings if the employee has one or more dependents. These benefits are paid from the first day of injury, and are unlimited in time.

Permanent disability benefit - The permanent disability benefit equals 70 per cent of the employee's earnings over the last five years of employment.

Partial disability benefit - This benefit equals a percentage of the full pension, proportionate to the degree of disability (if the employee is more than 10 per cent disabled). If the employee is less than 25 per cent disabled, the benefit may be paid as a lump sum.

Survivor's benefits for industrial injuries - The survivor pension equals 50 per cent of the employee's pension or 75 per cent if there are dependents. The pension is payable to the widow or dependent invalid widower. Children and parents receive the same benefits they would receive under the regular survivor's pension.

Voluntary schemes

Voluntary schemes may be offered by either the state or by private companies. The operation of voluntary schemes is not however common or widespread in Turkey. Where the employee satisfies the following prerequisites, he or she may apply for a voluntary scheme after leaving his or her employment:

- the employee has applied to the Social Security Institute for a Voluntary Scheme;
- the employee is not working under the provisions of a Social Security Scheme;
- the employee has paid premiums for 360 days per year.

Foreign employees

All employees, including foreign nationals must belong to a social security scheme which provides coverage for work related accidents, illness, sickness, pregnancy, disability, old age and death. The amount of contributions payable by the employee and employer is determined as a percentage of gross salary, and such contributions are tax deductible.

Citizens of countries with whom Turkey has negotiated a bilateral social security agreement (Table 6) are able to stay within their own national social security schemes and are not required to pay all the social security contributions. They will however, remain liable for the 5 and 6 per cent disability and sickness benefit contributions.

It should be noted however, that for specific cases the related bilateral tax treaty should be reviewed.

Table 6

Countries	Period of Detachment	
	When arriving as an individual	Period of secondment
Austria	Note 3	24 months
Belgium	Note 3	12 months*
Denmark	Note 3	12 months*
France	Note 4	36 months*
Germany	Note 2	Note 5
Libya	Note 3	Note 3
The Netherlands	Note 3	24 months*
Norway	Note 3	12 months*
Sweden	Note 3	24 months*
Switzerland	Note 3	24 months*
United Kingdom	Note 1	Note 1

*   Extensions are allowed.

Note 1:   The treaty with United Kingdom does not specify a time period in which the expatriate can remain in his or her own country's social security scheme.

Note 2:   The treaty with Germany does not specify a time period, the expatriate can select a country scheme in which he or she would remain within the first three months of work.

Note 3:   The social security scheme of the country in which the expatriate works will be applied.

Note 4:   The social security scheme of the country in which the expatriate works will be applied, but in addition, the expatriate can still continue to make contributions in his or her own country scheme on a voluntary basis.

Note 5:   When an employee is seconded to another country, the scheme of the employee's own country is applicable during the period of his or her secondment.

This chapter was written by Adnan Nas, Nas Yeminli Mali Müşavirlik A.Ş., Coopers & Lybrand International.

United Kingdom

Introduction

The law of employment and labour relations in the UK is partly derived from statute and partly from common law. Voluntary collective agreements also play an unusually important role in determining practice.

The statutory principles are to be found in more than 50 Acts of Parliament, and are supplemented by case law, statutory and non-statutory codes of practice and numerous supplementary regulations. On their own, the relevant Acts of Parliament will rarely give a complete picture.

Strictly speaking the employment law described in this chapter is that of England and Wales. The same statutory provisions apply to Scotland in most cases. Separate laws operate in Northern Ireland (although provisions are designed to produce the same effect) and the legal situation in the Channel Islands and the Isle of Man may often be quite different from that in England and Wales.

The distinction between individual rights and collective rights is less significant than it was. The former are largely regulated by statute and contract, whilst the latter have traditionally been regulated by voluntary agreements between employers and trade unions but are now increasingly regulated by statute also.

Individual employment regulations

Contracts

Contracts of employment may be concluded orally or in writing, however employers are required under the Employment Protection (Consolidation) Act 1978, as amended, to give employees a written statement of their terms and conditions of employment within the first two months of their commencing employment. In particular, the employer must give the employee a single document, known as the 'principal statement', containing the following information:

- the names of the employer and employee;
- the date on which employment with this employer began;
- the date on which any previous employment with this or any other employer commenced which is to be regarded as continuous with this employment;
- the scale or rate of remuneration or the method of calculating such remuneration and the frequency of payment;
- any terms and conditions relating to hours of work, including normal working hours;
- entitlement to holidays, including public holidays and rates of holiday pay (including any entitlement to accrued holiday pay on termination of employment);
- the employee's job title or a brief description of the work for which the employee is employed;
- either the place where the employee is required to work, or where the employee is required to work at a number of places an indication of that fact, together with the address of the employer.

In addition, the employer must provide the employee with information on the following matters, which may be provided in instalments either before or after the principal statement:

- whether the employment is for a fixed term and the expiry date;
- the length of notice the employee is required to give and is entitled to receive;
- rules relating to sick leave, and sick pay (or reference to a document where such details may be found);
- any collective agreements which directly affect the employee's terms and conditions of employment, and where the employer is not a party, the names of the parties;
- details of any pensions or pension schemes including whether there is a contracting-out certificate in force (or reference to documents where such details may be found);

- where the employee is required to work outside the United Kingdom for a period of more than one month, the period of such service, the currency in which remuneration will be paid, any additional remuneration and/or benefits provided while working overseas and any terms and conditions of employment relating to the employee's return to the United Kingdom;
- any disciplinary rules and grievance procedures applying to the employee (or reference to documents where such details may be found) - this only applies to an organisation employing more than 20 persons;
- the persons to whom the employee can apply for redress of any grievances or if dissatisfied with a disciplinary decision (or reference to documents where such details may be found).

Where there are no terms to be given under any of these headings, this should be specified in the written statement.

Employers are not required to give written terms and conditions of employment to employees working for less than eight hours a week, persons employed under contracts of employment for less than one month, employees working wholly or mainly outside Great Britain, registered dock workers or merchant seamen.

The employer must notify the employee of any changes to the terms and conditions of employment at the earliest opportunity, which must not be later than one month after the change occurs.

In practice employers frequently provide employees with written contracts of employment or staff handbooks which set out in more detail necessary information about terms and conditions of employment.

Wages and salaries

Minimum wage provision - There is no minimum legal wage in the UK. The rate of pay and frequency of payment are matters for negotiation between the employer and employee. In practice the 'rate of pay for the job' is often determined by collective agreements between employers or employers' organisations and trade unions.

Under the Equal Pay Act 1970, employers are prohibited from providing different rates of pay for different sexes.

Method of payment - All written statements of terms and conditions of employment must include details of the method and frequency of payment and how pay is to be calculated.

Deductions from pay - With few exceptions, the only deductions from pay which an employer can make without the express written agreement of the employee are in respect of income tax and national insurance contributions.

Itemized pay statement - Most employees who work more than eight hours a week have a right to an itemized pay statement at or before the time payment is made, showing in writing the gross amount, the reasons for any deductions and (where different parts of the net amount are paid by different methods) the net amount and method of payment.

Hours of work/shift work/overtime

There is at the time of writing no statutory maximum limits on the number of hours that may be worked per week, other than in the case of children.   Unless the UK's challenge to the legality of the EC Working Time Directive is successful, legislation will be necessary in the future to implement the Directive. There is nonetheless already a general statutory duty on employers to provide safe working conditions and a requirement for employees to work excessively long hours may be held in breach of this obligation.

Holidays

Employers are under no statutory obligation to allow paid (or unpaid) holidays. Holiday entitlement is determined by the contract of employment and is either agreed between the parties when the contract is formed or by collective agreement. Invariably full-time employees are entitled to several weeks paid holiday each year.

Maternity provisions

All employees regardless of their length of service or hours of work are entitled to 14 weeks' maternity leave. The employee must advise her employer, at least 21 days before commencing maternity leave, that she is pregnant and state the expected week of childbirth.

A pregnant employee is also entitled to reasonable time off work and full pay for ante-natal care undertaken on the advice of a doctor, midwife or registered health visitor. The employee is also entitled to the continuation of all contractual benefits, with the exclusion of remuneration, during her maternity leave.

Maternity leave cannot commence until the eleventh week before the expected week of childbirth.

Employees are entitled to different rates of maternity pay depending upon their length of service and level of national insurance contributions. A Statutory Maternity Allowance is paid to those employees who do not qualify for Statutory Maternity Pay (SMP). This allowance is payable for a period of 18 weeks at two rates:

- the lower rate of £44.55 per week (as at 11 November 1994) if the person has left employment prior to the fifteenth week before the expected week of childbirth or if the person is self-employed;
- the higher rate of £52.50 per week (as at 11 November 1994) if the employee is employed on or before the fifteenth week before the expected week of childbirth.

To receive SMP, an employee must have at least 26 weeks' continuous service with the employer, calculated at the fifteenth week before the expected week of childbirth, and must have an average earnings at or above the lower earnings limit for national insurance (£56.00 per week). SMP is paid for a period of 18 weeks at two levels:

- for the first six weeks, the employee receives 90 per cent of her average weekly earnings;
- for the remaining 12 weeks, the employee receives the standard rate of SMP (£52.50 per week).

Employees who have two years' continuous service at the eleventh week before the expected week of childbirth are entitled to maternity leave for up to a maximum of 40 weeks. Maternity leave cannot start until the eleventh week before the expected week of childbirth and only 29 weeks are ever available after the birth. Employees who take extended maternity leave are entitled to return to work after completion of maternity leave, either to the original job or to another equivalent job which provides no less favourable conditions.

The dismissal or selection for redundancy of an employee because of her pregnancy or maternity will automatically be unfair and the employee will be entitled to bring a claim for unfair dismissal, regardless of her length of service or hours of work.

Statutory rights to time off work

Employees who are officials of independent trade unions recognised by the employer are entitled to be given reasonable time off with pay to carry out their trade union duties, including collective bargaining, industrial relations training and so on. Health and safety representatives are also entitled to reasonable paid time off to discharge his or her duties or to undergo reasonable training.

Members of recognised independent trade unions must be given reasonable time off (although there is no statutory right to time off with pay) to take part in the activities of their union. Such 'activities' do not include taking industrial action.

Employees who hold certain specified public offices are also entitled to reasonable time off (without pay) to carry out the duties of that office. Employees who have been given notice of dismissal by reason of redundancy are entitled to seek a limited period of paid time off to look for alternative work or to make arrangements for training for future employment.

Disciplinary and grievance procedures

Written statements of terms and conditions must state any disciplinary and grievance procedures to which the employee is subject, or refer to the document or documents in which these procedures are contained. This may be an issue if a claim of unfair dismissal is made. If so the industrial tribunal may compare the procedure with the guidelines laid down in the Advisory Conciliation and Arbitration Service (ACAS) code of practice.

The procedure should specify how an employee is to be warned about misconduct and the arrangements for holding disciplinary hearings. Disciplinary procedures should also make provision for appeals by employees dissatisfied with a disciplinary decisions, identifying by name or job title the person to whom any appeal should be made.

Period of notice

Except where termination is for gross misconduct by the employee, or fundamental breach of contract by the employer, employers and employees are required to give a minimum period of notice upon termination of employment.

The period of notice which must be given the greater of the period required by statute or the period stated in the contract of employment. the statutory notice to be given to the employee is determined in accordance with that employee's period of continuous service with the employer, as illustrated in Table 1. It is common for the parties to agree a longer period of notice in the contract of employment.

Table 1

Notice period	Period of continuous service
1 week's notice	1 month up to 2 years
1 week's notice for each year of continuous service	2 or more years but less than 12 years
12 weeks' notice	12 or more years

Where an employee has been continuously employed for one month or more, statute requires the employee to give the employer one week's notice to terminate the contract of employment.

Either party may waive his or her right to notice or accept a payment in lieu of notice. Where there is a breach of the contractual notice period without compensation in lieu, the injured party is entitled to bring a claim for damages.

Termination without notice

Either party may terminate the contract of employment without notice if there is a breach which is sufficiently serious as to go to the root of the contract. Examples of conduct where the employer is justified in terminating the contract without notice include:

- dishonesty;
- refusing to carry out the employer's legitimate instructions;
- breach of confidentiality;
- incompetence.

Examples where employees have been justified in terminating the contract without notice include:

- unilateral reduction in wages;
- public humiliation by the employer;
- demotion.

The employee must terminate the contract in response to that breach, within a reasonable period of time. If the employee delays the termination for too long, the tribunal may deem the employee to have accepted the breach and as a result, varied the contract of employment.

Unfair dismissal

Employees with at least two years' continuous service have a statutory right to bring a claim for unfair dismissal. This right does not extend to persons who have reached the normal retiring age, or where there is no normal retiring age, have attained the age of 65. Nor do employees who ordinarily work outside Great Britain, crews of fishing vessels or police officers have the right to claim unfair dismissal.

If a claim of unfair dismissal is made, the employer must show that the dismissal was one of the reasons listed in Section 57(2) of the Employment Protection (Consolidation) Act 1978, namely:

- capability or qualifications;
- conduct;
- redundancy;
- contravention of a statutory enactment;
- for some other substantial reason.

The employer must show that he or she acted reasonably in treating that reason or if there is more than one, the principal reason as sufficient for dismissal and that the dismissal was carried out in a procedurally fair manner.

Where an unfair dismissal claim is established, the industrial tribunal may order reinstatement, re-engagement or compensation.

The ACAS code of practice provides guidance on how to deal with termination procedures in a procedurally fair manner.

Rights to a written statement of the reason for dismissal

Generally employees who have been employed for at least two years, at the date of termination, can request a written statement of the reasons for the dismissal. Employees who are dismissed because of pregnancy can request a written statement at any time, regardless of length of service.

Such a statement must be provided within 14 days of the request. If the request is unreasonably refused, untrue or inadequate, the employee may enforce this right by complaint to an Industrial Tribunal.

Redundancy

An employee is dismissed by reason of redundancy, if the dismissal is attributable wholly or mainly to:

- the fact that the employer has ceased, or intends to cease, to carry on the business for the purposes of which the employee is employed, or has ceased, or intends to cease, to carry on that business in the place where the employee is employed, or
- the fact that the requirements of that business for employees to carry out work of a particular kind, or for employees to carry out work of a particular kind in the place where he is employed, have ceased or diminished or are expected to cease or diminish.

A dismissal for redundancy is potentially fair. The employee can challenge the redundancy on the basis that there is no genuine redundancy or that the procedure followed to implement the redundancy was unfair.

It is good industrial relations practice to warn the employees and/or their union representatives well in advance of the impending redundancies and where more than ten employees are made redundant there are statutory duties to consult trade union representatives (see below). In addition, the employer should, where possible, consult with the employees and/or their union representatives about the selection criteria. The criteria used to select employees should be as objective as possible to ensure fairness. The employer is also expected to investigate the possibility of finding suitable alternative employment for the employees made redundant. Where an employer selects an employee for redundancy in contravention of an agreed procedure or customary arrangement, the dismissal will automatically be unfair.

An employee with at least two years' continuous service who is declared redundant within the terms of the statutory definition will be entitled to a statutory redundancy payment. The payment is calculated on the basis of a week's pay (with a maximum of £205 per week) for each year of service up to a maximum of 20 years' service. For complete years of service when the employee was 41 or over the week's pay figure is multiplied by 1.5p and where the employee was under 22 for all or part of the year the figure is multiplied by 0.5. Service under 18 does not count. The current maximum is £6 150 (£205 x 1.5 x 20).

In practice employers frequently pay more than the statute requires.

Lay-off and guarantee payments

An employee who is laid-off because of a shortage of work is entitled, as a minimum, to a guarantee payment not exceeding £14.10 per day (as at 31 August 1994). Employees must have been continuously employed for at least one month to claim such payments, and the maximum
entitlement is to five days in any three month period. Where the normal working week is less than five days entitlement is reduced accordingly.

In the absence of any express term in the contract providing for lay - off, employers do not have any general statutory right to lay-off workers without pay, although the courts may imply such a term depending upon the circumstances and established custom and practice in the industry. Generally the courts will not imply such a term into the contracts of white-collar employees.

Collective employment regulations

Trade unions

Any employee has a right to be or not to be a member of an independent trade union. Where the union is recognised by the employer, the employee has the right to take part in lawful activities of that union.

Dismissal because an employee is either a member of a trade union or refuses to join is automatically unfair.

Recognition of trade unions by employers is voluntary; there is no legal requirement on employers to recognise a trade union. Once an independent trade union has been recognised, it acquires a number of statutory rights, including the right for members and officials to have time off and the right to be consulted on redundancies.

Collective termination for economic reasons (redundancy)

Where an employer intends to make between 10 and 100 employees redundant at one establishment within a period of 30 days or less, the employer must consult any recognised trade union representatives at the earliest opportunity, and in any event at least 30 days before the first redundancies take effect. Where an employer intends to make over 100 redundancies at one establishment within a period of 90 days or less, the employer must consult the unions representatives at least 90 days before the first redundancies take effect. The employer is also required to notify the Secretary of State in writing, of the proposed redundancies within the specified time periods.

During the consultation period, the employer must provide the union representatives with the following information:

- the reasons for the redundancies;
- the numbers and descriptions of the employees whom the employer proposes to dismiss as redundant;
- the total number of employees employed at the establishment by the employer;
- the proposed method of selecting the employees for redundancy;
- the proposed method of carrying out the dismissals, including details about the proposed timetable;
- any proposals to reduce the number of redundancies;
- ways of mitigating the effects of the redundancies;
- the proposed method of calculating the redundancy payments.

This information must be delivered to the union or employee representatives or sent by post to the head office or to such other addresses as may be notified to the employer, at the earliest opportunity.

Failure by the employer to comply with these statutory consultation requirements may result in the industrial tribunal making a protective award, under which the employer may be ordered to pay the employees for the period during which consultation should have taken place.

Pensions, tax and insurance

Income tax and national insurance

Employers have a statutory obligation to deduct income tax from the pay of their employees (whether or not the Inland Revenue have so directed the employer) and to deduct earnings related Class 1 National Insurance contributions from pay. The rate of contributions paid by employee and employer varies according to the level of earnings and whether the employee is contracted into or out of the State Earnings

Related pension scheme (SERPS). Employers must account to the Inland Revenue for such deductions, and make appropriate payments to the Collector of Taxes within 14 days of the end of the tax month. The employer is liable for any failure to make deductions, including interest and penalties which may be charged for failures relating to deductions.

Sickness benefit

Subject to satisfying certain qualifying conditions, an employee is entitled to statutory sick pay in respect of days of absence due to illness. The qualifying conditions are complex and entitlement is limited to the first 28 weeks of incapacity for work during any period of three years. A proportion of statutory sick pay (SSP) paid by the employer is recoverable by way of deductions from employers' national insurance contributions.

Retirement pensions

Employees are able to establish occupational pension schemes for their employees. Such schemes are able to contract out of SERPS. There is considerable flexibility in the type and quantum of the benefits to be provided by such schemes, for example, they may be either defined contribution or defined benefit in nature or a combination of both. Furthermore schemes may or may not require members to contribute to the benefits which they provide.

Considerable tax advantages are granted to schemes which are 'approved' by the UK Inland Revenue. However there currently is a trend to offer highly paid employees the opportunity to benefit from 'unapproved' top up arrangements.

The rules which govern an approved pension scheme must expressly state what a member's normal retirement date will be, within the age range 60 to 75. However it is certainly possible for an employee to have a different normal retirement date under their contract of employment.

Health and safety

Health and safety legislation in the UK is of two types. There is general legislation which lays down broad obligations and general duties, and there is specific legislation which sets out precise requirements in respect of particular types of industrial premises and processes. In addition there are many regulations relating to premises, processes, operations, circumstances, types of machinery, materials and other substances.

General duties of the employer

Employers are obliged at common law to select reasonably competent employees, provide adequate materials and provide safe systems of working.

All employers have the duty to prepare and regularly revise a written statement of general policy towards health and safety at work, setting out the arrangements for putting that policy into effect, and nominating a responsible and competent individual who will ensure the implementation and monitoring of the policy. Premises are subject to inspection by officers of the Health and Safety Executive, who may issue improvement or prohibition orders or ultimately institute criminal proceedings for breach of these statutory obligations. Regulations make provision for compulsory recognition of safety representatives in certain circumstances, and for the compulsory establishment of safety committees in appropriate cases.

Employers' liability insurance

All employers must take out insurance against liability for personal injury and disease suffered by employees in the course of their employment. Copies of the insurance document must be displayed in all premises to which they relate. Cover of at least £2 million must be provided in respect of any one claim.

Unlawful discrimination in relation to employment

Race and sex discrimination

If an employer refuses employment or treats an employee less favourably on grounds of sex, marital status, colour, race, or ethnic or national origin, the person against whom this action is taken may claim compensation. In addition, in Northern Ireland, it is unlawful to discriminate on the grounds of religion.

The Commission for Racial Equality and the Equal Opportunities Commission can conduct 'formal investigations' of employers if they believe that discriminatory conduct is taking place. Failure to comply with recommendations made during an investigation can lead to legal proceedings being taken by the relevant Commission.

The Race Relations and Equal Opportunities codes of practice contain recommendations on the operation of equal opportunities policies which, although not legally binding in themselves, may be taken into account by a tribunal or court.

Official bodies

Advisory Conciliation and Arbitration Service (ACAS)

The principal function of ACAS is to work to improve industrial relations and to promote the extension, development and, where necessary, the reform of collective bargaining. It provides advice to employers, employers associations, workers or trade unions on any matters concerned with the wide range of industrial relations services, including arbitration, mediation, conciliation and general and specific advice on industrial relations matters. ACAS also produces codes of practice and guidance on matters of industrial relations practice. Industrial tribunals may take account of the provisions of such codes of practice when determining, for instance, whether a dismissal was unfair.

Health and Safety Commission (HSC)

The HSC has a statutory duty to ensure observance of the Act's provisions. It consists of the Health and Safety Executive (which provides inspectorate services in respect of dangerous substances, major hazards, and nuclear safety), the Employment Medical Advisory Service (medical aspects of employment) and Industry Advisory committees (concerned with health, safety and welfare aspects in particular industries).

Commission for Racial Equality (CRE)

The CRE has a general duty to promote the elimination of discrimination on grounds of race, colour or ethnic origin, to promote equality of opportunity and harmony between racial groups and to monitor the workings of the 1976 Race Relations Act. It may also assist applicants pursue claims of racial discrimination and may carry out investigations into an employers actions.

Equal Opportunities Commission (EOC)

The EOC has similar powers and responsibilities to the CRE in the area of discrimination on grounds of sex, and marital status.

Courts and tribunals

Industrial tribunals - Industrial tribunals determine applications relating to employment rights, the most important of which are the rights not to be unfairly dismissed; the right to a redundancy payment; and the right not to be unlawfully discriminated against on grounds of sex or race in relation to employment. The procedure is less formal than that of a court. Cases heard in tribunals may result in awards of compensation, reinstatement or re-engagement.

Employment Appeal Tribunal (EAT) - The EAT is a division of the High Court, presided over by a High Court judge. It hears appeals from the decisions of industrial tribunals on questions of law. Appeals from the EAT are to the Court of Appeal and from there to the House of Lords.

Foreign employees

Overseas nationals will usually require some form of immigration clearance before they travel to the United Kingdom to take up employment. Immigration to the United Kingdom is governed primarily by the Immigration Act 1971 and by the Statement in Changes in Immigration Rules which are published from time to time by the Secretary of State.

Citizens of the European Union and certain members of their families are free to travel to the UK to seek or take up work without immigration clearances as are nationals of those other countries which are signatories of the European Economic Area Agreement, namely Austria, Finland, Iceland, Norway and Sweden. There are also special provisions contained in the Immigration Rules which allow Commonwealth citizens with UK ancestry to work in the United Kingdom having gained prior immigration clearance from a British mission overseas.

The Employment Department will only issue permits for posts which require:

- a recognised degree level or equivalent professional qualification;
- senior executive/administrative skills;
- highly qualified technicians with specialised or rare skills.

Work permits may be issued for period of up to four years, after which an application may be made for indefinite leave to remain in the UK.

A training and work experience permit scheme (known as 'TWES') is also operated for overseas nationals. Permits under this scheme are only issued for limited periods of one to two years and applicants are usually prohibited from joining the work permit scheme after their period of training/work experience is over.

Other forms of immigration clearance must be gained from British missions overseas. These include entry clearances for sole representatives of overseas firms who have no other agent in the UK and persons wishing to set up, or join an existing company as a partner or major shareholder.

After spending four continuous years in approved employment in the UK, workers may be granted indefinite leave to remain in this country at the discretion of the Home Office. They may apply for British citizenship in due course if certain other qualifying criteria are fulfilled.

This chapter was written by Leigh-Anne Buxton, Coopers & Lybrand, United Kingdom.

Index

488